Olabode Ogunlana

Olabode Ogunlana, B.A.(Hons), M.A., M.B.A. is a Chartered Insurance Practitioner. He was the first Nigerian Managing Director of the National Insurance Corporation of Nigeria. Since his retirement from active insurance work the author has devoted much time to the study of Yoruba Culture and Language.

THE RARE LEAF
YORUBA LEGENDS
AND
LOVE STORIES

BOOKS
OF AFRICA

Publisher: Books of Africa Ltd

16 Overhill Road

East Dulwich

London SE22 0PH

United Kingdom

Website: www.booksofafrica.com

Email: admin@booksofafrica.com

   sales@booksofafrica.com

Copyright © Olabode Ogunlana 2013

ISBN 978-0-9926863-6-9

A CIP catalogue record for this book is available from
the British Library.

Printed by TJ International Ltd, United Kingdom.

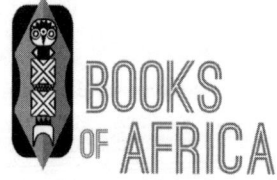

DEDICATION

This book is dedicated to His Royal Majesty Oba Okunade Sijuwade, Olubuse II, The Ooni of Ife, the spiritual head of the Yoruba people.

And also to my late paternal grandparents, Ogunlana Eleku and Molaye, his wife who introduced me to the lore and culture of oral storytelling.

THE RARE LEAF
YORUBA LEGENDS AND LOVE STORIES

OLABODE OGUNLANA

CONTENTS

Preface   10

The Quest for the Rare Leaf   13

The Legend of the Queen's Basket   40

The Legend of Orunmila   46

The Ebiripo Episode   56

The King's Gatekeeper   70

The Thief and The White Chief   76

Kasali Strikes Again   82

What's After Six?   94

What you sow, you reap   106

The Last Miracle   118

I Know   126

The Fruit of Patience   134

You Sweet Rogue   148

Predestined   168

Vindication   200

The Atonement   234

PREFACE

Yoruba, one of the major languages of West Africa, with approximately fifty million speakers, has down the ages been primarily an oral language: it only effectively came into a written form from the mid-nineteenth century, initially through the work of missionaries.

The author's father, a former school teacher, though not explicitly an anti-colonialist, brought his children up to value the indigenous culture, its language and its oral storytelling traditions, at a time when the culture was marginalised and undervalued. In his childhood, in the 1930s and 1940s, the author experienced at first hand, what in orality studies would be called the interface between primary oral culture and narrative, as understood within the western tradition.

There is a rich tradition of storytelling within Yoruba culture, with stories passed down through the generations but never written down, which is still underexplored by modern scholars. This book sets out to present a particular sub-group of these: oral stories which have some kind of historical basis, handed down in the Ogere-Remo area (now in Ogun State) in the Remo dialect of Yoruba.

As originally told, within the primary oral culture, such stories assumed that those listening would know the culture and traditions within which they originally arose and were passed on. A non-Yoruba reader cannot have that knowledge, but within the fast-evolving cultural and linguistic situation in south-western Nigeria today many Yoruba people, especially young people, are also experiencing that culture far less intimately or are simply losing touch with it altogether. In this context, to set down these stories in print for the first time becomes an act of "translation" not simply from the Ogere-Remo oral dialect into written English, but from the original cultural context of the story into a form that can make sense to a wider audience.

This work studies the problematic of this. It also examines in detail the author's own experience of the orality-literature interface in the context of the way in which Yoruba culture was undervalued in the colonial period and the subsequent rise of Yoruba studies. His research brings forward four Yoruba oral stories into a written form for the first time. The original stories had no titles, but here they are called "The Quest for the Rare Leaf". "The Legend of the Queen's Basket", "The Legend of Orunmila" and "The Ebiripo Episode." The context and background of each of these stories has been thoroughly researched prior to their transformation into modern literary form.

At the heart of the work is the author's desire that the Yoruba oral tradition of storytelling should be reappraised and preserved before it suffers any more erosion. The work provides glimpses into a rich oral storytelling tradition and will hopefully provoke others to work in this important area.

Some of the more modern stories featured in the second part of this book are not merely to amuse; more importantly they are intended to remind us of the high ideals of our forebears and to encourage us to transmit them to those who follow us. The last two stories are not at all traditional but are included to show the changes, sometimes imperceptible, in our beliefs and attitudes since our contact with the outside world.

Olabode Ogunlana

THE QUEST FOR THE RARE LEAF

Introduction

I vividly remember the return of cousin Sode who had been away in Burma serving in the West African Frontier Force. The school had just closed for the day. As we were coming out of the main gate leading into Broad Street some soldiers came marching along, towards the Racecourse. They were led by the military band. As the soldiers marched past the High School I saw him. At first I thought I was dreaming … but it was cousin Sode all right. When I shouted his name he turned his face to the right to see who was calling. He could not wave to me but his face lightened and I knew he had seen me. Most of us ran after the marching soldiers. At the Racecourse the Governor-General inspected the returning troops. When the parade was dismissed I rushed up to Sode. At first he lifted me up, then he put me down and we hugged each other. We then moved towards the army lorries parked near the cricket ground. After collecting his kit we walked all the way home, traversing half of Broad Street, from the General Hospital near the Colonial Church down to the Supreme Court Buildings on Tinubu Square, where we turned off into Alli Street. We took the short-cut through Edwin Lane behind the C.M.S. Church which led us into Isaleagbede Street, then into Aroloya Street and finally into Ojo-Giwa Street.

Great excitement greeted our entry into the compound. Nobody knew that the soldiers were to arrive that day, and there was a great hum of surprise. Family and neighbours all wanted to shake hands and talk with cousin Sode. Being the very first person to see him and to escort him home gave me a sense of pride. I took his kit into his room. I replaced my Win-the-War hat with his army felt hat which nearly covered my entire face. My Win-the-War hat was cheap and made of raffia palm; it had replaced the boater hat which could no longer be imported because of the war.

With so many handshakes I feared that Sode's right arm might be wrenched from his shoulder. Everyone wanted to hear about his experiences in Burma. He recounted how they were taken by boat from Ehingbeti Wharf on the Marina to Freetown in Sierra Leone, where all the soldiers from the British West African colonies had converged. They then travelled in a large troopship to Burma. With the three stripes on his arms, we watched him with pride as he told his story. Somehow all kinds of food, palm-wine and soft drinks appeared. An impromptu party started which went on far into the night. Poor cousin Sode was barraged with questions which went on until we all eventually went to bed in the early hours of the next morning. Fortunately it was a Saturday, and we did not need to wake up early. Cousin Sode decided that he would stay on in Lagos for some days to collect his discharge papers and pay-packet as well as to make some purchases before leaving for Ogere to see his family. Among other things, he bought an HMV gramophone and a Raleigh bicycle with speed gears, which at the time was a sign of opulence.

I was unable to have cousin Sode to myself until Sunday evening. I then requested him to remind me of Grandpa's story about Malomo the herbalist. As he seemed not to remember it, I had to prompt him. Even then he thought the story was about Bere and the bondsman. His recollection seemed hazy, like mine. So he suggested that we should ask my father who must have heard the story several times. When we both approached my father he promised to oblige us on the following day as it was already late. He also added that it was a long story.

The following day I reminded Dad, who was commonly known as Eseso, about his promise. He said that the story did not originate from Eleku, his late father. Grandpa had heard the story from Nodu Amoye, his own father. His father's full name was Gusennodu but as was customary in Remo it had been shortened. Dad said that, according to Nodu, the events which gave rise to the story took place some ten years before Eko – as Lagos was then called - was ceded to Queen Victoria. He then told us his version of Eleku's story.

From time to time, in those far off days, traders, both women and men, from all over Remo, made the hazardous journey to Lagos to sell *gari*, palm-oil, yams, *afon, esuru*, rice and other farm products and to bring back with them cloth, rare trinkets, mirrors, coral beads and such like things. The men would buy farm tools and building materials – corrugated iron sheets, for example – intending to sell them, although in fact only a few could afford them as most houses at that time were thatched. They trekked several days on foot along tortuous narrow footpaths amidst forests and jungles, going via Sagamu and Odogiyan, all the way to Ebute Ikorodu where they joined the *oko-aje*, locally made wooden boats steered by poles, which conveyed them to Lagos. They used to land at Ebute Eiyekole until later when the boats started to moor at Ebute-Ero which was very near the residence of the *Eleko*, the paramount chief of Lagos. At that time Ogere traders were referred to as 'the *Oluwo* Gbuyi's people'. Why will become clear as this story unfolds, said Dad with a smile.

Long before the arrival of the *Gesi* – as the British colonialists were called – the Yoruba had lived in towns. Each town, large or small, had a government of its own. While the *Oba* or king was the ruler, each town in Remo was run by the *Igbimo Ilu* or town council.[1] Now, while the *Oba* as king was the nominal head, the *Igbimo Ilu* governed, both at the legislative and executive levels. The *Oluwo* was head of the *Igbimo*, while the other chiefs – the *Olisa, Asipa, Apena, Likotun,* and *Balogun* as well as others – were its members. The *Igbimo Ilu* had overall authority over all spheres of life within the town including the markets as well as the supervising body, the *pampa,* of which the powerful *Iyaloja* was a

---

[1] Before this, the governance of a town was in the hands of the Osugbo which took over from the Agalamasa. Both of these latter bodies were considered by the people led by the Oloritun, the head of a quarter, as being partisan in their dealings; some even regarded them as secret cults.

member. The occupation of the Ogere people was mainly farming. Among other things, they grew a lot of rice, *esuru*, a type of yam and *afon*, the African breadfruit.

After a little pause Dad said, "Let us now begin the story of The Quest for the Rare Leaf."

* * *

The *Oluwo* of Ogere, Gbuyi, and his deputy, the *Asipa*, had been good friends from childhood. The *Asipa* belonged to the male section of the age-group of which the Oluwo's first wife was leader of the female section. This provided another bond between the two friends. In their desire to strengthen further the bond between them, as well as the bond between their two families, the *Oluwo* and the *Asipa* had agreed that Omoyeni, the *Oluwo*'s first daughter, would in due course marry Yera, the *Asipa*'s first son.

The wealthy and influential *Oluwo* was highly respected not only in Ogere but in all Remo and even as far as Lagos where he had lived with his late father. The Oluwo had four wives of whom Malomo was the first and most senior. Her eldest daughter, Omoyeni, was the one promised as the future bride to Yera, the *Asipa*'s son.

Malomo was a herbalist. She grew herbs as well as other trees with medicinal contents from which she prepared remedies for the cure of ailments and also condiments for cooking. Omoyeni helped her in the business and she had learnt how to grow and use the herbs, particularly for mothers during pregnancy and for the care of mother and child after the delivery. The *Oluwo* had introduced Malomo to contacts in Lagos who bought most of her products; thus she had become wealthy in her own right. Gbolaga, called Gbola, an *Iwofa* (bondsman[2]), had been passed to Malomo by the *Oluwo* to assist her with all the hard work requiring male

[2] Tied worker who can only be released by paying back a "bond"

strength. Alimi Alarobo, an intermediary in the trading business, supplier of the aso oke (best quality woven and dyed cloth) to the important personalities in Remo and district, had, from their first meeting in Lagos, become a good friend of the *Oluwo* who was also an important client of Alimi. To expand his business, Alimi had borrowed some money from the *Oluwo*. As was the custom in those days, he had sent his first son to the *Oluwo* to serve him as *Iwofa* for ten years in lieu of repayment of capital and interest. Gbola, who was then 12-years-old, was very handsome, well-built and light in complexion. He was gentle, softly spoken and hard working. Gbola was two years older than Omoyeni. Both of them grew up together like brother and sister under Malomo's care. As constant companions, it was natural enough that they should grow fond of each other.

One morning the *Oluwo* and the *Asipa* set out at dawn to inspect the repairs to a damaged *afara* (bridge) across the Ejigu river. They went by the Oko Ugbodo footpath, narrow, craggy, and twisted with its many bends. To the right were many cocoa trees, and to the left were kola-nut trees. The farms on both sides of the footpath were interspersed with *aiba* leaves, vegetable gardens and various kinds of fruit trees especially pawpaws. The morning was misty. All was silent and quiet. As they walked along, the *Oluwo* broke the silence, by relating the strange dream he had had during the night.

"In my dream Omoyeni, my daughter, was by the stream which ran by Malomo's farm, washing some herbs in a basket. Coming towards her was a frail looking horse with a nondescript rider on it. The horse was trotting slowly and silently, but just before it reached Omoyeni the horse, now a noble looking animal, gathered speed and the rider on top of it assumed a very different look. He had turned into a tall and handsome man! In the twinkling of an eye the man bent down, swept up Omoyeni onto the charger, and galloped away at a very fast pace. As the horse flew past me I was surprised to observe that rather than being frightened Omoyeni looked elated. She was smiling as she waved to me as if saying goodbye. I woke up bewildered, wondering what this dream meant."

"It's a strange dream", remarked Asipa. "You should consult Adifase."

"I shall certainly do so after the meeting today."

The footpath being narrow and not wanting to step on any of the newly made heaps for planting yams, the two men proceeded one behind the other, the *Oluwo* leading the way. As they approached their destination they started to hear voices, those of members of Taiye's age-group, conversing among themselves. It was the *Egbe's* turn to undertake the repairs to the dislodged bridge and also to maintain the footpath and clear the undergrowth from along the approach pathway leading to the bridge. The swollen river had caused a lot of damage. As the two chiefs came close, the young men at work prostrated themselves and gave the usual greetings.

"Where is your *Jagun* (leader)?" asked the *Oluwo*.

"He is on the other side testing the strength and efficacy of the lashings and straps", answered one of them.

"Which age-group is responsible for the stretch between the bridge and Akamiko?" enquired the Asipa. "That's Oye's age-group, but they are not due to start work until after the next market day."

The two elders expressed appreciation for the work being done as well as for its quality as they took their leave.

'*Olipakala a gbe wven*' ('Our founder will continue to support you'), added the *Oluwo*.

As the two elders left the Oko Ugbodo footpath and headed for the town the *Oluwo* suggested that they should seize the opportunity to call on the age-group at work on the new sanitation enclosure. By now the light which heralded a new dawn was ablaze in all its glory. The risen sun had dispersed the mists and all the dewdrops on the leaves of the cocoa trees in the farmsteads had started to dry up. Egbe Salau, whose turn it was to work on the sanitation ground, was already there. One group was digging the holes for the compost while the other was busy trimming off the twigs and leaves from the felled tree trunks. The usual greetings were exchanged between the elders and the youngsters who made the customary salute and doffed their caps. After a brief inspection they entered the town by Panoda market so they could see the members of the *pampa* who were already at work. The *Iyaloja* was in charge that day. The usual greetings ensued with the men prostrating themselves and the women kneeling to show respect for the chiefs. Soon work resumed. The various food items were inspected for quality. Gari (cassava flour) and palm-oil were tasted and other farm-products examined. After the inspection, the two chiefs separated. Both later came back for the meeting of the council.

When the meeting was over, the *Oluwo* went to see Adifase, the town's leading *babalawo*, its Ifa priest and diviner. As the *Oluwo* knocked at the door he called out, "Adifase, I hope you are in."

"I am home, *Oluwo*. I hope all is well", replied the *babalawo*.

"I am here to ensure that all will continue to be well," replied the Oluwo. After the exchange of greetings, both of them repaired to the thatched-roofed hut overlooking the fields.

"What is this urgent matter that has brought the *Oluwo* himself to me? Your coming out here is strange. Usually you send for me."

"On this occasion it has to be so. As the elders say, 'When an adult is seen taking giant strides he is either chasing something or something is chasing him.' Besides, 'It is he who has a thorn in his foot who visits the one with a knife.' Overnight I had a dream which puzzled and frightened me."

"Let's have it! This is why Orunmila (the Yoruba god of divination and wisdom) lives here."

When the *Oluwo* had related his dream Adifase went into

his room to fetch the sack which contained his *Opele*, divining equipment. As the *Oluwo* was sitting on the only *ipeku* (stool) in the room, Adifase spread out a mat to sit on. He removed his *abeti-aja* (cap) before throwing the *opele* on the mat. Then a puzzled expression appeared on his face. He threw the *opele* again and again. When he looked up he asked, "*Oluwo asape*, are you by any chance contemplating doing something contrary to the traditions of this community?"

"No," replied the surprised *Oluwo*.

Once more Adifase threw the *opele*. He looked up.

"Are you sure? Ifa says that as custodian of our tradition you are trying to bend it to suit yourself! Please explain this."

"Would Ifa be referring to the arrangement between me and the *Asipa*?"

"What is that about? Please explain."

"I hoped that Omoyeni, my *Bere*, would in due course marry Yera, the *Asipa's Dawodu*, to further strengthen the friendship which has existed since our boyhood days."

"Has Yera shown an interest in Omoyeni?"

"Not really. We both just felt that it would be a good match."

"*Oluwo*, you and *Asipa* need to take great care and tread carefully. Not all things desirable are permissible, otherwise customs, traditions and culture would never have come into existence. Half a word is enough for the wise! Don't overstep the bounds. In the interest of the community let things take their normal course." So cautioned the Ifa priest.

"Thank you very much," answered the *Oluwo*. He was thoughtful as he left Adifase's abode.

* * *

Malomo, the *Oluwo's* senior wife, had her main farm about three miles from town. It was quite large and extended over many acres. She cultivated all sorts of herbs and trees with medicinal properties for the production of medicines and spices. While Gbola would undertake the heavy duties – digging, planting, cutting, pounding and drying the roots and bark before making them into paste or powder – while Omoyeni would attend to the winnowing, grinding, and sifting. Malomo herself handled the treating, steaming, and mixing, and the general preparations were undertaken at *oko etile* (a farm behind their compound in town).

There was a good rapport between Omoyeni and Gbola. The two became close and constant companions, so much so that they soon fell in love, what with the *Bere*[3] already behaving like a seductive young girl and the flame of manhood already starting to stir in Gbola's loins. When Malomo became ill, an illness which became protracted, and she was almost crippled with arthritis, she could no longer go to the main farm. Thus it fell on Omoyeni and Gbola to run the business, with overall supervision in Omoyeni's hands. She pointed out to Gbola which root was to be pounded, which was to be shredded, and so on. After the day's hard work Omoyeni, dainty maiden that she was, bathed herself in the stream behind the farm before completing her toilet, which comprised rubbing her skin with *ori* (shea butter), applying ground *osun* (a paste obtained from African rosewood) to the base of her feet, and the *tiroo* (galena, made with lead sulphide to brighten them) between her eyelids. Gbola in the meantime busied himself cleaning and storing the implements and tools, and preparing the bundles and baskets of herbs ready to take home.

On one such occasion Gbola heard Omoyeni yelling for him. She had twisted her ankle while getting out of the stream and was lying on the grassy bank in great pain. Gbola found her there, naked, writhing in agony. He quickly fetched a mat, laid her on it and dried her with one of her wrappers. Covering her with the wrapper he quickly uprooted some giant *gbegi* grass, ground its

---

[3] *Bere* is the name given to the eldest daughter in a family

bulb into paste and mixed this with shea butter. With this mixture he started to rub and massage her ankle as well as her leg. While he did so Omoyeni started to moan, though not entirely in pain. In fact it was less agony and more passion: her desirable thin lips were quivering. Slowly, the moaning turned to gasping. Then she started to whisper, "It's so soothing, don't stop, please continue. It's so soothing and pleasing; please move upwards, yes, up my leg, up and up." And she started to coo like a dove.

It was a very cool harmattan evening. Omoyeni whispered, 'I am cold. Please carry me into the hut, I need some warmth.' As Gbola gently lifted her, and nestled her in his arms and against his chest, Omoyeni clung tightly onto Gbola's neck. The position being so comfortable and cosy, Omoyeni implored Gbola to leave her there awhile. Contented, Omoyeni continued to moan; then her body started to pulsate slowly. As Gbola bent down to lower her onto the mat, Omoyeni's hold on his neck became tighter. The pulsation became more pronounced and her face had a sweet broadened smile. Her lips parted and her whispers became inaudible. In that moment she became bewitching and everything became blurred. The embers of affection that had smouldered for so long were ignited in a flash. The flame sparked. The accident then turned into an incident: Omoyeni the maiden was transformed into a woman. From that day onwards Omoyeni started to glow and to purr, especially whenever the two were alone. For his part Gbola doted on her even more, anticipating her every wish.

* * *

Six weeks later Omoyeni discovered she was pregnant. In trepidation she told Malomo about the accident and the incident on the farm. While showing her dismay, her mother was in fact inwardly pleased, for she did not approve of the proposed union between the pretty, dainty Omoyeni and Yera, the crude and lazy bore. Besides, she was fond of Gbola. At the same time she was apprehensive of the scandal that would ensue, especially in such a small community. How would she and Omoyeni live it down? The shame would kill them both. Then another thought surged to the front of her mind. How would her husband, the *Oluwo*, react, with his strict adherence to traditional customs and values?

Almost certainly, the heavens would fall! However, Malomo was consoled by the fact by insisting on the union of Yera and Omoyeni he had not followed tradition and many had started to whisper. 'Maybe it is all for the good,' she thought quietly. And suddenly she became silent, lost in deep thought, while Omoyeni looked on anxiously. Then she smiled and said to her daughter, "For the time being keep quiet. I know what to do. Off with you. I will see you later. In the meantime, you and Gbola must behave normally and go about your work as usual. Until I sort this out, both of you should spend more time on the farm."

Then, still deep in thought, Malomo started her plan. She said to herself, 'Asipa, my age-mate, is *Oluwo*'s best friend as well as his confidant. He is the key to the solution. He will assist me. I shall lure him with something delectable. But first I must fire Yera's longing for the best prize. I shall do more. Yera must be stampeded into immediate marriage with Omoyeni. As a bait I shall dangle before Yera the prospect of marriage with Oburo. That will take place soon after the first one with Omoyeni. With that, Yera will understand and will not even want to consummate his first marriage – if it can be called that – and Omoyeni will be left unmolested to continue in the herb garden. There is nothing new in having two wives at the same time. With help from me, he will have the means he needs for that.'

Accordingly, she sent for Yera at a time when Omoyeni was away at the farm. Before then she had requested her niece, Oburo Orokelewa (the fair beauty), to come and cook the lunch for her visitor. She had also primed this pretty girl to take exceptional care with her toilet and put on an elegant head-tie. She confided in her niece that the intention was to turn Yera's head. The innocent and unsuspecting girl opened her eyes wide in amazement.

"Auntie, that is the young groom intended for Omoyeni."

"Shut up and do as you're told. Don't you want an ideal groom like him - and he's the son of the *Asipa*?"

At first Oburo smiled coyly but then she reacted: "'I don't want to pinch Omoyeni's man! I love my cousin."

Malomo replied sharply, "Are you deaf, do as you're told." Then, with her mesmerising smile: "You will never regret it. Omoyeni and I will always be grateful to you. We shall contribute generously to your trousseau. You will be the envy of all the other girls."

And so Yera came to lunch. He greatly enjoyed the meal with Malomo and Oburo; perhaps even more, he enjoyed the company, the smiles and the attention of Malomo's niece. After the meal when Oburo had retired to the backyard to wash the dishes Yera asked shyly who the sweet young maiden was.

"Do you like her? Isn't she prettier and more pleasant than haughty Omoyeni?"

"She is indeed lovely. No one could see her and not desire her." Yera's eyes were glowing.

"She is my niece and the Apena's daughter. If you really prefer her I can persuade her to consider your suit. More than that, I can persuade Omoyeni to give you up for her," she said with her sweet, crafty smile.

"Please do so. For this elegant prize I shall do whatever you and Omoyeni want. The only difficulty I see is my father. He has set his mind on my union with Omoyeni. Can you handle that as well?"

Malomo whispered silently to herself, '*Awodi to nre Ibara, efufu ta n'dipe o ni okuku mu ise ya,*' that is to say, 'The tail of the hawk that is bound for Ibara is lifted by the wind; it says "Now

to business".' An order to do what we want to do anyway hardly needs encouragement!

With a big smile Malomo said, "Just leave it all to me. I know your taste. You know how close your late mother was to me. Let's just say I am representing her. I shall talk to the *Asipa*, but a little cunning will be required. To compensate Omoyeni you will agree that the marriage with her will take place very soon. Of course you realise that there will be no consummation. You will be keeping her safe from scandal and for Gbola, so to say," she added with a wink. "Soon after that your true wedding with the one you love will take place. Oh, what a joy that will be! It is not new in our society to take two wives almost at the same time. The generous gifts of money from Omoyeni and me will enable you to bear the expense of keeping them both. You will be the envy of your age-mates who have been sneering at you."

Yera left in a happy daze and with great anticipation!

* * *

The next victim of Malomo's guile was Apena, Oburo's father. Malomo had no difficulty with him, because of his ambitions for himself and his pretty daughter. Anyway he thought that becoming an in-law to the highly favoured *Asipa*, next in command to *Oluwo* himself was worth any sacrifice. To further soften Apena's mind and make him more pliable, Malomo said with a very crafty smile, "Apena, let us be honest with ourselves. The procedure by which matches are now arranged for young couples without regard to their feelings, and without consultation with them, is foreign to our custom. How compatible is it with the tradition of our ancestors? How fair is it to the young ones? After all, the youngsters will spend all their lives together. Shouldn't they have a say in the matter? You know the old custom. After a young man has fallen for someone, he will request his parents to ask an *alarena* (marriage intermediary) to undertake the necessary enquiries as to the suitability of the girl for marriage. How wise our forefathers were! At no time did Yera tell the *Asipa* that he was interested in Omoyeni, whereas he had been singing the praises of Oburo and hankering after her. You have confirmed that he has opened his heart to you about this. Please give Oburo your support; the two are in love. What can be better than such a match? Arrange for your *alarena* to get on with her duties."

The approach to *Asipa* was subtle. Prompted by Malomo, Yera requested his father to ask *Oluwo* for an early marriage between him and Omoyeni. When approached in this way the unsuspecting *Asipa* was overjoyed. He readily agreed, as his dream, in spite of the murmurs of the detractors, was about to come true. Even when he became aware of his son's interest in Oburo, he brushed it aside. He thought to himself, 'One cannot account for the whims of this new generation!' Suddenly his son, who had never shown much interest in anything, now wanted for himself two of the most attractive young women in the community! He concluded that as long as his wishes and those of his best friend were met, it did not matter if Yera took a second wife. Omoyeni, *Oluwo's Bere*, would in reality be a mere second. In addition he would have both the *Oluwo* and Apena as in-laws! What could be better?

As for the *Oluwo*, there was no impediment since he had set his mind on the union. As a result he readily agreed. Thus the marriage between Yera and Omoyeni took place.

The storm broke when Omoyeni's son was born early. Such a premature birth, by almost two months, seemed very strange to the community. The *Oluwo* became suspicious. He asked questions and made enquiries. Although he is regarded as the custodian of the community's tradition he could not afford to examine this matter closely since he had compromised himself by not honouring tradition over Yera's union with Omoyeni. So he gave in easily in order to avoid a scandal. However, all too soon he learnt that Gbola was the father of Omoyeni's son! He became furious.

'Here is a more serious scandal,' thought the *Oluwo*. 'How can a mere *Iwofa*, a bondsman, become father of my grandson? Such a catastrophe must be prevented at all cost.' He then took a very rash decision. He asked Gbola to leave the town immediately to go and procure for him *ewe mi riyiri*, the rare leaf. The elders knew that in reality Gbola was being sent into exile, never to return. He had been sent on a quest that was bound to fail, for no such leaf in fact existed. Very few people knew the background story. Oburo's marriage to Yera had been celebrated after his first wedding with Omoyeni. Yera and Oburo were greatly in love and, because they knew the true state of affairs between Yera and Omoyeni, , they went off to live happily forgetting all about Omoyemi whom most people believed was Yera's senior wife. 'Let her busy herself with her herbs while leaving us to enjoy our match,' seemed to sum up their attitude. As for poor Gbola, he started to wander from village to village and from town to town, on the fruitless quest for the 'rare leaf'.

* * *

For seven long months Gbola travelled on many dusty, rugged

and twisting footpaths. He had seen more villages, hamlets and towns than he had ever thought to see in his life. He started to get weary and frustrated. Omoyeni and their little son were always in his thoughts. Towards evening one day as he was ascending a hill he decided to rest. He came to a big *araba*, a white silk cotton tree as the sun was setting. The many colours of the setting sun – golden yellow tinged with orange, light grey, and crimson – gladdened his heart and put new life and hope into him. He remembered what they said the Ifa oracle had predicted about his life. Would it ever come to pass? he wondered. He was musing about this when he thought he heard someone sighing - or perhaps it was just his imagination. Then he heard the sound again. It was followed clearly by a voice.

"Who is there? What are you doing in this lonely spot so late in the evening?"

Gbola tip-toed silently to see who it was. Reclining against the tree was a cheerful looking man, smiling to himself.

Gbola addressed him: "Who are you too? And if you don't mind me asking, what are you doing in this lonely place?"

The merry faced man, still smiling, answered calmly, "I am *Eniko o mo*, messenger of the *Irunmales* (Yoruba gods), and it is my business to move around the country. You look so weary. Fortunately you are near a haven of rest, but you won't find the way unless I point you in the right direction." With a twinkle in his eye he continued, "When you get to the top of the hill you will see a clump of thick *koko* leaves, green, large and lush, on your left. Push them aside. You will come into an open space. Follow the narrow footpath. It will lead you to the home of an old wise man. There you will find shelter for the night and much more."

Before Gbola could thank him the stranger jumped up, whistling a funny tune and disappeared into the approaching night.

Although Gbola was doubtful about the man's sanity, he decided to put his suggestion to the test. Sure enough he found the cottage. He was very tired and footsore. He was about to collapse when he saw an old man dressed all in white, with hair and a beard both also completely white. He was reclining on a *taraga (a* couch made with cane). On seeing Gbola's condition the old man quickly called for someone from within to come out and assist the staggering stranger. There was a prompt response. When the stranger had been seated the old man requested some cold water to be brought for him. Though Gbola wanted to speak, the old man signalled that he should hold his peace.

"You must be really exhausted. Please rest and get back your breath before speaking. You must be famished too."

He then called for food enough for two. Again Gbola indicated his wish to speak. "Not yet. You can speak after the meal, not before," said the aged man.

Before long two women appeared carrying earthenware bowls and platters. They were placed on an *ipeku* (stool) in front of the old man. A big earthenware bowl of water was brought to enable the two to wash their hands. The old man asked Gbola to proceed, but he invited the old man to do so first. The old man smiled and washed his hands. Then Gbola did the same. When the remnants of the meal had been cleared away the old man asked for a gourd of palm-wine to be brought. A young man came in with a gourd and two drinking calabashes. First he prostrated himself before the old man, then he squatted and poured the two calabashes full with white froth, before handing them over with a bow, first to the old man and then to Gbola. They were then left alone.

For the first time Gbola observed his surroundings. The moon was already high in the sky; the stars were twinkling; the breeze was cool and fresh. The serenity here was astounding: there were palm trees, sugar-cane stems, bananas, plantains and other forms of vegetation. There were very tall, ancient-looking trees, the tallest being a white silk cotton tree with immense girth and leafy, majestic branches. The old man then motioned to Gbola that he should now speak. So Gbola told his story, starting from the very beginning. After hearing him out the old man sighed deeply and shook his head.

Pointing to his head the old man asked, "What do you see here?"

"Hair, white like cotton," replied Gbola.

Again the old man pointed to his chin and asked "And this?"

"A white beard, full and long."

"You are right, my son. But what do they stand for?"

"It is obvious, revered father, that you are very old. Your face has the stamp of age and wisdom."

The old man nodded. *"Beni, Ewu logbo, irugbon lagba* (Yes, wisdom comes with age). Indeed, as one goes along the journey of life one picks up events and experiences which later become stories to be told when one gets old – making history, one might say. If I tell you what I have been through before attaining this ripe age and acquiring this white hair, you might pray to die young! So I won't." He was still smiling. "A man must learn to bear the burden of life with courage. Intuition tells me that you have before you a glorious life and future. The *Oluwo* must have

30

felt deeply offended to send you on this fruitless quest." And now he chuckled. "Whenever an elder requests someone to go in search of the 'rare leaf' it means 'get lost in exile and never come back.'" Then he added, "*ogbon ki i tan l'aiye k'awa lo s'orun* (the world cannot become bereft of wisdom to entail a journey to heaven). For now, go in and have a good night's rest. We shall discuss things further in the morning."

The sage was already reclining on his *taraga,* a cane couch, when Gbola made his appearance next morning. It was a beautiful day. The sun was just rising. It was cool and calm. The birds had started chirping. There was peace and quiet, which reminded Gbola of the haven to which *Eniko o mo* made reference. He was marvelling at the world around him when he remembered where he was, prostrated himself before the old man and in response to his greetings and enquiries as to whether he had slept well and had breakfast he answered in the affirmative.

"My son, go to the *Iroko* tree in front of you. Underneath it is what looks like a thick shrub. Bring me one of its twigs with as many leaves as possible. Tomorrow, dry the leaves in the sun. Do so every day until they become very dry. Then take the dried leaves to the *Oluwo* and tell him, "I cannot find the 'rare leaf', but in its place, here is a leaf equally valuable. It is called *Ewe kagba gba a, kowo, koye. Gbigba lagba ngba a,* meaning an elder overlooks a troubling and baffling episode. That, my son, will be the end of the matter."

Then the old man asked Gbola to kneel in front of him. Placing his two hands on Gbola's head, he blessed him. "You are a very fortunate young man, Omoluwabi[4]. Go in peace. Wealth, honour and peace will be your lot. The Almighty Father will be your support and defence all the days of your life. Amen."

He then took an *ado,* a miniature gourd containing a potion, from underneath his seat.

[4] The name means "from the stem of Noah"

31

"Take this valuable medication. You will need it soon. Whenever you are told that a person is suffering from a disease without cure then give it to that person. Put sixteen drops of it into *eko* (steamed maize flour) and mix it with water for the person to drink. The person who drinks this will not only become well but will become new again. Guard it. It is precious. Continue on this footpath before you until you get into a glade. From the height you will see a valley. Go there. Good fortune awaits you there." Once again Gbola prostrated himself before the old man and thanked him profusely.

Now he walked briskly and confidently along. Very soon he reached the glade mentioned by the old man. The sun was blazing but due to the shade provided by the trees the whole place was cool. The sky was clear and blue. The local birds, *elulu, orofo, adaba,* and *atiala-atioro*[5] were flitting from tree to tree. The setting was so serene and inviting. This would have been a good place to rest, thought Gbola, but his mission gave no room for rest. As the old man had said, the plateau overlooked a very beautiful vista. Right before him was a farm in a valley. He could see a number of people in it; from where he stood they looked so small. Beyond the farm some thatch-roofed huts dotted the area. Eager to reach the farm to test the truth of the old man's words, he quickened his pace as he descended. Soon after, he reached the entrance to the farm. A man standing there seemed to be expecting someone. Before Gbola could speak the man asked if he was the man sent from the vegetable farm. Gbola answered in the negative. "Then you must be one of those men seeking work here." Gbola replied that he was new in the village, adding that he could do with a job. The man informed him that the place was a special farm devoted to growing herbs, medicinal trees and plants. Gbola smiled saying that this had been his occupation for the last ten years. He was invited in to meet the owner of the farm. First the man went into

[5] The Senegal Coucal, Sierra Leone Green Fruit Pigeon, West African Red-eyed Turtle Dove and the Allied Hornbill

a room and Gbola could hear him talking with two people, a man and a woman. He was then invited in. A young lady, with a puzzled look, was sitting in front of a long trestle on which there were many plants and herbs.

"We are told you know about herbs," said the lady.

"Yes," replied Gbola.

He was then invited to move nearer and help identify the plants on the trestle. Gbola moved closer, wondering what was afoot. Seeing the look on Gbola's face the lady went on to explain that the man in charge of the farm had suddenly fallen ill and although they were the owners of the farm they did not know much about herbs. Gbola then sorted out the herbs. He asked for water to sprinkle on some of them. "The others would need to be soaked," he added. After some discussion on the growing of herbs and their treatment Gbola was conducted round the large farm which appeared to be flourishing. He was persuaded to stay the night with the couple so that they could resume their talk the next day. On the following day Gbola agreed to stay only for a month or two. All too soon he had forgotten the old man's prediction.

The elderly man was in fact merely visiting the farm to assist his niece to get settled and take charge. Now that an expert had been found he planned to leave soon, which he did. As agreed, Gbola began work at the farm the next day. Watching how Gbola set to work and how he got on with the workforce, the woman was highly impressed. Later that evening the lady made an attractive offer, asking Gbola to stay indefinitely to help organise the farm and make it more profitable. She offered Gbola half of the resulting profit. She went on to explain that after the death of the farmer the family had wanted to sell the farm, but now she had found an expert she would stay on, learn on the job and become an expert herself, so that she could then run the farm when Gbola eventually left. Gbola agreed to stay for a while. He taught the workers all about herbs: when, how, and where to grow all the species; how to harvest them, and the various processes; the treatments required; storage and everything else that needed to be done. Above all, Gbola promised to introduce them to buyers who knew the value of good herbs.

Gbola had been given a hut to live in. After a year he felt that he had saved enough to repay what his father owed to the *Oluwo* should this be necessary, as well as to pay for the dowry and other expenses of the marriage with Omoyeni. When he mentioned his plan to leave, the lady looked sad. She requested Gbola to stay on as she would be unable to run the farm without him. Later that evening she came to Gbola's hut to discuss 'a very important issue', as she put it. She came straight to the point: "Gbola, you have great expertise with herbs and your skill with people is excellent. Under you the farm has taken a turn for the better. All the employees are happy working under you. You have shown me the value of what we have in this farm and that we are on to something important here. I am being candid, *tomo eni ba da a ka so* (do not hesitate to praise a good person). We are both single and, although it is unheard of for a woman to propose to a man, my desire is that we get married. Then you will never have to leave *Ido Oyin*, this farm and me."

Gbola was taken aback. He explained that the reason he wished to leave was to return to his beloved fiancée and their child from whom he had been separated for almost two years. The lady seemed stunned. "All the workers say you are unmarried. Are you saying all this to put me off? Am I not beautiful enough? I have no ties whatsoever with anyone in the world. I know my proposal is odd and sudden. Please think about it overnight," she pleaded. Gbola replied gently: "There is nothing to think over. I have told the truth." To Gbola's embarrassment the lady broke down and started to sob. After calming down she appeared to have dropped asleep. Gbola had to tap her on the shoulder. "Let me walk you to your hut. We shall talk some more tomorrow." All she could do was nod. She walked as if she was half asleep while Gbola supported her.

The next day, first thing in the morning, Gbola called on her. He asked her not to be despondent. He offered to go to his home and talk to his fiancée to try to convince her so his family could come and settle at Ido Oyin provided they could jointly own the farm on an equal basis. Morin, for that was the name of the lady, beamed with a smile. She said, "You mean that, honestly? You are not running away." "No, I assure you," was Gbola's reply.

* * *

To the consternation of Malomo, and others within the household, late one evening the *Oluwo* suddenly felt very ill. Malomo thought that he was suffering from *lofutu*, arthritis, and treated him accordingly. They all went to bed in great anxiety. First thing next morning Malomo went into his room to enquire about his illness. *Oluwo* said he felt much the same as the previous evening, only now he could not lift his right arm, which felt wholly lifeless. Malomo made the observation that it was obviously not *lofutu*, as the balm comprising of ground *gbegi* bulb and *ori* would have made him better. She added that she had requested Omoyeni, who was now as knowledgeable as herself, to come and examine the *Oluwo*. As they were talking Omoyeni entered. After a brief examination she confirmed that it was not *lofutu*. She suggested that Tunda, the traditional doctor, be invited to see her father. He agreed and asked that Malomo should also send for Adifase, the Ifa priest. As father and daughter sat silently the *Oluwo* said this: "Omoyeni, you still wear this grief on your face even after almost two years. Something tells me that all will be well. Cheer up."

Tunda agreed that the Oluwo's ailment was not *lofutu*. "What it is, I do not know. Let's wait and hear what Adifase has to say." Not long afterwards Adifase arrived. After his normal greeting he added, "The *Irunmales* will support us. Lipakala will uphold us." He spread out his mat and produced from his pouch the *opele*. He whispered into it before the first throw; then he made a second and a third throw.

Looking up he blurted out, "'Ha! Ha! I said so! May the *Irunmales* forgive you, *Oluwo*! But for Malomo your suffering could have been worse. What you called her guile was what reduced your pain. Ifa says you will get well. Malomo, our good mother, I and Orunmila thank you."

He continued, "The *orisas* and *Irunmales*, guardian spirits of this town and the entire community, have levelled three charges against you. Firstly, your treatment of Omoyeni and Gbola was uncalled for. Gbola was no ordinary bondsman. You assured his father, Alimi, your friend, that Gbola would be treated as your own child. You gave him your word. Yes, a worthless *Iwofa* may be sent into an exile of no return, but no sane person would throw out a ward. Secondly, you forced Omoyeni and Yera into a union distasteful to them both which was not in accordance with our custom and tradition – you, the *Oluwo Asape*, custodian of Ogere culture! Thirdly, you acted contrary to what fate had decreed for Yera and Gbola. Everyone, including the *Asipa*, Yera's father, knew the type of person he was. He was lazy and cowardly, so much so that he refused to train or serve as a warrior. He had been so petted and cuddled he behaved like a spoilt child! Our elders said *Ile ni iku wa l'eran Ajayi; Ayanmo-ipin eran Olugbode*: 'The-home-is-where-death-lurks, the name of Ajayi's goat; One's-fate-is-set-at-one's-creation, the name of Olugbode's goat.' No one was surprised when he died suddenly in his own home under the *afon* tree. Who are you to alter his fate? As for Gbola, Ifa says that at his birth it was shown that he was a great star who would rise high in the firmament, add lustre to his family heritage, and become a useful citizen of the world. To save your own face you sacrificed him and sent him into exile! This is what you must now do…..

"Send your messengers out to find Gbola and bring him home. After all the necessary preliminaries, hand over Omoyeni to Alimi, to be passed on to Gbola as his wife. To propitiate the *Irunmales* and the Ogere community you will at your own expense procure two hornless cattle which from today will roam around this town as was instructed by Lipakala himself when he founded this town of sixteen rivers and sixteen hills. It is not for nothing that the figure sixteen tallies with Orunmila's sixteen *odus. Be e ni; erendogun Ifa ni i fo ire,* meaning only sixteen *odus* can bring good things. This action will promote trade and commerce in this land as well as bringing lasting peace to the community. Orunmila further says that help is at your doorstep and Ifa adds that you will fully recover and give further service to this community. Never again, until you are gathered to the abode of your ancestors, do anything contrary to the traditions of Ogere! *Aki i gbo buruku l'enu abo're. Abo mi re. Lipakala agbeni ma dehin a gbe gbogbo wa. Ase – Amen*: '(He who propitiates the gods never utters evil words. I am done. May Lipakala continue to support and defend us. Amen.)' "

At this point Malomo went out to fetch *Oluwo*'s meal. As she got into the yard which separated his quarters and hers, she came face to face with what she thought was an apparition. Her face became drained of blood, and she stared like one seeing a ghost.

There was utter silence.

"Elewe omo, it's me, Gbola. I am not a phantom."

Still visibly shaken, Malomo gasped, "Have you found the rare leaf?"

"No, but a sage gave me a substitute which is equally good and perhaps better. Where is the *Oluwo* so I can put it in his hand? Where are Omoyeni and the child?"

"Both are quite well. Come in and see the *Oluwo* who is unwell."

Just then they were interrupted by a wailing noise from under a tree in the compound. Looking in the direction of the noise Gbola saw that it was Oburo. She was sitting on a mat, wailing and weeping and some people were waiting on her. Gbola was informed that Yera had died that morning; a ripe *afon* (African breadfruit) dropped on him and broke his neck. Gbola went over to Oburo, consoled her and handed her over to her age-mates who had come to console her.

At this point there was yet another interruption. Alimi, Gbola's father, entered and asked Malomo what was happening. She told him everything. Just then Omoyeni came out to find out what was delaying her mother. She could not believe her eyes when she saw Gbola! They flew into each other's arms. After calming down they all proceeded into *Oluwo*'s quarters. The once vibrant chief was now laid low with a useless right arm. To their surprise he started to make apologies to both Alimi and Gbola. Adifase, the *babalawo*, then explained what had happened. There and then Gbola asked for cold water and *eko* (steamed ground corn flour wrapped in leaves) to be brought. He prepared a mixture which he passed to the *Oluwo* to drink after his meal. He also made a bowl of it for Malomo. He said this was to be repeated daily, and within three months the *Oluwo* was restored to his former health; Malomo too was healed of her chronic arthritis.

When Gbola, Omoyeni and their son left for Ido Oyin they were accompanied by Oburo who was now a childless widow. A month earlier Gbola and Omoyeni's marriage had been celebrated. Omorinsola (Morin's name in full) was delighted to welcome Gbola and his family to Ido Oyin. Omorinsola, now Gbola's business partner, later married Gbolawoye, Gbola's younger brother. In this haven of peace Oburo found another husband. The herb business grew enormously, offering employment to many in the village. No one was surprised when Gbola rose to become a chief in Ido Oyin.

Eseso concluded his story with the words *abo mi re*, which means 'Here ends the story.; 'I am done.'

—————————◆—————————

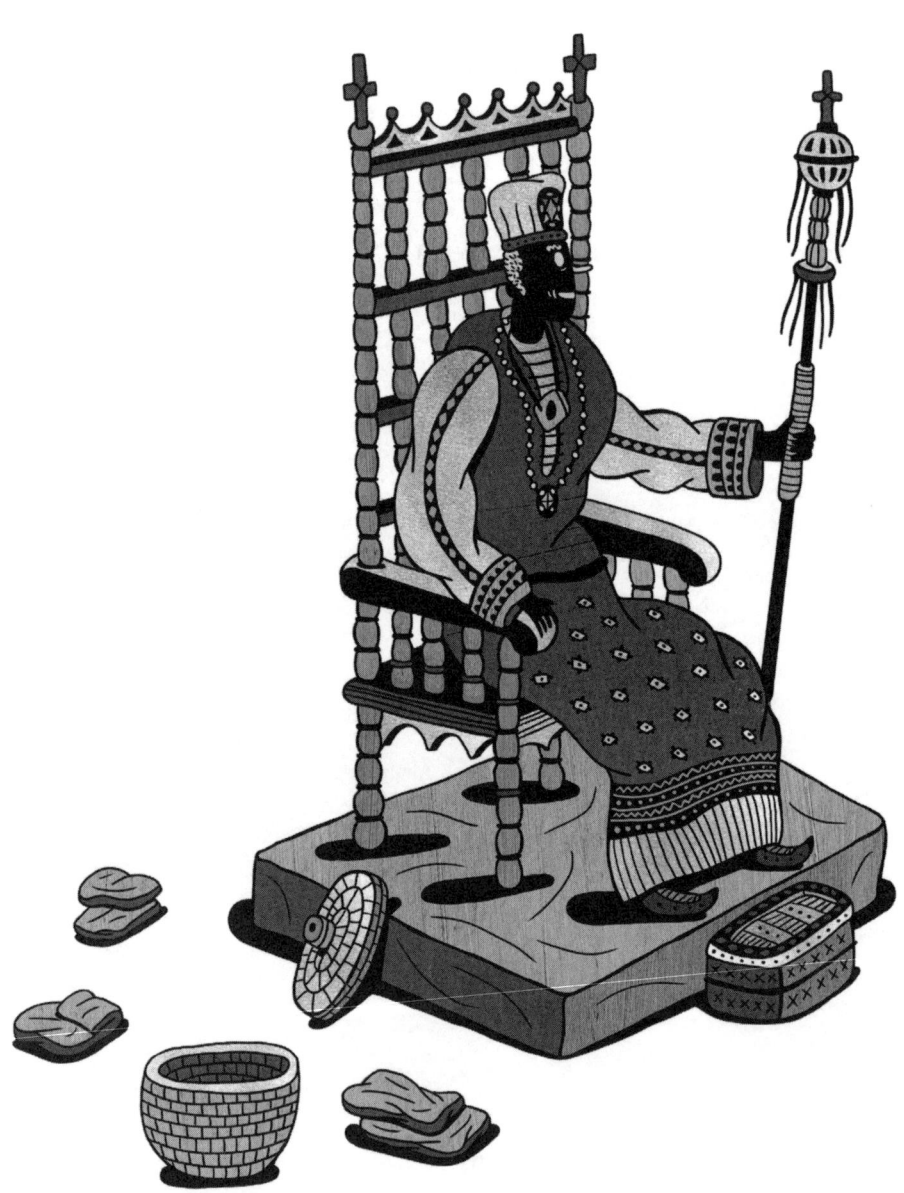

THE LEGEND OF THE QUEEN'S BASKET

When we were children we used to visit the village, often spending the long vacations there during the rainy season. At these times the moon appeared only rarely and when it did we were all so glad. On such nights my grandfather would tell us stories. "I want you to listen to one of them which I found very fascinating," my grandfather said to us on one such night.

My late nephew, Tade, was forever probing and asking about the history of the family. He had a great ally in Iya Alaro (dyer), an old woman who was said to be a distant relation. One time, Tade paid Iya Alaro a visit, a pre-arranged one. He got the usual warm welcome.

"Do you have your writing materials as I directed?" asked the wise old woman. "Yes, revered mother; I have them here," replied the young man. "I also warned my wife that I shall be with you for some time. You may, therefore, proceed. Please take all the time you need."

"Sit down, my son and record the events which took place long before your mother of blessed memory was born. Olabosipo, sometimes called Olabopo (or Labo for short) was the first daughter of Oba Afun. She was generally known and called Bere. In later years she was given the title of custodian of the Queen's Basket. She was a very graceful and beautiful woman. She was as wise as she was fair, and also a dyer of great repute. Legend has it that a goddess taught her. In addition, she excelled in the craft of weaving on the loom the local fabric known as *aso oke*. I was her ward and she taught me the craft of dyeing. That was how I became Iya Alaro. For the sake of completeness I should explain that among the Yoruba all first born females in a family are called Bere while their male counterparts are called Dawodu."

One morning Oba Afun did not emerge as usual from his *akodi* (the inner chamber of the royal apartments). The courtiers and others had been sitting patiently for many hours, some of them since the cock crowed. By then the sun was already overhead, beating mercilessly down on the bald heads of the old, wizened men who formed the majority of the revered assemblage. No man was allowed to wear a cap within the royal precinct. They were at a loss as to what should be done. It is forbidden for anyone to enter the venerated chamber unless sent for. Not even his senior wife, the *Yeye Olori* or indeed his *babalawo* (the king's diviner and priest, also known as *adifa oba*) are allowed to breach the protocol.

In the end it was the *Yeye Olori* who pointed the assemblage in the right direction. "Please send for Bere," she advised, and when she came the situation was explained to her. "As your father's favourite child, we authorise you to enter the chamber to find out what is wrong. We know that it is against tradition, but your father dotes on you. Please save us all from this dreadful suspense. The last time in living memory a similar thing occurred was when the reigning *Afun* joined his ancestors. May the *irunmales* (the Yoruba gods) forbid it on this occasion."

Understandably, it was with great trepidation that Bere entered the royal chamber. The Oba was staring into space. In front of him was an oval shaped raffia basket. The lid was by its side. Bere knelt on her knees with her hands firmly on the ground and her face bent downwards. The Oba appeared to be unaware of the intrusion. The silence was punctuated by ominous sighs and groans issuing forth from *Kabiyesi* (his majesty). After some time had passed, Bere summoned up the courage to whisper, "I hope all is well, *Kabiyesi*? The entire court has been in a state of suspense and fear. What is the matter? What is the problem? Is wisdom not the daughter of old age? After all, any problem to which you have no solution can only be solved by the *irunmales* (gods) and others in the great beyond."

This appeal evoked a response from *Kabiyesi*. He said: "My

daughter, a horrendous thing has happened. All my powers have gone. They have crumbled like dust. Step forward and see for yourself. This kingdom is doomed. My words, hitherto charged with supernatural powers, no longer have force. My *Ase* (potent words) have disappeared. Who has done this? What has caused it? Come forward my daughter and behold with your eyes."

"I dare not," replied Bere. "Who am I to look inside the Queen's basket. Everyone knows its powers. Please, father, do not press me to do this. Just tell me what has happened. Between us and with guidance from the *irunmales* and our ancestors, a satisfactory solution will be found."

"As everyone knows, and as you have testified, this basket is sacred, extremely so," the Oba responded. "It was entrusted to me by my mother, the late Queen. It belonged to her mother before her and her mother before that. It has always been passed down by the reigning Queen to her successor, from time immemorial."

In reply, Bere observed that if the basket was so ancient and potent why should the contents crumble? Would the physical state of the contents really matter to the extent that it would eradicate or diminish the powers of the contents of the basket?

"I have my doubts, father. What really matters is the strength of your faith, your faith in the powers bequeathed to you by your ancestors."

"You do not understand, my daughter. I derive all my powers from the contents of the basket. Whatever I say when my hands are resting on it will come to pass. If I bless a person the blessing will rest and abide with him or her for all time. Similarly if I curse, the curse will persist. Without the Queen's basket I am nothing. Every morning when I wake, the first thing I do is to touch the basket and pat my bald head with my hands while at the same time blessing myself and asking for the wisdom to undertake all my duties for the day. I have done this for years without ever removing the lid of the basket. Even when I put in new contents the lid will only be half-opened. Because of the weighty issues to be dealt with by the council today I thought I would obtain extra power and discernment by touching the contents. What a costly error," the Oba continued. "I know what the contents are! All I had to do was to lift up the side of the basket and throw in the new package. Instead I touched the contents inside! Let us see now - how many additional packages have I deposited into it during my reign? All told 37 or 38."

"If I may ask, father," said Bere, "how is it that your mother entrusted it to you when the tradition had been that it went down from mother to daughter?"

"I think it was because my mother was greatly fond of me," the Oba replied. "She thought that the powers possessed by the basket would make me a great ruler. Besides, when she was called home to her rest, her Bere, my sister, was away. As you know she got married to the Oba of Ajiran far away in the city beyond the Delta."

"If I may ask, father," his daughter requested, "what do the packets dropped into the basket contain?" *Kabiyesi* then explained: "They are the trophies of the virtue of our womenfolk. Whenever they got married their *ibale* (i.e. *Iba-ni-ile*, the sign of virginity being intact) were sent home as proof of their virtue and the high standard of their upbringing. This was the white cloth stained by blood during consummation of the marriage. I am hoping that after the festival of the new yams when you are married to the tall warrior from the town of sixteen hills and sixteen streams, yours will be added. The *ibale* was regarded as a good omen and it provided a solid foundation for a blissful, fruitful and prosperous marriage. Mothers whose daughters lived up to these high expectations were greatly honoured and applauded. Similarly, such brides were respected by their husbands and by both families. The brides were given valuable presents. Such brides became the envy of all the girls and their parents. How terrible was the ignominy of the bride who proved otherwise! May the *irumales* never inflict such a girl and such ill-luck on our family."

"What preservatives are used to ensure that the cloths remain intact?" asked Bere. "We were told that in ancient times they were soaked in special dyes," the Oba explained, "but over generations the art of making the dyes was lost. The cloths were, therefore, no longer so treated."

"Are you surprised then that they disintegrated? What matters, father, is your faith in the efficacy of the basket and its contents. As I see it, the state of the contents is of no significance. Nevertheless I shall spare no effort in finding the correct dye. As you know I had always assisted grandmother with her herb garden. With a thorough search I shall soon find which roots or leaves or combination of both are used. Now father, replace the lid, put your hands on the basket, pat your head, and bless me. In particular ask the gods to give me the wisdom to detect quickly the right roots and herbs."

Kabiyesi signified his consent with a smile. Then he added that the ancient tradition would be restored there and then. "You, my daughter, as the Bere, will now become the custodian of this powerful and famous basket; but it will be kept in the Senior Wife's quarters. Beres must get married. Then the basket will be inherited by the new Bere. Since it will still remain within the royal compound its power will still be there for me as before. Pick it up my dear child. May the *irunmales* always bless and protect you."

Thereafter the King in all his majesty emerged from his chamber leaning on the arm of his beloved daughter, Bere. The entire court cheered, with all the women kneeling while the men prostrated. The *kakaki* (trumpet) was blaring. This was how Bere became the custodian of the Queen's basket.

THE LEGEND OF ORUNMILA

Introduction

Rev. Canon John King, chaplain to the Bishop of Lagos, was the director of the Lay Preacher's Course for the 1965-66 session in which I participated. He made it mandatory for every candidate to select and study an aspect of one indigenous religion for the purpose of comparison with Christianity. A brief report of each candidate's findings was to be submitted to him by the end of June 1966; the course ended in September 1966. I decided to study Ifa (the Yoruba god of wisdom and divination), including worship and the act of divination itself. Accordingly, my father arranged for an old friend of his, Pa Fagbemi, an experienced and renowned Ifa priest, to have me as a pupil for six months. Pa Fagbemi was about ten years older than my father, and at that time he had four full-time pupils. I was not part of that group, so he gave me two separate sessions per week, from 3-5pm on Tuesdays and Thursdays. As the men's Bible class in my church was held on Thursdays at 6pm I usually went to the class direct from Pa Fagbemi's residence.

One Thursday I arrived early and spent the waiting period reading my Yoruba Bible. I normally read my Yoruba Bible aloud to myself to ensure that my pronunciation and inflections were correct, as after the course I would be expected to give one sermon every month in Yoruba. It was, therefore, essential that my Yoruba should be perfect, including the usage of appropriate proverbs, adages and sayings. On this occasion I was going through the portion to be studied at the Bible class later that evening, Matthew 6: 25-34. As I reached verse 33, "But seek ye first the kingdom of God, and his righteousness; and all these things shall be added unto you", I heard from Pa's room, his voice being clear and loud, *okare omo; be e gangan lo yo loju opon mi*, meaning "Bless you, my

47

son. That was exactly what was revealed on my divining plate." I smiled and thought to myself, Pa must have misunderstood or misheard what I was reading or he must have been discussing something entirely different with his client.

When the client left I was invited in by Pa. "Bode," he said, "I dare say you smiled when you heard my voice." I could only smile again when I said, "I thought that you were addressing your client." He then repeated that what I was reading coincided with what his previous divination had revealed. With incredulity showing on my face Pa said, "Let me explain myself." He then told me the most astounding story (as I then thought) I had ever heard in my life.

"You must have forgotten that at the very beginning of time mankind came from Adamo (Adam), the father of all men. After the great flood, man then started to trace his new beginning from Noah, and that was why any man of good and proper behaviour amongst the Yoruba was, and still is, referred to as *omo-luwa-bi*, a corruption of *omo-Noah-bi*. It was after the flood that men, in their misguided wisdom, decided to build a tower which would reach up to heaven, so that if God decided to visit the earth with another flood they could all climb up to his abode. God came and inspected the tower, and then he made the common language in use at the time no longer intelligible to them; as a result they parted ways and scattered all over the face of the earth. From then until now men have worshipped that same 'almighty being' as each and everyone knew best. It was only those misguided ones, who did not believe in him, who failed to do so, as a result of which they denied the existence of their maker." Pa ended on this note: "Why do you think that the white priest sent you to learn from me?" He then asked, "Would you rather go to your Bible Class now, or listen to the story of Orunmila?" I opted to listen to him. So Pa Fagbemi continued.

* * *

A long time ago, before the *irunmales* (Yoruba gods) first visited Ile-Ife, an incident occurred in a village near Usi. Just before nightfall, an old man with white hair and a white flowing beard, dressed all in white, walked into the compound of the *Bale* (Head of the village). Although leaning heavily on a white walking stick, his sedate strides could best be described as majestic. He had a commanding presence with the appearance of a sage. On seeing him, the *Bale*, who was reclining on his couch, quickly got up to welcome the visitor. After having been offered a seat the old man introduced himself as Omo-Onire of Obameri, on the outskirts of Ile-Ife. He said that he had come to make a request from the *Bale*.

"*Alagba* (revered elder), what may that be?"

"My servants after a long and hard search reported to me just this morning that this village would be the most suitable place for me and my sons to live."

"What is special about this small village, which gives it a preference to *Obameri* which is obviously a much larger village?"

"That exactly is the reason; *Obameri* is much too large for my youngest son."

"*Alagba*, please explain that to me."

"I have four sons; the youngest of them is a thinker."

"What do you mean a thinker?"

Right from the age of eight he started behaving as an adult. At six, when the neighbours started to call him *atikekere sogbon* (the young but wise one), at first I took no notice. By the time he was ten he started behaving like a wise old man! Often he would sit apart with a far-away look, like someone deep in thought; he seemed to be seeing things that we could not. Then he started using the voice of an adult. Again, as he didn't talk much, at first this went unnoticed. To hear him speaking, without actually seeing the speaker, you would think that you were hearing the voice of an old man! His wisdom and logic far exceeded his years. By the time he turned sixteen, which was about a month ago, he spoke with the wisdom of an older person. He was always seeking remote and quiet places for his meditation. It was then that I became convinced that there was something unique about him. So I asked my servants to seek a much smaller village with fewer people than in Obameri. It was reported to me only this morning that a small village surrounded by hills, sheltered and serene, had been found; they thought it was ideal. So I got here about two hours ago, along the side of the stream with the bamboo grove on its bank. Guided by one of my servants and one of your villagers who is his friend, I strolled around the entire village. I was struck by the peacefulness. I became convinced that they were right. Therefore I thought that I would seek your permission before I return home later this evening."

"If you don't mind me asking, what do you do for a living?" said the *Bale*.

"Have you ever heard of Ijana[6] palm oil?"

"Everyone knows about it."

"I own the forest where the oil is produced. The farm as well as the entire Ijana forests adjoining it have belonged to my family from time immemorial. I earn the best part of my income from both of them. In addition I breed ducks and pigeons, both of which are known for their good quality. The climate here as well as your ponds will suit both the ducks and the pigeons."

Following this the *Bale* and the sage discussed a number of other things, presumably so as to know each other better. Intuition told the *Bale* that the coming of the sage would bring a lot of good to his village and to its people. Accordingly he granted the sage's request.

Two weeks after this initial visit, the sage and his four sons and other members of their families and servants arrived at the village. The *Bale* allocated them a large tract of fertile land towards the

---

[6] I have often wondered if there is any connection between the name of Omo-onire's youngest son, Ajana and Ijana forest.

bamboo grove. Though the *Bale* had indicated that no payment was required, he took the money offered for the land, at the insistence of the sage. The sons of Omo-Onire who settled with him in the village were called: Oju-Ekun, *omo alara*; Arogbodo-Lewa, *omo ajero*; Gegelasa, *omo inu igbin kanko*; and Ajana.

The eldest son, Oju-Ekun, was a man of commerce with a great zest for the acquisition of money, wealth, and possessions. He was forever striving to become wealthier and wealthier. The second brother, Arogbodo Lewa, was a handsome playboy, too keen on the opposite sex, and as vain as *Okin*, the peacock. Gegelasa, the third one, popularly known as *Olomo Yindoyindo*, 'the one with an uncountable number of children,' was a great lover of kids. He was always looking for stray and neglected children so that he could cuddle and care for them. The youngest son was Ajana, the thinker. He was of a serious nature, and enjoyed conversing with old men. He was always seeking after knowledge. When he was not doing that he kept himself to himself.

When Omo-Onire had become old and frail, and thought that he was about to join his ancestors, he called his eldest son and said to him: "My child, I am about to be called home for my final rest. I have summoned you so that I can bless you with my *ase* (potent words), and so that you may ask for anything special you desire."

"Father, I wish to have wealth surpassing that of anyone else."

"Don't you think that you already have enough?" asked the old man.

"You asked for my wish and I have stated it."

His father blessed him confirming that his wish had been granted. The sage then sent for Arogbodo-Lewa. He posed the same question to him. He asked for beautiful women. "Don't you already have them to your heart's content?" the sage asked. "Father, you wanted to know my wish: I want women!" The father then asked if Arogbodo-Lewa was aware of the saying of the Yoruba elders that "a man who is overly fond of the opposite sex is likely to die by their hands."

"I am, and I'm willing to take the risk!"

The old man blessed him, adding that his wish had been granted.

The sage next sent for Gegelasa and repeated the same question. He asked for more children. He too was blessed and his wish granted.

When sent for, Ajana's request in reply to his father was this: "Father, my wish is to find the way that leads to *Olodumare*'s[7] abode, to enable me to offer him my services as his messenger, to interpret his messages to all men, so that the world may be made better."

His father was amazed: "What put that into your head?"

"I am certain that such a request will benefit all of mankind." The sage nodded, smiled and blessed him. He ended by saying, "My son, your wish has been granted." Not long after this, the sage died and was buried. He was mourned by the entire village.

In accordance with his wish Oju-Ekun became very wealthy. All kinds of people, from far and near came to borrow money from him. He accumulated many bondsmen[8] and extended his farms. Many of his debtors blessed and praised him while many others uttered *epe* (potent curses). No one was surprised when he died in his prime. In accordance with the prevailing custom, all his possessions – wives, wealth, children, and bondsmen – were divided into three equal parts and given to his three brothers. It is said that one of his descendants became the Oba Alara of Ilara Ekiti.

Similarly Arogbodo-Lewa was next to die due to the stress of his life with so many wives and concubines. All he possessed was divided in two, with equal portions going to each of his two remaining brothers. It is said that one of his descendants became

[7] The supreme Yoruba God
[8] Tied workers who can only be released by paying back a "bond"

Oba Ajero of Ijero Ekiti.

In due course, Gegelasa also died. The main cause of his death was the anxiety and strain of managing his countless children, biological, adopted, and inherited.

Now Ajana, the only surviving brother, had inherited all the possessions of his three deceased brothers: wealth, wives, children, bondsmen, and many other things. Ajana asked the messengers who brought the inheritance, the male children, as well as all the bondsmen, to build some huts, in fact as many as would be needed to house them all and to contain all the inheritance - hence the saying *Ajana olojule egbeje* (Ajana the possessor of 1400 huts). He released the bondsmen, and giving them farms and huts, liberating them, in fact. He allowed all the women to take husbands of their choice. From amongst the young men, he selected some who were willing to learn at his feet, and they became his pupils. And so he continued to think, and meditate, and to strive for peace and unity among all men. It was reported that after some time he disappeared from the village, which had increased enormously in size and wealth. Where he went no one knew, but he was greatly revered by all.

When the *irunmales* later paid their first visit to Ile-Ife, the place believed by the Yoruba to be the cradle of mankind, it was said that Ajana was one of them, now identified as Orunmila, god of wisdom and divination. He revealed the ways and wishes of Olodumare to men, through his divination. Among his names was *Eleri Ipin* (the one who witnesses the choice of destiny by each and every human being).

Comment

I was astounded by Pa Fagbemi's story, especially because of the features which seemed similar to Christianity. I was impressed that an old man of seventy-five could remember so vividly a tale he had originally been told forty-five years earlier and could recall it so well. There were no hesitations in his delivery, no faltering at all. When I asked for clarifications in some parts which appeared obscure, he gave me further explanations in an easy and candid way. His lucidity was impressive. I then asked for the secret of such a retentive memory and power of recall. He said that there were three main reasons for the quality of his memory. Firstly, he had understudied a very knowledgeable and experienced master, the *araba* of *Usi*, the most senior Ifa priest of the time, under whom he had served ten years, the last three as his *amu'gba legbe* (personal assistant). Secondly, he used the '*isoye*' provided by the *araba*. When I asked him what '*isoye*' was, he explained that it was a herbal preparation which aided retentive memory and the recall of information as and when required. He added that he was still using it. He gave me some, which I accepted merely out of courtesy. In my ignorance, and due to my lack of faith, I later threw it away believing that I needed no aid to memory. Thirdly, he said that the *araba* who had told him the story of *Orunmila*, also taught him various formulae to aid retention and recall. Pa emphasised that the most important thing he had learnt from the *araba* was the need to remember the critical order of sequences; so, for example, in divination: who it was who came for divination; what was the purpose or cause; what Ifa revealed; what steps needed to be taken (usually these were sacrifices); what should be the types and nature of the sacrifices. Expressed in another way, the diviner, the one seeking divination, the purpose, the revelation, and the sacrifices prescribed.

Pa Fagbemi stressed that once you remembered the sequence, other things naturally fell into place. Here was a classic case of how high-level memorization functions within a primary oral culture. My own childhood training – for example, my father's requirement that I memorize songs from the traditional festivals such as *Oro* and *Balufon*– has helped me too to have a strong memory. In setting down the oral story which I have crafted into this written tale I did not need to refer to my original report given to Canon King in June 1966 – except on one point, the name of the village near Ife which Omo-Onire came from. In this way I hope I have kept something of the original feeling of an oral transmission through the generations.

The Similarities between Ifa and the Scriptures

I still find remarkable the references made by Pa Fagbemi to various passages in the Bible. These include Genesis 1:26 (The creation of man); Genesis 6:9–13 (Noah and the flood); and Genesis 11:1–9 (the tower of Babel). The central parable-like passage in his story, where those concerned too much with wealth, sex, and the preservation of their line, make choices leading to their own disaster, finds many echoes in the New Testament, notably, for example, Matthew 6: 25–34, quoted above and which may have provoked Pa Fagbemi to tell me the story, and Galatians 5:10-26, which contrasts the fruits of the spirit with those of the flesh.

I also find striking in the legend the emergence of Ajana as Orunmila – that is to say, the good man becoming a god. Clearly, these matters could only be studied properly within the context of comparative religion and I do not have space to treat them fully here. They are part of my ongoing interest in oral culture, which I shall continue to research in this and related areas. In view of the ancient nature of Pa Fagbemi's oral story, passed down through many generations, I decided to give it the title "The Legend of Orunmila", though, as should now be clear, it could equally be called "The Parable of Orunmila."

THE EBIRIPO EPISODE

Introduction

We lived in Lagos, but while we were in the village during our holidays we stayed with our grandmother, who was called Iya-Agba. She was on her own since her husband, our grandfather, had died, except, of course, that she had servants and lots of relations staying with her.

We spent a lot of time with Granny in her kitchen which was in effect also her living room. One day we sat there watching her prepare the *dipon*, a mixture of beans and maize cooked with palm oil, which was to be taken to the *aro* – that is, a group or collective that helps with farm-work – for them to eat the next day.

Dupe, my cousin, was always asking questions. It was she who started the conversation about *ebiripo*, steamed grated cocoyam with palm oil and pepper.

"Grandmother," she began, "when we were at Ikenne yesterday we ate some delicious *ebiripo* which we enjoyed so much. I wanted to buy some more when we visited *okerobu*, the market-on-the-hill, today. You can imagine my surprise when the woman said: "You won't find it in Ogere market". Bunmi chipped in, thinking that they'd misunderstood something, but then another woman said, "It's taboo to sell *ebiripo* in the market or anywhere else in public in Ogere. Ask Granny when you get home. She'll back me up."

Grandma smiled saying that the woman was correct: "It is forbidden, and that has been the case since the *ebiripo* episode ages ago."

"Why is it forbidden here, especially when such a delicious food is freely sold in Ikenne and all over Remo?" asked Dupe. Grandma replied with a chuckle: "You children are fond of ferreting things out." The actual words used by Grandma in the Remo dialect were "*Ewven omode wve wven le topenpen urhun rhe nidi koko ju."*

"But Grandma, what's wrong to ask what everyone seems to know anyway?" retorted Dupe, clearly upset that she could not get an answer.

"Who says you have no right to know?" interjected the old woman. "I'm merely referring to your nosiness!"

"We don't normally live here; shouldn't we ask questions?"

"All right, I'll tell you," Grandma said. "All of you, come and sit down."

So Grandma started her story.

* * *

"Long, long ago Olipakala, an Ife prince, established Ogere[9] as a village by drawing together some smaller hamlets, sixteen in all. The new village encompassed Agbele, the largest of the hamlets, in the valley between it and what came to be known as Iperu, and other hamlets right up to Logorun, which then had its famous market lit at night by many earthenware lamps, and its outskirts went right up to the Ogun River. The story I am about to tell you arose from an event which happened about thirty years after the establishment of Ogere.

Ogere became well known for *esuru*, a type of yam common in the Remo area, which local people like to eat, and *afon*, African breadfruit, which is spherical in shape, about eighteen inches in diameter and weighs up to fifteen kilos. Its delicious cooked seeds were commonly eaten with a relish; it tastes good and is used for the prevention and cure of guinea-worms. The Ogere market also has its special rice ...

"What's special about Ogere's rice Grandma?" the irrepressible Dupe interposed. "If you keep interrupting I shall not continue the story," Grandma said sternly. Dupe apologised and Grandma

---

[9] An article in the *Punch* of Friday 16 October, 2009 (pp. 29–31) affirms that Ogere was established in 1401.

continued her tale.

The rice grown in Ogere farms has a special flavour which is equalled only by that in Ofada village, one of Ogere's neighbouring villages a few miles from here. The two villages have a special quality of soil that produces rice with a unique flavour. As a result, all and sundry flock to Ogere market for its rice as well as for its *afon*.

Suddenly our neighbours in Sinwun and Owode laid claim to the Ogere farms beyond Ogun and Edu rivers. At first, our ancestors thought it was a joke, but the incursions into the farms by the Sinwun farmers continued. On two occasions this led to serious confrontations. The intruders were met with so much force that they desisted for some time and Ogere thought that that was the end of the matter. But it was not so.

The last of the incidents almost turned into full-scale war. It took all the hunters and the entire troop of young Olopere warriors, the youths responsible for security and defence of the village, to repel the rapacious invaders. Again, it was thought that an end had been put to our neighbours' provocations.

Ten years after Olipakala had established Ogere, the tribesmen from the hills beyond Owode had sought an alliance with the Ogere warriors in order to repel some invaders from Idaomi, also known as Egun or Ajase, who wanted to take over Ota, an Egba settlement, with its large fields of sugar cane. A long war between the two factions resulted. So Ogunware, the foremost blacksmith in Ogere at that time, had to establish a new smithy at Ota for the on-the-spot fabrication of weapons of war. This earned him the nickname *agbede Ota ni ile onireke* meaning the eminent blacksmith of Ota in the land of sugar cane.

In fact Ogunware was a renowned hunter as well as a blacksmith. He was originally from Lagere in Ife. He was a member of the body that came over from Ijebu Ode to Ogere under the leadership of Olipakala, the founding father of Ogere. He was credited with establishing four smithies, in Lagere at Ife, in Ikoyi Ile, to the north of Ogbomoso, in Itunmaro in Ogere, and at Ota.

Shortly after this, the tribesmen from the hills, with the support of Ogere warriors, defeated the Idaomi invaders. With that victory the people of Ogere thought that all conflict had finally ceased, but unfortunately their neighbours at Sinwun and Owode were still hankering after the Ogere rice fields.

Some time after the Ota episode, the *Bale* of Owode sent an emissary to Alegunsen, the then Ologere (*oba*), to request assistance to repel the raiders from Idaomi who they claimed had again invaded the Papa farms just beyond Ofada. No one suspected that it was a ruse, as before then the Owode people had become seemingly friendly with the Ogere community. They bought most of Ogere's production of *esuru* and *alo*, a type of yam, thin, yellowish in colour and slightly sweet in taste, which was as popular as the rice. What is more they paid higher prices than other buyers. Thus the Ogere people were lulled into a false sense of security. Alegunsen and his people heeded the call for help from the supposed friends against the Idaomi. A strong force of the Oloperes and hunters then left for Owode to give the required support.

Here Grandma paused to take a sip of water and to gauge the interest in the young people around her. They were sitting wide-eyed and impatient for her to continue the tale. Grandma took another slow sip of her water, and then continued.

* * *

The incident which is famous in our history took place a day before the annual Balufon festival and dance, for which all the maidens and other women had prepared for months. *Balufon* is the abbreviated form of *Obalufon*, the god considered to be the inventor of weaving and cloth. He is worshipped in Ijebu and Remo areas, and his favourite colour is purple.

Before the festival the women had consumed a lot of *awuje* (Lima beans) cooked with rich palm oil. They believed this made their skin shine for the public display which took place at the festival. The *balufon* drums had all been restrung and retuned; these are the special drums made with the skin of *ekiri,* wild goats. Male members of the four ruling houses of the new Ogere are the custodians of the drums.

The Ogere fighters left for Owode the day before the festival, much to the regret of both the warriors and the girls, for it was at this festival that partners were appraised and chosen for marriage. So the entire community was in something of a subdued mood.

All the women traders, with the exception of greedy Efunbola, chose not to go to the Ajura market on the day of the Balufon. Efunbola was reluctant to miss the market and decided to slaughter four goats, instead of the usual two, to meet the demand created by the absence of her fellow traders. She and her niece, Ninse, were the only travellers going from Ogere to Ajura that morning. What enticed Ninse to accompany her was the tryst between her and her admirer from Lapoyo who was to meet her at Ajura. It was just as well she went! Had Ninse not gone to Lapoyo in search of her admirer (who had failed to show up at Ajura) the history of Ogere might have been very different. Some even say that Ogere might have been wiped out of existence.

A pleasant surprise awaited Efunbola at Ajura. Something that had never happened before, some strange men came and purchased her entire basket of *edenru* (roasted meat), much to the chagrin of her usual customers. When she asked others in the market who the men were, no one knew. All she was told was that they had arrived the night before, buying up everything and eating all the food in the town. Of course all the market women were pleased to make a lot of money off the strangers.

Efunbola was not complacent by nature and she was highly sensitive. Her intuition told her that something was amiss, and shrewdly she asked her niece to enquire discreetly what was really going on. In the meantime she went to buy a few things to take home.

Ninse who had been racking her brains for excuses to sneak away to find her young admirer who had failed to turn up as arranged, was delighted. She said to herself cryptically, '*Awodi to nre bara, efufu ta ndi pe oni okuku muse ya*', ('the hawk that is Ibara bound is lifted at the tail by the wind; it says, now to business'). She was very pleased at the encouragement to do what she had wanted to do anyway. She went quickly on her way to Lapoyo village. She met her admirer who was cautiously leaving the village and asked him why he failed to meet her in Ajura.

He explained that the Bale of Lapoyo had banned all travel for two days, adding that it was with a great deal of difficulty that he had been able to escape his father's strict watch and leave the village. Ninse asked why such a ban should be imposed. He replied that, at first, he did not know exactly why but while eavesdropping the night before he had heard a neighbour telling his father that Ogere people were not to be told about the imminent invasion.

"Invasion?!" asked Ninse, with a terrified look. Her boyfriend then explained that apparently the Bale of the village had been given a huge bribe by the Owode chieftain to ensure that no one travelled to Ogere to warn them about the attack that had been planned. This was because Owode was aware of the friendly relationship between Lapoyo and Ogere. Lapoyo had the lion's share of the Ogere's rice in exchange for their palm oil.

Ninse's boyfriend then explained: "Besides, the Bale had assured the elders of Lapoyo that Owode soldiers could be easily defeated by the tough Ogere fighters. I was, however, dismayed when I later heard my father telling another neighbour that the Ogere warriors had been lured out of town. It was a carefully laid plan since there was no invasion by the Idaomi."

"What can we do?" asked the Ninse, very worried. "I don't know. Besides, it's rather late in the day and it will be dark soon," answered her boyfriend.

"That should not deter us; we must set out with all speed to Ogere immediately," countered Ninse. Thus the young lover had to run alongside Ninse. With the cunning of a hound, he suggested that they should keep to the forest in case the Ajura-Ogere footpath was being watched. They both ran all the way to Oke-odo near Agbere before they stopped, out of sheer fatigue.

After a little rest they reached and crossed Joboyo stream as the sun was setting. In their effort to avoid being seen from the Ogun river end, they got into a large enclosed area where there was a thatched hut. With the crackling of the dried twigs and leaves the inhabitant of the hut heard their movement.

Out of the hut a woman's voice inquired, "Who are you who dare to approach this ground, sacred to Yemogun!" They were rooted to the spot. They could hear the snapping of twigs and leaves as a gaunt woman emerged. "This is forbidden ground, don't you know? Don't you see the *marigho* (palm frond) hanging up there? You are approaching a sacred grove. You are lucky I stopped you just in time; otherwise the goddess herself would have struck you dead," said the woman sternly.

Ninse was now shaking, and she fell at the woman's feet and held them in the manner of a suppliant. Both said to the woman, "Good mother, please help us to save Ogere."

"Save Ogere from what!?" asked the astonished keeper of the Yemogun grove. Ninse was still panting as she recounted what she had learnt, and her friend echoed her words. The old woman, whose initial anger had now calmed, invited them in and gave them cold water from an *amu* (a clay pot). She then asked them to repeat their story slowly. After hearing their remarkable tale again, she remarked: "My children, you must be right. Since this morning I have had the premonition of danger, especially when the wind suddenly started to howl, with all the birds hurtling and fluttering over the grove. To make matters worse, the dogs also joined in the howling; theirs were such blood-curdling howls, I wondered then what it could be. Now I know. Eat some *afon* and *eja-aro* (catfish) as you must be hungry. Then I'll send you to the *Iyaloja* who, as you know, is the most powerful woman in Ogere."

Grandmother paused again to take a few sips of water. By this time, the children around her were desperate for her to continue with the exciting story.

After the two finished their meal, Grandmother told them, the old woman spoke almost in a whisper. "Listen carefully; go slowly and look cautiously left and right before you cross to the other side of the footpath to Mapagha. Do you know the house of Iyaloja? Go there. Show her this staff of office. Ask Iyaloja, and the Iyalode, the leaders of the elders, to come immediately. Tell her it is extremely urgent, but don't tell her what you have told me. Go. May Lipakala guard you both."

Fortunately the *Iyaloja* was at home, and she was not yet asleep. Before they knocked on the door, she had enquired who was approaching at such a late hour. She then peeped out carrying an earthenware lamp as it was already dark. "We have a message for you, respected Iyaloja, from the old woman at the grove. She gave us her staff of office to assure you that we come from her, and she told us to leave the staff with you. You and Iyalode Efuntolabo must go to see her tonight as soon as possible," they explained.

"The matter must be extremely important and urgent for her to entrust this ancient staff to such youthful hands as yours." Pointing to Ninse she said, "You must be a virgin, otherwise you could not have taken seven steps without having toppled over."

"Yes mama, I am."

"Who is your mother?"

"Moloko, of Maro compound," Ninse replied.

"*Ah Egbe mi* (a member of my age-group)" the old woman

intoned. "Greet her for me. I hope to see her in the morning."

The entire village was thrown into turmoil to hear the *Oba*'s village crier at the first cockcrow clanging his gong with the metal bar. This was a clarion call, by the authority of the Ologere, to all women of Ogere, young and old. "Following this announcement you should all assemble promptly in front of the Iyaloja's residence. It is important and urgent that you all do so. Failure to comply will have terrible consequences." Within half an hour of this call the entire compound of Iyaloja was filled with the women, many of them without their head-ties *(idiku)*, but all with their *oja* firmly wrapped around their waists. They were surprised to be confronted not with Iyaloja alone, for beside her was Iyalode Efuntolabo, the *Jagun* of the foremost female *egbe*.

While they were still wondering what was so urgent, out of Iyaloja's front door stepped the *Yeye* herself, mother of the community, the *Alase* of Yemogun, decked in her purple *aso-oke*, a locally woven traditional dyed wrapper, over which was her white *oja* firmly in place, white *saki*, insignia of her position, and over her right shoulder a longish white horsetail fly-whisk with a handle covered in white beads. Another white *saki* was worn as a headdress over her white hair. She was clutching the *opa ase onide*, the ancient brass staff of her office, with the effigy of a dove as a handle. Though frail looking she was a sight to behold. Her unblinking eyes, which seemed to take in all that was around her, were shining. Her genial manner and comportment confirmed that she was indeed a high priestess. She was a sight to behold. Her presence was awe-inspiring.

Despite her gaunt frame, the *Yeye* exuded authority as the *Alase* of the revered goddess. A great hush fell when, before speaking, she raised her right hand, now holding the white fly-whisk. Her staff of office had been transferred to the left. Her sonorous voice vibrated with emotion, yet it was calm and clear as she spoke –

so much so, that the old men looking from afar off could guess the meaning of her words, designed to urge and motivate, and to instil in the women the spirit of Yemogun. She ended on a note which all the women echoed: "Yes", they all shouted loudly, 'The one who supports us and never deserts us, Lipakala, will be with us. He will disgrace and defeat our enemies. Amen. Amen."- in the Remo dialect, *Lipakala, 'agbeni me dehin e te'ni nehin, e to owvon osika n'oju; wva ngha.* Soon after, they all dispersed in a jubilant mood.

The remaining menfolk in the village were inside their own compounds and the whole village was hushed. The atmosphere was charged. Suspense and an air of expectation hung in the air. The entire village was quiet except for Iya Ojuroye's compound where all the women had converged. The compound was as busy as a beehive. Some of the men and women, old and young, were busy peeling the skin off the coco-yams, others were busy grating them. Many women were engrossed wrapping the blended cocoyam in *aiba* leaves. Soon these were arranged into large earthenware pots. Underneath them were portable ovens consisting of pots with parts cut away for inserting firewood. The fires were blazing. Within the hour all the women except Ojuroye and Iyaloja had disappeared.

After an hour, the women were back with braided hair and smart purple wrappers and *oja* (waist bands). Later, they carried oval-shaped covered calabashes on their heads, and then filed in an orderly procession towards the Ogun river by way of the *panoda,* where paths crossed. There was a hush as they crossed the narrow bamboo bridge that spanned the Ogun River, coming down on the Oke-odo side. Soon many stalls appeared, manned by beautiful women, all decked in purple.

* * *

It was time for Grandmother to take another few sips of water, letting the tension rise among her attentive young audience. After what seemed an eternity to the children, while Grandmother coughed, patted her chest, and wiped her mouth, she continued her narrative.

At Owode as dawn broke it was quite a job waking up all the sleeping men, the group that had suddenly appeared the previous evening, Their leaders had to drag and kick them to get them up. Many were holding their heads in their hands. Several walked unsteadily until one of the leaders started splashing cold water on all of them, on their heads, faces and chests. The smell of *akara* (fried bean balls) and *moyinmoyin* (steamed blended beans wrapped in leaves), helped to complete the task of waking them.

They all descended on the food laid out on the grass beneath the trees. After eating, they started their military march. By the time they got around the Ajura bend leading straight to Ogere many of them were already tired. Oke asked if they had had breakfast. When some answered yes, he replied sharply, when? "Just now," he said, "but I feel empty. I need to eat some more." Most of them felt the same but were ashamed to admit it. The enormous quantities of goat pepper soup accompanied by *kekeye* (a strong alcoholic drink) that they had consumed so happily the night before had taken its inevitable toll on them. The *eko* (ground corn wrapped in leaves after steaming) and *akara* as well as the *moyinmoyin* served earlier that morning could not satisfy them.

By the time they reached the bridge at Agbere they were puffing and panting. The man leading the vanguard opened his eyes. He thought he was dreaming. Right in front of them were stalls behind which were pretty women unwrapping what looked like *ekuru* (steamed ground beans without oil) but with a more pleasing aroma. Whatever it was, it had an unusually arresting and enticing smell. *Oke abolonjeku*, 'Guzzle Guts' himself, the front man, was the first to taste the delicious *ebiripo*. "We have reached the abode of the dwellers of the enchanted vale," he yelled. "Come and eat," he encouraged the others. The entire body of men went scrambling for the *ebiripo*. When they had satisfied themselves they became exceedingly thirsty. In one mad rush they made for the River Ogun. Down they went on their knees and bellies, lapping at the water. They were all so mad with thirst that those behind surged forward in a frenzied haste to reach the water as well. Thus they trampled over those in front. As they all drank, some slid forward, others slid straight into the river, yet others were pushed into it from the rear by their comrades who were desperate to satisfy their thirst.

It was a scene of utter chaos. Then came a hush. The resulting quiet was indescribable. The remaining few in the rear looked on mesmerized. It was as if they were in a trance. Though they had the urge to flee, their legs seemed like lead. Amidst the confusion, like men dreaming, they saw more beautiful women – to some of them, it was like a hallucination – emerging from the bushes around them, urging them to eat and refresh themselves. The scent of the tempting food was like something from outside the world of mortals. Completely mesmerised, they fell on the neatly folded parcels of food, now being unwrapped by the shapely hands of the women whose smiling faces enticed them to eat more.

Having eaten their fill, like those who are possessed, they all made their way towards the river, causing yet another stampede and confusion. They were, however, hampered by the piles of bodies that had previously been trampled on and who lay dead or dying in front of them in all kinds of strange postures. They stumbled over these bodies. All too soon there came a great hush, like the silence of the grave. The much-anticipated battle never took place. Instead the attacking force was defeated by those who are sometimes described as the weaker sex. The women had won the day. So ended the *ebiripo* episode, with the complete rout of the invaders.

Thus came true, though with a twist, the saying of the Yoruba elders, *b'okurin ri ejo ti obirin pa a; ani k'ejo sa ti ku*, meaning 'what does it matter if a man is first to see the snake which is later killed by the woman', an expression usually used for cowardly males, though that was certainly was not the case on this occasion. What mattered, in this critical instance, was that Ogere was saved.

Some said that Yemogun, the revered wife of *Olipakala* herself, had appeared to inspire the women. To commemorate this momentous event the *Oba* and *Igbimo* of Ogere forbade from that time on the public sale in Ogere of *ebiripo*, the fatal food that had saved Ogere and its people. The ban remains in force, from that day to this.

———————➤◆◀———————

THE KING'S GATEKEEPER

There was a well-known market in the domain of Oba Wasere which was popularly known as Ilu Idera. Idera market, right in the centre of the town, was large and offered an extensive variety of the goods. The local inhabitants, however, fondly called their market *'emi Idera'* meaning the heart of Idera community, which it was indeed, as everything, except the *oba's* palace, revolved around it. It was not merely a place for commerce, it was also a centre for local entertainments, with its *sakara, alugba* and *ogidigbo* forms of music. It was great fun to listen to and dance to these melodious tunes in the evenings. It soothed the nerves, made you forget your worries and gave you new energy.

Idera was also famous for its stilt dancers and acrobats. It was also the place to exchange news and disseminate information, especially about foreign and distant lands. The section of the market for *aso oke* – the locally woven and dyed cloth – as well as for rams and goats, was the most popular in the entire district. Idera was indeed the heart and centre of Idera township.

Oba Wasere, whose full name was Awaye Wasere (meaning one sent into the world to make it better) was a very popular monarch. He was widely known for his generosity and geniality; he was greatly revered. He wished everyone within his domain to be happy and contented. He had what is generally referred to as open arms and an open heart. It delighted him no end to receive and entertain his subjects as well as strangers.

Anyone who wanted to see the King, no matter how lowly, was allowed to do so, provided whoever it was came at the prescribed time and was willing to wait, no matter how long it took. One other attraction was that no visitor, no matter how humble, left the palace without a gift.

This generous practice by Oba Wasere was considered strange, because it was contrary to the practice at that time among other *obas*, who believed in and followed to the letter the old custom of kings receiving presents, so as to induce favours. This practice was once referred to as *somi, somi la ngbo n'ile oba*, meaning 'help me off-load from my head the present for *kabiyesi* (his majesty)'.

Unsurprisingly, the king's gatekeeper was always kept busy and he enjoyed his role tremendously. Nite, the gatekeeper, was a law unto himself. Nobody, except the high and mighty, was allowed into the palace without a solemn promise that at least one tenth of whatever was received from the king, or its equivalent in cash, would be passed on to him.

Almost everyone knew about this obnoxious practice, yet they all condoned it, as they would want to come back, again and again, to a warm welcome from Nite. So they all submitted to his odious ways; no one wanted to bell the cat! Although the gatekeeper's real name was not Nite, his unpleasant character had earned him, from the populace, this notorious nickname deriving from *Alainitelorun*, one who was never contented. The number and weight of curses heaped on Nite daily can be imagined.

One day, a man named Nimbe – whose full name was Olorunmbe, (God exists) visited the palace. As usual he promised a tenth of whatever present he got from the King to the gatekeeper. Nimbe was a very poor peasant who lived a long distance from the palace. He walked with a limp that made the long distance difficult and tiring for him. As a result, he visited the King only once a year. Aware of his circumstance, the King was always more generous with him. In addition to money the King would give him food such as yams, corn and fruit. On this occasion as in the past Nite took his share of the king's largesse.

Nimbe eventually got home after a very exhausting journey to and from the palace completely fatigued. His friend and neighbour, Alatunse (meaning he who makes amends) helped him to unload his basket and to put its contents inside his hut.

While doing so Alatunse observed the odd number of yams and other items. There were only three yam tubers and eighteen oranges. Also a few bananas were missing from the bunch. On asking how this came about Nimbe explained that it was due to the 'toll' exacted by Nite.

The following week Alatunse decided to visit the King's palace. On arrival at the palace Nite exacted from Alatunse the usual promise of payment. Alatunse, as customary, was received graciously by the King. When he was leaving the King asked him what he would like as a present out of the range of gifts on offer.

"None of these" he said.

"What is it then you wish for?" asked the King.

"Twenty strokes of the cane," he said.

"That's odd" observed the King. "May I ask why?" he added.

Alatunse then explained the bargain between him and Nite. The King was astounded and furious. He, the benevolent monarch, could not believe that such a dastardly practice of extortion could be happening within his domain, let alone in his palace.

He then admonished everyone present, adding, 'Did not our elders say *Bi ara ile eni ba nje kokoro buruku, ti a ko so fun, huruhere e ko ni i je ka sun loru,* which means if a member of one's household is eating bad insects and is not cautioned, his or her hacking cough will not permit one any sleep during the night'. If you do not advise your brother you will share in his misfortune.

With righteous indignation the King ordered Nite to be brought immediately before him. When questioned by the courtiers and confronted by Alatunse, he confessed. "How long has this practice been going on?" asked the King. All those present within the King's audience room chorused that the practice had existed for as long as Nite had been the gatekeeper.

The King was exceedingly sad to hear it. He then asked for one of the guards to be called in to administer the flogging; not on Alatunse but on Nite and not twenty strokes but twice as many. In addition Nite was immediately sacked as gatekeeper and banished from the King's domain. Alatunse was highly commended for bringing Nite's corrupt practices to the attention of the King. He was also presented with very handsome gifts. In making the presentation the King's chief Counsellor said:

"This incident has reaffirmed the truth of the Yoruba saying '*ijo gbogbo ni t'ole; ijo kan ni ti onihun*', which means 'whereas its every day for the thief the owner has only one, the day of reckoning, which is both important and salutary. You have indeed lived up to your good name, Alatunse (he who makes amends). May many others in this land emulate your conduct."

THE THIEF AND THE WHITE CHIEF

Oganla village with its hills and valleys is very picturesque. You can approach the village from different directions but the main route from its nearest neighbouring village, Ipele, is by far the most beautiful. Coming from Ipele one has to descend into the valley before climbing a very high hill to enter Oganla The ancient trees on both sides of the rough stony road cast their leafy branches over the entire stretch forming a shaded tunnel. A tired visitor would be tempted to sit beneath one of the trees to take a rest before entering the village. This haven of peace is one of the many attractions which make Oganla a well loved place.

Many of the men in the village are farmers but there are also a few traders and craftsmen: blacksmiths, masons, bricklayers, carpenters and wood carvers. The village has one famous gold- and silversmith and also a second-hand clothes dealer, who is a very popular man. He is jocularly referred to as the friend of Kasali, who is one of the most flamboyant and popular characters in Oganla. Tall, handsome, and amiable, Kasali is liked by all, especially by the opposite sex.

Many of the women in the village are housewives. Those of them who carry on one trade or another usually do so from home. By far the most popular trade is cooking and selling food such as rice, *dipon* (a mixture of beans and corn cooked with palm oil), *moyinmoyin* (steamed blended beans with palm oil wrapped in leaves), *amala* (steamed yam flour), pounded yam, *ogi* (pounded maize soaked in water prior to being made into paste) and *awuje* which is made from lima beans.

Oganla is a very lively and happy village. With its rapid development it is on the verge of becoming a town. It hosts many festivals: *oro* which some say is an *orisa* (a god) - *oro*, the roaring bull which makes its loud voice heard by all. In ancient times its worshippers formed a guild called *osugbo*. There is also the *Agemo* or *Agemon*; this is also an *orisa* worshipped mainly in Ijebu and Remo. Its worshippers are known as Alagemo. *Agemo* is a cult performed in secret and hidden from women. Also popular are Eluku (a type of masquerade) and Balufon, or Obalufon, the name of the god who is considered to be the inventor of clothing and the art of weaving; and *Egungun*, a masquerade which is also well-liked and is generally considered to be the reincarnated spirit of an ancestor. Its dress is *ago* (an especially decorated costume which is a great work of art) and it has an unnatural accentuated voice. Another thrilling masquerade which is equally admired is *asa* which is peculiar to Remo; it is called *agere* in other Yoruba towns and villages. The performer walks or even dances on stilts, a pair of upright poles with supports for the feet, high above the ground.

Kasali is very sociable. Everybody, young and old, is fond of him and likes his company. Like most of the men he works on his farm in the mornings. In the evenings he is to be seen with a *sakara* musical group. He is equally as good with the drums and on the *agidigbo*. In between singing, dancing and generally entertaining those around he regales the company with stories. He is well known for his numerous jokes and banter. In spite of all his good points everyone knows that Kasali is a thief, indeed, an experienced and clever rogue. Some refer to him as a professional thief. It is generally believed that he has a special *juju* that aids him. One good thing about him is that he never steals from Oganla. He always brings his 'goodies' from other towns and villages. He has a handful of assistants who are euphemistically referred to as his 'apprentices'. They are ardent students in the art of thievery.

It is in the lively setting described above that Kasali and his band operate. Kasali is indeed an extraordinary rogue. If one were to write about all his exploits, it would fill many books; it suffices to recount only two of them here.

Oganla boasts of four churches, or 'missions' as they were known locally in the old days. Of course, the worship of the many indigenous *irunmales* is still widely prevalent. Yet, remarkably, adherents of the various religions mix and interact together cordially. Oganla might be described as a most tolerant and harmonious community.

One of Oganla's missions has a white minister who has lived in the area for over three decades. He was honoured with title of chief by the paramount ruler of the district many years earlier. His residence is about seven miles away from Oganla, and he is also responsible for the entire district comprising of more than thirty towns and villages. Friendly and well known to all, he is generally referred to as the 'white chief'. He is an eloquent speaker and is fluent in Yoruba; thus he has a great rapport with the people.

The white chief and Kasali met some time ago at one of the social gatherings at the mission house. Although Kasali is not a Christian, he is very sociable and generally participates in the mission's social functions. The mission maintains an open door policy in the hope of making new converts. During a conversation between the two men, the priest jokingly referred to Kasali's reputation.

"I am intrigued by the powers attributed to your unique *juju*," the white chief remarked.

"Do you believe the stories?" asked Kasali.

"You may fool simple folks with such tales, but a man of God like me cannot be intimidated or impressed by them," the white chief affirmed.

"So why don't we put it to the test?" asked Kasali.

"How?"

"I can come and operate in your mission house for instance."

"You will fail if you try."

Kasali assured him that he will 'visit' him shortly.

The mission yard in which the white chief lives is by far the largest in the area. This is understandable as it is the district headquarters of the mission. In addition to the chapel, which the local inhabitants call the 'prayer house', it has many other buildings such as the school house, the mission offices, private residences for the teachers and church workers as well as a clinic. The entire mission compound has high brick walls. At night, guards are always on duty. By local standards, the compound is considered impregnable. Apart from the chapel, the residence of the white chief is the most prominent. It is a large brick and timber structure with, various offices and meeting rooms on the ground floor and living rooms and bedrooms on the first floor. The rooms with balconies are spacious and look out on the many tall trees in the compound.

One Friday night, Kasali decides to pay the white chief a visit. It is a dark and moonless night. It is a particularly cool night and all the good people within the mission yard are enjoying the sleep of the just. Kasali has no difficulty in gaining entrance into the yard. Having been to the clinic on several occasions, he knows the compound well. Quietly he climbs one of the tall trees that surround the white chief's residence. In no time he quietly lets himself down onto the chief's bedroom's balcony. As the windows are all wide open, he has no difficulty in making an entry.

The white chief is asleep on his comfortable bed covered by a mosquito net. Beside him is a coffee table on which are various bibles, hymnals and other books. His spectacles are lying on the open bible. Beside it is his favourite pocket watch as well as his wallet. After looking round Kasali decides to take the spectacles, pocket watch and a Bible. He quietly leaves the room through the window by which he gained entry. Using the tree again, he climbs over the fence and melts into the night.

When the white chief wakes up in the morning his pocket watch and spectacles are missing as well as the Bible he was reading before he fell asleep. He wonders if they are in the study on the ground floor and, just as he is about to call his housekeeper, his servant appears at the door to announce a visitor. "At this hour of the day? Who is he? Has he been here before?" asks the white chief. Getting no satisfactory reply from the servant, he decides to go downstairs to investigate. There he finds Kasali, calmly sitting. As the white chief enters, Kasali rises and greets him respectfully.

Since the day of their last conversation the white chief had not given Kasali any thought. "This is a great surprise," says the white chief in response, "and to what do I owe the honour of this visit?"

"I am here, white chief, to enquire after your health and to return to you some property of yours."

Thereupon Kasali brings out from the deep pocket of his *agbada* (robe) a pair of spectacles, the pocket watch and the Bible.

"How did you find them?" the white chief asks.

"I removed them last night when I paid the visit I promised you when we last met. As I did not call professionally, I did not take your wallet which was on the table. What I did, I did for the fun of it and to prove to you, white chief, that the gods of our people are still powerful."

The white chief looks at Kasali in disbelief. "You were actually in my bedroom last night and I did not wake up?" stammers the white chief.

"If there had been one hundred of you in the room I would have entered unseen. White men do not possess all the powers," Kasali responds with bravado.

"Please pardon my ignorance," the white chief replies with a wry smile. The two shake hands and Kasali leaves.

Later that afternoon the white chief recounts the episode to the *Babaijo*, the lay president of a nearby church. He asks him what he thinks of the incident. The *Babaijo* replies promptly. "Kasali is the best of them all. He is widely known in these parts and beyond. We must thank God that he is your friend, as it will not do to have him as an enemy. All the white chief could do is mutter, "We live and learn".

KASALI STRIKES AGAIN

Baba Akin was the *Olorode*, chief and head of the hunters, of Igbehinadun district as his father had been before him. He was very tall and fair-skinned. He had great presence and was highly respected. Usually, the hunters would congregate at his compound in the early evenings about the time the night market began. They discussed matters of common interest. Such gatherings would break up about the time the night market was closing. This was to enable those going on night-hunting to be well fed by their wives.

One night after the hunters had left, my companions and I who were home on holiday decided to visit the *Olorode* who was my late mother's eldest brother. The visit was partly because of the bush meat which visitors were offered in his compound which we city dwellers enjoy eating, and partly to be entertained by his enthralling stories. When we got there Kasali and another man were with the *Olorode*. Soon after our arrival, however, Kasali and his companion left. I supposed this was to enable us enjoy the company of the old man undisturbed. As Kasali was leaving my uncle deliberately wiggled his nose and said '*sio*', a word and gesticulation commonly used in the locality to show disdain; but this apparent disrespect, in this instance, seemed to show a trace of admiration. We thought that this was funny and puzzling. Needless to say, we made no comment.

A few minutes after this, Sanya asked if the old man who had just departed was the notorious thief, Kasali. My uncle nodded. "Is he as clever and as dangerous as was widely reported?" I asked.

"Very much so," answered my uncle. "Why is he different from all the other robbers?" I again asked.

"He relies on the *ofo* and *ogede* (incantations) he learnt from his late father, Bamise, who was in my age group. He was the leading herbalist in this area. Kasali worked under him as an apprentice for many years and he learnt a lot from him. Kasali has more knowledge of spells and charms than most people in these parts.

"What exactly are *ofo* and *ogede*?" I enquired. "They are potent words inherited from our ancestors who used them in warfare and for hunting. When used their opponents would be reduced to near idiots or would just lie down and sleep; sometimes ferocious animals have been known to have cowered or suddenly developed lockjaw or have their claws broken at crucial moments just before being attacked," my uncle explained.

"Did that really happen?" I asked incredulously. "Of course, I know and have used the *ogede* and *ofo* myself. How do you think I succeeded as the best hunter for years before being elevated to the position of *Olorode*?"

"Please tell us about Kasali. We want to know whether or not the stories about him were exaggerated," I entreated.

"Have you heard an account of his last operation, before he disbanded his gang?" asked my uncle. We all said 'no'. "That was an interesting episode," the old man said.

He then went on: "Years ago in the days of Eleku, your paternal grandfather, there was a bold robber, a stranger, who lived in Oganla village. Where he came from no-one knew. He was charming and extremely pleasant. He was very popular because of his cordial relationship with everyone. The elders say '*awolu mate o mo won ara re ni*' (a stranger who behaves will not be disgraced). Kasali was his foremost assistant. He taught Kasali many things until he too became a master thief. The powers he had acquired from his father added to Kasali's cleverness as a professional master thief. He had a number of assistants, euphemistically called apprentices. As everyone knew, Kasali was and still is a musician. He plays the *agidigbo*, and he is one of the best at *sakara* (a form of Yoruba dance and music). Up till now he is still the leader of a *sakara* band. He played most evenings at the night market, which still does. When dancing had ceased late in the evening he would switch to his main business which normally began about midnight. He chose teams for operations at random from his band of 'apprentices'. None of them ever had more than a few hours' warning before any operation. He did all the spade work and planning himself. One good thing about Kasali was that he never operated in Oganla. His philosophy was '*ka ma ko ere oko wale*', bring the good things from elsewhere to Oganla.

Before any operations Kasali usually made a good study of his victims: the house and the area in which they lived as well as what they had by way of possessions. The *Balogun*[10] of Idi-Isin had for some time been high on his list of intended victims. This was because of his wealth: his collection of *aso-oke*, other rare costumes, and rare valuable ornaments; besides, his assortment of gold and coral beads was one of the best in the district. As previously mentioned Kasali did not warn members of the gang and he varied the selection of members for each operation. In the case of the intended onslaught against the *Balogun* of Idi-Isin, he selected only four from the gang. They were informed only on the morning of the operation. They were asked to assemble at the market place early in the evening. Between then and nine they sat at the palm-wine bar drinking. As an *agidigbo* band was in attendance they did some dancing. They also enjoyed the bush meat for which the bar was popular. As most of the market women started to leave for their homes two members of the gang left the bar. A little later the other two departed. Kasali waited for another fifteen minutes before he sauntered out after them. Their rendezvous was the dreaded *Igbo-obi* (the forest of kola nuts, a notorious spot) where three roads met down in the valley between Oganla and Ipele. From there they walked briskly past Ipele village towards Idi-Isin town. Just before the main entrance to Idi-Isin they made a detour. It was at this juncture that Kasali told the gang the target

---

[10] Although now used for the head of a society or a body, the title is strictly that of a commander of the veteran warriors.

for the night's operation. Although the *Balogun*'s house was near the market a small cluster of trees separated the market and his compound.

Two members of the gang acted as look-out men. Kasali himself was accompanied by the other two. It was a dark and windy night. It was misty and it had started to drizzle There were no stars in the sky; neither was there any sign of the moon.. Just the perfect conditions for this operation, thought Kasali. They scouted around the area to check on the movements of the many *asode*, the night watchmen. Only after that the operation commenced. Kasali helped himself to a tall ladder from the nearby sawmill. He then instructed a member of the gang to hold the ladder firmly against the high wall. The other followed Kasali up the ladder. At a point Kasali signalled for him to stop. The gang member had the two large sacks which had been brought for the operation. Kasali clambered silently up to the roof and dropped down, similarly noiselessly, into the courtyard. At this point he stood still, gently inclined his head and started to whisper one of his most potent *ogede*: ... he ended on the note,

Asun fonfon n'tifon;
Asun mapa'rada niti igi aja;
Gbogbo eni ti owa ninu ile yi e sun;
Mo ni k'e sun.

(All those in this abode go into deep sleep like the beams of a roof.)

He then took a small gourd of charms from his pocket and tipped a small quantity of its contents onto his left palm; this he blew into the air. He then proceeded cautiously. Obviously he knew his way around. He went through passages treading very quietly like a cat. Eventually he reappeared at a window, just above where his assistant was stationed. He signalled him to be at the ready. About fifteen minutes later he let down the first big *agbada* (the largest Yoruba outer robe). It was soon followed by

the matching *dansiki* (tunic) and pair of *sokoto* (trousers), *aso ibora* (wrapper) and embroidered *fila* (decorated cap). Others followed in rapid succession. This went on for about forty minutes until all the targeted pieces had been passed down.

The operation was completed without any hitch and the party departed without any interruption. On getting back to base Kasali asked his men to produce the loot. He then discovered that the best pieces were missing. "How come? I personally lifted and passed on the various items including the special ones down to you," he said, pointing to the assistant stationed on the ladder. "I, therefore, should know what was lifted," he continued. To be absolutely certain he again enquired, enumerating one by one the items passed down:

The set of *alare* (scarlet coloured *aso oke*).

'Not there' was the answer.

The *Etu* (navy blue *aso oke*),

Not there.

The *Sanyan* (beige *aso oke*),

Not there.

The light damask.

Not there.

Dandogo eleya (the large pleated robe),

Not there.

Where is the package containing the gold and coral beads chains?

Not there.

They all looked at one another in bewilderment. Completely exasperated, Kasali left them in a huff. The following morning he summoned all members of the gang, including those who did not participate in this operation. He recounted to all present what had happened the previous night. He ended by asking if anyone had a change of mind. Still there was no reply. Kasali then said "I will give you one more day to rethink. If there has been no development by the end of tomorrow, every member of the gang is to report at the usual rendezvous for important meetings, first thing in the morning, the day after tomorrow, about the time farmers depart for their farms."

Kasali received no further report on the following day. So, on the appointed day everybody reported at the usual meeting-place. Then Kasali threw the bombshell.

"Ogbon ki i tan l'aye ka wa lo s'orun", that is, the world is not so bereft of wisdom to warrant a trip to heaven. The testimony of the owner is crucial; we shall all now proceed to Idi Isin to pay the *Balogun* himself a visit. This will give him the opportunity to confirm the things removed from his residence on the day of the incident."

There was utter silence. Then one member of the gang, visibly shaking like one having the ague, asked with temerity, "Master, you mean we will ask the owner himself what items of clothing and other valuables were stolen from his house?" "That's precisely what I have in mind", answered Kasali. The member now perspiring profusely further interjected with shaking voice, "How could we do that without giving ourselves away?" Promptly Kasali answered, "At this stage it is essential we obtain the testimony of the owner unless you have an alternative suggestion." He went on further "*Bi omode ba gbongbon kiku iya re a gbongbon sin sin re.*" This means if a child has the wisdom to die, the mother will find the enlightenment to bury it. All they could do was to look askance at one another. Had it been possible to read minds, a lot would have been discovered within the breasts of the individual members as they marched steadily towards Idi Isin. Unfortunately none had such a gift.

So they proceeded towards Idi Isin; members of the gang still thought that the master was bluffing. On they went, going via Igbo-obi and past Ipele. As they approached Idi Isin, all of them with the exception of Kasali, started to fidget. Kasali made a beeline for the Balogun's residence without a backward glance, passing through the cluster of trees. He knocked loudly on the main door. When it was opened by one of the servants, he greeted the man cheerfully and told him that members of the Oganla community had come to pay their respects to the *Balogun* in order to commiserate with him for his recent loss. The *Balogun* was a member of the Moslem community in Oganla and had sometimes led the Friday *Jumat* prayers. It was, therefore, no surprise that they came to sympathise with him. They were duly conducted to the *Balogun*. To greet him they all prostrated themselves before him with respect for his age and standing in the community. Kasali then said that he and his colleagues learnt that the *Balogun* had been visited by robbers. When the *Balogun* said that this was so, he gave the customary greeting suitable for the occasion:

May you live long.
Your loss has purchased
for you lengthy life.
The owner will continue to have,
while the thief will never

gather enough to become wealthy.

The Balogun thanked them profusely. Kasali then said, "I hope that magnificent damask robe you used at the last Ramadan festival was not taken."

"It was." "Good gracious; I hope they overlooked the *Alare* – the scarlet coloured outfit."

"Of course not."

"My goodness, that irreplaceable garment. Let's thank God, you still have the native woven gown."

"Who says? That was taken as well."

"With the navy and beige robes you still have you will be able to manage until the stolen ones are replaced."

"My dear young man, they made a clean sweep; all is gone, including my favourite velvet pleated robe which I used on the occasion of my last visit to you."

"Good heavens; they must be a hard hearted gang."

After a few minutes more and following another prayer said by Kasali they left the Balogun's house. They were all uneasy as they filed out silently from the compound. Hardly had they gone twenty yards when Kasali repeated the words of the Yoruba elders: *'Bi yio bale bi yo bale ni labalaba fi nwogbo lo: ara aibale ni t'awodi'* (It would land is the way a butterfly would fly into the bush; restlessness is the lot of the eagle). Everyone remained silent. They were at the main entrance into the village when Kasali asked them all to come to their usual meeting place. When they had all arrived Kasali cleared his throat. He then said, "In the past we all believed that *agbajo owo la a fi nsoya*, (unity is strength}. But going by recent developments things seem to have changed; it appears now that it is now everyone for himself. There is no doubt that *ni isenyin ba'se je ti wo arin wa; igi woroko ti i nda'na ru* (at present we have in our midst someone who is like a crooked piece of stick which scatters the fire, just as an evil person spoils a feast). As you all know *ti awo ko ba gbe awo ni igunpa, awo a te* - if members of a cult are not supportive of one another the cult will crash. Our elders also say 'ki oju ma ri ibi ese l'ogun re' (for the eyes to see no evil, the legs are the medicine). Medicine as used here is like a talisman. The meaning of this last proverb is that the legs bear the responsibility of transporting the eyes (and its owners) away from locations that might harbour evil. My advice is that you should all leave this village before cockcrow tomorrow; of course, none of you will dare to return until after my death".

One of them replied, "I am sure, highly respected master, that the guilty ones have already become wise. I am in no doubt that by nightfall all the garments and other valuables will be returned to you."

On this note Kasali left them and went to the palm-wine joint to cool off. On getting home later that night his most junior wife was waiting on the front veranda. She reported that three of the boys had been and left three bags. "These two," she said pointing, "are the missing things. They are returned with profuse apologies. The third one contains the *itaran ati owo ngbe nde agba,* a self imposed fine for the inconvenience caused to an elder.

A few days after the events related above Baba Akin went to his *etile* farm, that is, a farm near the village. On entry into the farm he at first thought that he was in the wrong farm, but on looking up, the four *ose* (baobab) trees, the boundary markers, were still in place, and so were the newly planted *serigu*[11] fences. All the same he wondered; who or what could have weeded the farm, straightened the pathways between the mounds and replaced the canes for the yam tendrils. All his children and grandchildren were busy on their own farms and he no longer had farm workers. He walked to the barn. As he was about to sit down he thought that he heard a movement in the attic. Yes, there it was again.

"Who is there?" he asked. "It is me, Deru, Baba."

"Deru, what on earth are you doing here? Your old mother has

---

[11] Serigu is a Remo word for *botuje* – a Yoruba word. In full it is *olobotuje* = *ewe ayaba* = *lapalapa* (Jatropha Curcus). It is also called ringworm because the oil causes irritation on the skin of the children.

been frantically looking for you." As he was speaking Deru came down the ladder which had been let down through the hatch. After prostrating himself to greet Baba Akin , the young man squatted and said, "When Kasali disbanded the gang, he gave us until the following morning to leave the village. As I had no other place to go I went into my mother's store, took four tubers of yam, a bunch of plantain and a small keg of palm-oil and came here. I had been praying and hoping that you would come. Thank God you are now here, *Baba*, what do I do?"

Sit down and tell me what happened, the whole story." When Deru had completed his story Baba Akin assured him that he would intercede with Kasali to allow him to continue to live in the village, which he did. Since then Deru has become my retainer. He works on my farm and he is very well paid. That was the young fellow you saw with Kasali earlier this evening. He now plays with Kasali's *sakara* band. The *Olorode* ended by saying "*Ore kikikiti, iyekan katakata, ijo ore kitikiti ba ku iyekan katakata ni yio gbe sin*" which is, Deru and Kasali are now hand in glove, only death will separate them.

WHAT COMES AFTER SIX?

Driving into Oganla from Ipele I noticed an imposing new building at the top of the rocky hill. I wondered when it was built. Fortunately my cousin, Labajo, the current *Olorode* of Oganla was sitting beside me. When I pointed to the building asking who built it and when, he told me that it had been built about seven years earlier by Tunde, the son of one Lanuyi, now deceased, who was a contemporary of Teacher Taiwo, his late younger brother. I noticed that while speaking his face had a tell-tale expression. This provoked me to ask him to tell me all about Lanuyi's son, Tunde, when we got home.

Later that evening, as we sat with Sanya and two others by the barbecue, cousin Labajo told the interesting story of late Lanuyi's family. Lanuyi, an only child, lived in the village, where he had his primary education. As he did not attend the middle school, he did not have enough qualifications to be a pupil teacher, which was the employment to which most young people of his time resorted to in and around the village. Although he had the elementary rudiments of farming, he did not know enough to make a living out of it, nor was he inclined to take agriculture as a career; but having had the good fortune to inherit his father's farm and house, he reluctantly took up farming. He gradually discovered that farming was not as dull as he had once thought. For the first time, he became aware of the pristine beauty of the forests and trees; the singing birds, especially the distinctive song of the Senegal dove, or laughing dove, which the locals call *oderee koko*; the meandering rivers which shimmer in the sunlight; the squirrels darting here and there; and the fresh smell of the forest. He also grew to appreciate the clean, cool and fresh air; the beautiful blue sky peeping through the huge ancient trees; and the shrubs and hedges tinted with all sorts of colours. With such beautiful scenery confronting him day in and day out, Lanuyi felt contented with his lot, at least for the time being.

Relying on his meagre income from farming and his late father's goodwill he got married to a woman from the village. They had two children, a boy and a girl. As the children grew older, however, he found that his income could not sustain the family, let alone educate the children. So he decided to, do what some of his friends had done before him, leave the village for Lagos to make his fortune. He was lucky to find employment there with a good master, an ex-serviceman who had started a business with his discharge pay. He was in the business of selling building materials and ironmongery. During his apprenticeship, Lanuyi was given a room in the master's house and a small allowance, the greater part of which he sent to his family back in the village each month. He was able to visit the village once every three months. He learnt his new job quickly and was soon promoted to the position of salesman and was now able to earn a commission in addition to his small salary.

He was so good at communicating with people in a friendly way that he started to make good sales that earned him sizeable commissions. He saved much of his earnings since he lived frugally. Soon, he became a sub-distributor and moved to the outskirts of Lagos, to serve those who would find it difficult to travel on the poor roads into the city. In addition, many dreaded the turmoil and crowds in Lagos. Besides, the outskirts provided better and cleaner accommodation, costing less than the high rents charged by the unscrupulous landlords of Lagos.

Before long, his business grew to such an extent that he needed another hand. His first option was to ask his wife to leave the children with her mother and come to Lagos. His wife grumpily refused to move, claiming she was the type of plant that grew only in the home soil. In the circumstances, Lanuyi employed a young lady, Tanwa, as a sales assistant. She was from another village and in Lagos there were many such people. She was clever, skilful, helpful and willing to learn. Soon she was able to attend to all the routine work including typing and keeping the stores and sales records. Tanwa, prior to being employed by Lanuyi, had been living with her mother, a widow. They were able to make ends meet, as the mother was a roadside trader and she supplemented Tanwa's wages. After being employed by Lanuyi, their position improved, but unfortunately before long Tanwa's mother fell ill and died.

All alone in the world, Tanwa was devastated and was unable to cope with the ever soaring cost of living. As a temporary measure, Lanuyi gave her a room in his house. In return she did all the housework including cooking, in addition to her duties as sales assistant. But one thing led to another and Tanwa became pregnant. Lanuyi, a kind person, took her as a second wife to preserve her respectability. The cantankerous nature of his first wife doubtless contributed to his decision. The action would be in accord with a song once popular in the rural areas, which went as follows:

> Agb'oko l'eri ki ipa'tete;
> *To ba p'atete ategun agbokolo.*
> *Be e ategun ki i gbe iru e pa da.*
> *Oro awa di pagidari igi da*

> She who can a good man catch;
> Never plays with such a catch;
> Otherwise she may risk a snatch;
> And never again find such a match.

Besides, in those days, being a polygamist could make economic sense. Lanuyi gradually reduced his visits to the village. He continued to work hard to improve his business and to train Tunde, his new son by Tanwa, as well as to provide for those in the village. Despite these circumstances, Lanuyi did not wish to sever relations with his family back in the village and with his roots. He constantly remembered his father's advice: "Always think of the future. This is what the elders stress whenever they say that what's 'after six is more than seven'. Working away from home is like going to work at the farm. The farmer, of course, brings home the farm produce. Besides, yesterday, today and the future are inextricably linked. The events of yesterday are the stories of today that will become history in the distant future. Your roots will always be in the village. Our elders say *'Ko si ibi to 'da bi ile'* (there is no place like home). When a ship goes to sea it always returns to the harbour; never forget it."

He, therefore, had to bring Tanwa and their son to the home village. At first, it was just on occasional visits, but as his fortune improved he rebuilt his father's house. He then spent more time in the village, leaving the city business in the capable hands of Tanwa, who spent the best part of her time attending to the business. But the relations between the two wives were strained.

Tunde, Tanwa's son, grew up quickly. As he was clever like his parents he was successful in all he did. But, unfortunately for him, during his last year at secondary school his father, Lanuyi, died after a brief illness. The night before his death, Lanuyi again impressed upon his son the need for him eventually to return to the village to live, stressing that he did not wish his forbears and the family name to be forgotten there. "Besides, something tells me that doing so will considerably improve your fortune and future; you will have the last laugh over your antagonists. Promise me, my son."

"I promise, father; I shall do so." answered Tunde. "Thank you my son. You will never regret making the promise."

Out of necessity, Tunde became an adult overnight. He had to console his mother and help her with her work. As the business in Lagos was jointly owned by Lanuyi and Tanwa and was firmly in the hands of Tanwa, it was not possible for the first wife to interfere. She, therefore, as a reprisal, decided that she should inherit the rebuilt house in the village and a large part of the family farmland. She did not heed the advice given by members of the extended family. She reluctantly conceded to Tanwa and her son, Tunde, the single room in which she had lived during Lanuyi's life, and the rocky and near-barren part of the farmland near the cliff. Everybody in the village knew that nothing grew there. The small area of land was a little less than one acre, while the larger portion retained by the first wife was about five acres and yielded good crops. It was clear to everyone in the village that Tanwa and Tunde had been given a raw deal, but no one would dare to face up to the bad-tempered first wife. She was the only one who did not know that 'what is after six is more than seven'. They all knew the words of the elders, *ase'le l'abowaba,* (everyone would reap what they sowed).

In the effort to retain a connection with the village Tanwa and Tunde came home from time to time. Tunde was always singing his late father's favourite song, *'Ko si ibi to tabi ile'* (*'There's no place like home.'*) On such occasions they would be confined to their one room as the first wife did not allow them the use of the living room. They used the kitchen only at night after the first wife and her children had retired for the day. The bad-tempered first wife and her children made life difficult for Tanwa and Tunde. But for the intervention of distant relatives and neighbours, the peevish woman would have driven them out of the family home. Tanwa and Tunde persevered until in the end they could stand the ill-treatment no longer.

They resorted to renting a room and parlour in the village with a kitchen attached. Much as they tried they could not make anything grow on their farmland. But for the business in Lagos they would have become destitute, which was what the unpleasant woman intended. She did not want 'the strangers', as she referred to Tanwa and her son, to live in the village. She wanted them to go into oblivion.

As their farmland was near the village, Tanwa and her son decided to build a cottage on it to save the rent and to have a permanent home of their own in the village. They started by fencing the area. It took another two years before they had saved enough money to start building. In the course of the work they discovered that they needed to break part of the rock to create enough space for the house. This cost them a lot in terms of toil, as they could not afford to hire the modern machinery and expertise required. They had to depend on local labour and their own efforts to undertake the work.

As the rainy season had started, the labourers could not make fast progress with the work. Tunde became discouraged; he was always nagging about the delay caused by the rain. Tanwa's remark on such occasions was 't'olorun ba nse ore a lo'n se ibi' (we are inclined to misconstrue God's intervention). One day after a very heavy downpour they had to send the labourers home early. When the rain eventually eased in the late afternoon the labourers were nowhere to be found. As a result Tanwa and Tunde had to continue the work on their own. Very late in the evening, they decided to call it a day and return home. As Tunde climbed onto the edge of the rock to recover his *dansiki* he felt his feet sinking into the soft soil. He wondered how this could be on such rocky ground. What had happened was that a very large tree had become uprooted on that spot decades previously, leaving a large deposit of soil that had become covered with tall grass and other plants and the ground had compacted over time. As Tunde fought to free himself, he got more deeply embedded into the earth and the more he tried the worse it became and the deeper he sank. With a mighty heave, and with both arms clutching the solid ground on both sides, he thought that he would manage to pull himself up; but instead he fell into a cavity inside the rock. He had to shout very loudly, over and over again, to attract his mother's attention. Tanwa heard him and came to help. Tunde cautioned her not to come too near. He explained what had happened and asked her to go home to fetch a lantern and a coil of strong rope which he had in his room.

When Tanwa returned with the lantern and rope, she grumbled that she could not persuade anyone to come with her. Tunde's remark was, "Just as well," as he did not wish anyone to know about their predicament or the cave. He then asked his mother to tie one end of the rope securely around an *iroko* tree standing nearby and to throw the other end down to him. With a great deal of effort by both of them, during which poor Tanwa slipped several times and bruised herself and Tunde's hands became badly chafed by the rough rope, he was eventually pulled out. Fortunately he had found some huge stones in the cave; he had arranged them into a pile and stood on them. The pile made it easier for him to clamber up the wall of the cave while Tanwa pulled, but it was still an ordeal.

Early the following day, Tunde came to the farm and covered the opening as best as he could. This was to prevent any chance passers-by from noticing anything unusual. He again cautioned the mother that no-one was to be told about their discovery. He said that while in the dark cave he had felt some things with his feet. He would, therefore, like to explore the cave thoroughly.

The workers and the other labourers were dismissed rather early that day. As soon as the coast was clear, Tunde removed the leaves and branches, put in place a ladder he had borrowed and cautiously descended into the cave holding a lighted lantern. Meanwhile, Tanwa sat down to wait patiently. Tunde could not believe his eyes: littering the floor were piles of rubble covering what proved to be bags and wooden boxes, all coated and caked with dust. The first box he opened was rotten, so were all the other boxes and bags. They were all filled with clothes, but also contained a huge amount of money in the form of coins as well as jewellery, valuable necklaces and hand chains made of coral and gold. He pinched himself to make certain that he was not dreaming. He then noticed a narrow path leading towards the end of the rocks. He followed it and found at the end a well-studded strong door. Of course, he knew it could not be opened as it was overgrown with weeds and shrubs. He turned back. He then recalled his mother's reaction when he went on about the incessant rains.

When he told his mother what he had found, she too was astounded. While he kept watch, he requested the mother to go to the night market and purchase some jute sacks. On her return he climbed back into the underground cavity and carefully placed as much of the treasure as he could into the bags. He made several trips up and down the ladder before he could bring up all the bags. All night they washed and cleaned the coins, jewellery and other items. While at this joyous task Tunde referred to his mother's reaction to his previous nagging. Tanwa's spontaneous reply was, 'God's ways are inscrutable'.

As all the items of clothing had become rotten they were all returned the next evening to the cave, so as to conceal them. For many evenings they repeated the search and removed the remaining useful and valuable things. It took them several more evenings to fill the cavity with earth and rubble. Fresh grass was carefully planted on the spot, to obliterate all traces. Tunde cut some tree trunks which he arranged as a form of barrier; on top of the trunks were placed the *marigho*, palm fronds which was generally regarded as a spell; these they thought would scare nosey neighbours. A long time later Tanwa and Tunde discovered that they had stumbled upon Kasali's respository which he used during his many years as a robber and they learnt that he was the most notorious and daring bandit in the area.

On the following day, the main market day, Tanwa purchased

lots of fruit of different kinds, which she said were being taken to Lagos for sale. She hired a lorry into which she loaded all the baskets, making sure that those containing the valuables they had discovered were hidden under the fruit. She and Tunde were the only travellers in the lorry. They sold the valuables, a little at a time, in Lagos.

A few years later Tunde acquired another plot of land not far away from the cottage, near the top of the hill. On it he built a more imposing house – the mansion which triggered this tale. Soon after he and Tanwa had moved into the new house, Lanuyi's old house was burnt to the ground by fire. As a result, Lanuyi's first wife and her children had to move back to her old family house in a remote part of the village, a dilapidated and overcrowded structure. Having become used to a much better standard of living they found life there really arduous. If only they had not been indolent; if only they had not alienated themselves from the extended family; if they had used the greater portion of Lanuyi's land which they had grabbed, they might have avoided this predicament. Who knows, their plight might have proved right the Yoruba saying: *sikasika gbagbe ajobi, adaniloro gbagbe ola* (the mills of God grind slowly, yet they grind exceeding fine and sure). Understandably, no-one sympathised with them; everyone thought that they were reaping what they had sowed. Fortunately Tunde and his elder half-brother, who had kept in touch with him, had a cordial relationship. Tunde made him a monthly allowance on which he, his mother and sister survived. In the meantime Tanwa and Tunde continued to work hard at the business in Lagos. They were thus able to eventually rebuild the burnt family house and enable Tunde's half-brother and the others to move back into it, to their great relief.

Tunde, meanwhile, had opened a small branch of the building materials business in the village to serve it and the other surrounding villages. His half-brother was put in charge of it.

Having learnt from Tunde, he made a success of the new branch. Thanks to the rebuilt house and a steady income from the branch, the half-brother and his mother as well as his sister were able to live in reasonable comfort. The wicked woman and her daughter, thoroughly mortified, had no alternative but to call on Tanwa and Tunde one evening to ask for forgiveness for their past misdeeds and express appreciation for their rehabilitation as well as for their continued means of livelihood. In a good spirit, Tanwa and Tunde accepted their apologies and the family resumed a normal relationship.

Tanwa and Tunde were applauded by everyone in the village for their generous gesture. One of their elderly neighbours had this to say: "The events of yesterday have now become news today as they are sure to become history in the years to come. In conformity with the saying of Yoruba elders *'eyi ti owa lehin ofa oju oje lo'*, -'what's after six is more than seven' – very much more."

This seemingly simple story shows that the effects of every action or event may have momentous consequences; perhaps more than can be understood or discerned. Yes, what's after six is definitely more than seven; it could stretch to infinity.

WHAT YOU SOW, YOU REAP

Prologue

Had the Second World War not taken place I might not have joined the Boy Scouts and I might have missed the best version of this story told by the late Chief Banjo, the *Lisa* of Sagamu, who was then Headmaster of St Pauls C.M.S. School and also Group Scoutmaster. Thanks to Hitler's War, as the Second World War was generally referred to in those days, I joined the school Wolf Cub pack in February 1942 with Teacher Soda as its *Akela*, the cub master and leader of the pack. Scouting changed my life: it provided me with a fascinating introduction to nature and the environment; it introduced me to storytelling, amongst other things, and fired my enthusiasm to master the Remo dialect of the Yoruba language. Yes, I have a lot to thank Hitler's war for. Every grey cloud has a silver lining.

In December 1941 there was a big blast in Apapa where Lagos harbour now lies. At first it was thought that the blast resulted from a bomb sent from 'German Cameroon'. It later turned out that it was due to an accident at the Apapa oil company. There had been some previous incidents, however, and so great was the fear and alarm that a number of schools and students were evacuated from Lagos. So, early one morning in February of 1942, I found myself on *Harmony*, one of the boats in the Rickett's fleet which plied between Lagos and Agbowa-Ikosi. I was with my Godmother and her three children. We were fleeing from Hitler's War! It provided us, the children, with no end of thrills. It was a memorable experience, though the crossing itself was uneventful. Throughout the journey the sea and the sky were blue; the waves and the foam were white with a bluish tint. It was exciting to see the puny canoes of the local fishermen alongside *Harmony*. The smell of the various foods carried by the traders was pleasant and mouth-watering.

The passengers, many carrying loads on their heads, trekked from Agbowa-Ikosi Beach to a noisy market to board the lorry which would take us on the second leg of our journey, to Sagamu. The lorry was an old and rickety contraption that had seen better days. As it was unable to climb the *Oke-Oriya* hill with its full load of goods and passengers we all had to climb down and make the ascent on foot. Occasionally the two drivers' mates threw large wooden blocks behind the tyres of the lorry to prevent it from slipping backwards! While this looked funny to us children, my Godmother did not look amused. We had to stop on a number of occasions to get our breath back. It was a great relief when the climb was completed. The awkward movements of the passengers as they attempted to clamber up into the rickety vehicle caused us children much amusement. The arduous descent was equally frightening because the hill was so steep.

We travelled on a winding, crooked and bumpy laterite road. There was not much to see for miles but trees and undergrowth; the vegetation near the road was caked with dust. But occasionally we saw squirrels and other creatures darting across the road. I had never seen so many pawpaw trees in my life! Birds were pecking at the ripe pawpaw fruit. The lorry was raising as much dust as the smoke and soot belching from its exhaust pipe. Everyone in the lorry was puffing and coughing. It was most stressful for my poor Godmother. Whenever a lorry came from the opposite direction the dust became even thicker and more irritating. It was quite a relief to get to our destination. This was a sparsely populated area which I later learnt was called Makun. It had vast green fields and many trees. It was all very peaceful, unlike Ebute-Ero wharf in Lagos where we had embarked on *Harmony* that morning.

On the following Monday we registered at St Paul's C.M.S. School. There I joined the Wolf Cub pack at my Godmother's prompting. At my first camp, the group scoutmaster, Mr (later

Chief) Banjo, widely known for his stories, told us a tale during the "yarn period", which echoed one I had previously heard from my late grandfather in 1939. A year later I was to read another version of it in *Reader III* at St Paul's Breadfruit C.M.S. School on our return to Lagos, but Pa Banjo's version was by far the best and the most interesting. It is the one that has stuck in my mind ever since.

Pa Banjo started off with a number of riddles, preceded with the usual *alo*. This ritual is the rallying call to start a story-telling session. We all responded resoundingly with *"alo"*! Then, with a smile on his genial face, and without further ado, he launched into the story, which was as thrilling as it was entertaining. It was the tale of a very good man and his wicked neighbour.

* * *

Atunda, a fast growing village on the verge of becoming a town, is on the brow of a hill which commands a good view of the surrounding area. It is perhaps the most picturesque village in the whole district. The village overlooks a very fertile area of land used for farming. The Ibu River divides this large expanse in two: the part immediately beneath the hill is used for farming, while the other side, Igbo-Eri, "forest by the river," is a huge plantation with different varieties of banana and plantain; oil palms and two other varieties of palm which produce palm-wine (*oguro* and *aran*); and trees known locally as *gedu* which provide hardwood timber. The forest teems with game and other animals. Multi-coloured birds can be seen twittering, singing and flying between the trees. Monkeys of all sizes and colours jump from tree to tree. The forest abounds with innumerable butterflies of varying colours.

Most of the men in the village divide their time between farming and hunting. The village also has some full-time fishermen. There are a few others who also fish for pleasure as well as to provide for their own needs. The farmers grow maize, cassava, yams, groundnuts, tomatoes and vegetables.

Atunda market is very popular for palm oil, farm products, game and fresh fish. The village also has blacksmiths who make farming tools – hoes, cutlasses, knives, traps, buckets - as well as fishing hooks and *sakabula*, the locally made gun. In addition, the village boasts of other artisans – bricklayers, painters, carpenters and tailors. Many migrate from neighbouring cities to live in the rural areas due to the high cost of living. This has boosted the number of artisans in Atunda and increased its population. The women not involved with farming sell farm products: fresh and smoked fish; fresh and smoked game meat – this is the most popular - ; and home-cooked food such as *moyinmoyin*, *sagidi* (cooked and blended beans) and *edenru* (roast meat). Atunda is a very dynamic, friendly and lively community, which welcomes visitors and strangers. So it has a lot of 'foreigners' – the indigenes call them *ajeji* – living side by side with the locals.

By far the most popular man in Atunda is Asore "the one who takes delight in being good". This nickname is the result of his friendliness, helpfulness and great hospitality. The normal greeting when he is seen is '*Asore ma seka*' (He who does good and never evil). His usual answer is '*Eni se rere se fun ara re, eni se ika se fun ara re. Atore atika ikan ki i gbe*' (He who does what is good or evil will reap the appropriate benefit). He is the sole distributor of snuff for Atunda and its environs and from this he earns a good income. By local standards everyone thinks he is rich. Like most men in Atunda he also farms.

His nearest neighbour is Maku whom nearly everyone refers to as *Osika alawada* (the wicked joker who rejoices in evil), a nickname which is apt because of his wicked ways. Although he is a tailor, he also farms. Maku is a mischievous person, fond of senseless practical jokes. Because of these and his other bad qualities he has become notorious. Osika is also well known for his negativity.

After attending to customers in his store in the mornings until just before noon, Asore goes to his farm which is near the village. Whenever anyone passes by his farm, Asore will greet him and invite him to take some snuff from his pouch, which he usually hangs on a tree nearby. He makes no charge for the snuff: it is a sort of promotion for his snuff business. Thus the fame of Asore, the good man, spread far and wide. Perhaps the only person who does not like him is his neighbour, Maku, the bad man. The more popular Asore becomes, the more envious Maku is of him. Though pretending to be Asore's friend, he is only waiting for the opportunity to harm him.

On this particular evening most of the men are already home from their farms. Braziers and fireplaces are already glowing and the sweet smell of food is wafting in the air. While the women are busy with their cooking, the men, as usual, are in front of Maku's house for the first round of the evening's *ayo* game.

Ayo is played on a board about twenty-four inches long by six inches wide. There are six holes each on both sides of the board. At the start of the game, each hole has four *ayo* seeds in it. The main aim is for one of the two players to accumulate as many of the seeds as possible. Each plays in turn. Each tries to block the other by making it difficult for the opponent to accumulate seeds, that is by having more than one seed at any given time in any one hole. Whenever this happens the player collects the two or three seeds as the case may be. The winner is the one with the most seeds in the end. Although the game is between two players, each player has a number of supporters on his side. There is usually a running commentary on each side during the game by each supporter's group to motivate and encourage the player whom the group supports as well as to intimidate the opponent. Some groups even play drums. The activities of such supporters' groups can sometimes become rowdy. When a player has been beaten, another takes his place. This goes on until a champion player emerges. There are varying forms of the game and versions of it are played all over Africa.

Maku is one of the most skilful players. He comes out as champion most nights. Not only is Maku an adept at the game, he also has a stock of jokes. On many occasions it is Asore who provides the large gourd of palm wine, which passed around during the game - this drink is very good for lubricating the throat . Usually there is a break during which the men go home for the evening meal. More often than not the game continues after the meal until very late.

On that eventful day Asore plans to finish harvesting his crop of yams by the evening, but feeling tired he decides to go home early. So he starts putting all his implements into his basket: hoe, cutlass, and fly-whisk, and also his farm clothes. He is just about finishing when he hears the shuffling of feet; then a head appears. Almost immediately, comes the usual greeting: *asore ma seka*. It is his neighbour Maku. "It is rather late. I hope there's no problem?" says Asore.

"There are a few things I need to complete, as I shall not be around tomorrow," replies Maku. Asore offers him water and snuff as is his usual practice. The special thing about Asore's water is that it comes from an *amu,* a clay pot, which makes the water cool. After drinking the water Maku goes behind the tree to help himself to some snuff. He returns and bids Asore goodbye.

Soon after, Asore hears someone else approaching from the farm. Agbe, Maku's son, appears. He looks weary and very much unlike himself. In reply to Asore's question if all is well, he flops down on the green grass leaning his back against a tree. He explains that he is feeling faint and lifeless. Asore goes into his hut and brings him some water.

"Did you bring sufficient food to the farm?" he asks, "You look terrible."

"You are right, I feel terrible," Agbe replies.

Asore then also offers him some palm-wine as he thinks that will give him some energy. He then presses him to have some roasted yam as well. This is because he suspects that the young fellow is starving. Agbe accepts the kind offer, eats the yam and drinks the palm-wine. "I am sure that with the refreshment and a little rest you will soon feel better," says Asore. He then goes off to finish his packing. "Call me whenever you feel you have had enough rest and think you have sufficient strength to start the homeward journey." Soon after, Agbe calls out to say that they should start for home.

"May I have a little snuff to cheer me up?"

"Of course, help yourself," answers Asore.

He is just placing the basket inside the hut when he hears Agbe screaming, "I've been bitten by a snake." Asore quickly throws down the basket and rushes to the scene. On asking where the snake is, Agbe points to the hanging pouch. "Show me your wrist," Asore says. He then sits Agbe down and goes into the hut for his *agboyi,* a shaving knife. He bleeds Agbe, applies ground snake-poison antidote, and then tightly binds the wrist as well as his hand just below the elbow. He then asks Agbe to lift his hand and hold on to the back of his neck as if wearing an arm sling. He opens Agbe's mouth and from his medicine horn pours into it a small amount of liquid snake-bite antidote. He also binds the snuff pouch tightly so that the snake doesn't escape. They then start the homeward journey along the crooked, rough footpath with Agbe leaning heavily on Asore. Fortunately as they get on to the footpath leading to the village they see two young lads who offer to carry Agbe. Within a few minutes they get into the lane where Asore and Maku live.

That night the *ayo* game is a special one due to the presence of *Alagba* (Revered elder) Kale, the former *ayo* champion. On his arrival the old man greets them saying *"Mo k'ota, mo kope"* (" I greet both the champion and the underdog.") They answer

"Ota nje, ope ole fohun", (" The champion thanks you while the underdog is unable to speak.") He then sits down to watch the contest. Everyone can hear Maku's ringing voice asking Ade to wake up and play. The latter replies, "Take it easy. I need to think."

Maku: "He who does not understand *Ifa* divination always looks blank."

Ade: "Be patient; more haste makes less speed."

Maku: "Go and learn how to play this game. You ought to have done so before coming to play."

Ade: "Osika, you are being yourself; I know all about your ways. Don't try to stampede me. The snail is known for taking measured steps."

Maku: "You don't know who you're playing with. A child like you cannot lift the skull of an elephant, let alone carry it."

Ade: "Yes, an elephant may give a monkey a disdainful look; but everyone knows that a monkey is not a beggar."

Maku: "Oh, come on, play, dear talkative one. By the time I finish with you no one will recognise you."

Alagba: "Softly, softly. One does not play with one's child and go out into the bush to cut branches to make whips."

Maku: "Revered elder, Ade does not know his opponent. I once told him that a baby elephant calf should not trumpet whilst its parent is doing the same thing. Let me teach my untutored opponent some sense."

Looking towards Ade, he adds in his jeering voice with its peculiar ringing tone, "You need to practice some more before you play with a master player. That's what I am!" He again looks up, and turns his head. "Ah, here comes my good neighbour, but why the crowd? Why is he being carried? I hope he hasn't fainted." Turning to his opponent he continues, "Come on. Stop wasting time!"

The procession with Asore in the lead walks past Asore's house towards Maku's house. When Maku sees Asore on his feet he jumps up from his seat and runs to meet him.

"Maku, there has been a disaster. Agbe has been bitten by a snake," reports Asore.

Maku hastily brings out a mat on which they gently lay the groaning Agbe. Asore then goes on to explain all about the incident, adding that Agbe has been given snake-poison antidote both in powder and liquid forms.

"Quickly, call the traditional doctor," shouts Maku.

Ade runs speedily to fetch the doctor who arrives immediately and starts treating Agbe. While doing so Agbe's other hand falls limply to his side. After turning him over and looking into his eyes, the doctor pronounces Agbe dead.

There is a great hush. Then everyone starts to shout and to ask anew how it all happened. Asore recounts what happened all over again . . . ending by saying "Maku was the last person before Agbe to take snuff from the pouch."

At this point Maku slumps to the ground, and starts weeping and wailing.

"What have I done? I have with my own hand killed my only son, my very dear son."

"What do you mean?" asks everyone simultaneously.

With a haggard look he confesses his crime: "I put the snake in the pouch with the intention of killing Asore."

First observer: "You have reaped what you have sown. He who sets out to hurt another may injure himself."

Second Observer: "Ashes flow towards the thrower."

Third Observer: "The wicked man who lurks in ambush to murder someone else may end up committing suicide."

Alagba: "Fellows, this is a disastrous thing. Yes, very bad. While we sympathise with Maku we must learn lessons from this happening. We must avoid doing evil and instead concentrate on doing good. As this incident has demonstrated, you reap what you sow. Maku, may God console you. May he have mercy on us all. Amen."

First Observer: "Our elders say that the baldness of the vulture has nothing to do with the barber."

The crowd disperses slowly one by one, leaving Maku with the great grief which has now replaced his previous jests and jeers, and also leaving him with the corpse of his only son. His usually shining face with its twinkling eyes now looks dull, subdued and gloomy. Just one solitary person, Asore, remains to console the wretched, grieving father. Asore's parting words are these:

"Time has come for you to change. Do not lose heart: while there's life there's hope. Pull yourself together; work hard at being good. The Almighty Father will be with you in your trying moments. He will have mercy on you. He will forgive you. As for me, I have already forgiven you." In the Remo dialect this is even more beautiful, and runs like this:

Maku asiko ti to neyin nati tun wa se o. Ma bara je; ke e ku use tan, so o ma sara girin. Edumare ninu anu re a duro te e, asanu re, adari je e. Emi nite mi mo ti fori je e.

THE LAST MIRACLE

It was my first picnic at the High School in Lagos. We were at the Bar Beach, the famous Bar Beach with its white sand. It was Easter 19…. and it was a gorgeous day. It was bright and the sun was high up in the sky which was clear and blue, as was the sparkling sea. After the hustle and bustle of the events scheduled for the morning, after lunch we were given an hour of free time to rest. I felt restless and walked rather aimlessly towards the Kuramo Waters end of the Bar Beach.

As I walked along the side of the lagoon with its mango, cashew, paw-paw and sharp-sharp trees, I felt a sense of utter peace. It was all quiet and serene, unlike the noise of the seaside. As I emerged on the lagoon side I saw an old man sitting on a boulder near a crag at the point where the sea and the lagoon met. Separating the two was a rippling line of froth, bluish white in colour. It was a most beautiful sight to see the meeting point of the lagoon and the sea: one side green with its gentle emerald tinted ripples; the other blue with its white froth and a touch of azure. It was like a dividing line drawn by nature itself. It was all calm, cool and peaceful. There sat the old man precariously as if he would fall into the foaming sea any moment. He was scantily dressed and on his head was a cap perched at a jaunty angle.

Although, the sun was warm, curiously enough the old man was shivering. As I walked towards him I heard a sound like the uneven ticking of a clock. With concentration I soon discovered that it was the chattering of the remnants of the old man's teeth. He looked weary and unreal, like something from another world. Was this the old man of the sea? I then stood still, petrified and rooted to the ground. I pondered whether he was indeed human, or perhaps he might be a phantom. While still contemplating his other worldliness, I was startled, when the old man suddenly shouted:

"Young lad, what are you looking at? Haven't you ever seen a lonely old man before? Why are you staring at me?" I was so taken aback and paralysed with fear I could not say a word. "Are you dumb? Speak, say something," he added.

I answered almost in a whisper, "I am sorry sir, terribly sorry. You caught me by surprise." While speaking, I quickly doffed my school cap as the Reverend Roberts, the vice Principal, had taught us to as a mark of respect to elders.

"Ah! What a good boy, courteous too", the old man said, surprisingly, in a cultured voice. "Come nearer; who are you?" he asked. I told him that I was member of a group from my school on a picnic to celebrate Easter.

"Ah! Easter! Are you a Christian? What do you know about Jesus Christ?" he asked. I thought silently to myself: 'What would I know about Jesus Christ'. "I am neither the Vicar nor the Sunday School Superintendent," I muttered under my breath. Although the old man's peremptory manner of speaking had disconcerted me,. I reeled out what I had learned at Sunday School for the benefit of the old man – how Christ was born in Bethlehem of Judea, in the manger; how the large and luminous star heralded his birth; how the wise men from the East came to worship him and brought him gifts; how Mary and Joseph, his parents, ran away with him to Egypt to prevent wicked King Herod from killing the infant; how He grew up and taught in the synagogues; how He went about with His disciples preaching and healing the sick; how, out of envy, He was arrested and taken before Pilate; how He was tried and condemned to death by the Roman Governor; how He was crucified, buried and was raised up on the third day; and how He finally ascended to heaven.

As I was recounting these events the old man was nodding his head; he had a faraway look on his face; occasionally he would smile and his face became tender. I saw him being gradually transformed. The grotesque and frightening old man metamorphosed. In his place was a new person, a wise man with a benign face. He beckoned to me and said, "Come and sit by me. I am impressed by your knowledge of the Holy Book and you are so tender in years. I may as well entrust you with the treasure. You know what a treasure is?" he asked. I explained as far as my understanding of the word went at that time, that a treasure is something valuable and not easily come by. I lost my former fear of the old man and sat down by him as he bade me.

"Yes, you will do", he said as if speaking to himself. "I will entrust the secret to you. I want to pass it on as I have the premonition that my time is fast approaching. It won't do for the secret to go with me. I am going to tell you a story that perhaps no other living being in this world knows. I was told this story by an angel when I was a youth. He asked me to pass it on to a young lad when my time comes.

"Something tells me that now is the time and that you are the lad. I want to be sure though," he then added. "Before I go on, I want you to answer me a question. Which was the last miracle that Jesus Christ performed?" I quickly remembered the incident which took place on the Mount of Olives, when the ear of Malchus, the servant of the Chief Priest, was cut off, adding that after Jesus had admonished the offending disciple, who wielded the sword, He put the ear back in place and Malchus was healed.

The old man smiled. "That is what many would say. But that was not the last miracle of our Lord."

He said slowly. "Come with me, back in time to Jerusalem. There on the road that led to the market place not far from Golgotha sat a blind beggar. He was begging rather noisily for alms. Then he heard the footsteps of someone approaching. "Good day friend," he said "What has happened to Jerusalem? I have sat here from early morning as is my normal practice and until now hardly has anyone passed this way. It is most unusual; I have taken no alms this day. What has gone wrong?" he lamented.

"Are you a stranger in Jerusalem? Why should anyone come this way when all the fun is on the way to Golgotha," the person replied.

"Golgotha, that loathsome place. Why would people want to go there?" the beggar asked.

"You must be the only ignorant fool in Jerusalem. That preacher and rabble-rouser who called himself the Messiah, the Christ and son of God is being crucified. Had you sat on the road leading to Golgotha this day you would have made good takings," the speaker observed.

"Good son of Abraham lead me there. It is not yet too late" the beggar begged.

And so the mocker led the beggar as they moved towards the place of the skull.

At last they reached the vast field.

"How goes it son? Is it all over?" panted the beggar.

"No, a Roman soldier is descending the ladder. The show is still on," replied the mocker.

"May the God of Jacob reward you; please lead me closer. Although I cannot see, I want to get the feel, so that in days to come, I shall be able to say that I was there when the blasphemer was crucified. Indeed, he will destroy the temple and rebuild it in three days. That was what the Chief Priest reported that he said. The precious temple that our fathers toiled to build in forty years and six. He deserves to die."

Slowly the mocker led the blind wretch by the hand as both tottered towards the sacred spot on which the Saviour was crucified. Nearer and nearer, they went to the cross as if drawn by some unknown power.

"Holy Moses," said the mocker.

"The criminal is still talking. I can see his lips moving."

"What is he saying?"

The soldiers and others are laughing. The mocker was talking to himself. Then he shouted loudly.

"Old man, please walk faster or else I shall leave you to the mercy of the crowd. I do not want to miss what remains of the fun."

"May the God of Abraham reward you abundantly dear brother; have patience with a blind old man".

At that point, the mocker shouted. "Hey! He has been pierced on the side with a spear."

"By whom?" asked the blind man.

"By one of the soldiers. It must be part of the punishment ordered by Pilate. Holy Moses, so much blood and water gushing from his side. Who would have thought that such a thin fellow had so much in him," added the mocker.

"Gentle son of Isaac, please lead me to the foot of the cross so that I may have the pleasure of striking him, only on the foot. I still have enough strength in this old arm to do justice to such a felon," begged the beggar.

Curiously enough, the soldiers and other onlookers did not stop them. The blind old wretch clutched the mocker's hand tightly. He raised the other hand and slapped the Lord on the foot just as the mixture of water and blood was trickling down. Both splashed unto the sinner's eyes. Suddenly the beggar loosened his grip on the mocker's hand and reeled backwards.

"What is the matter now?" bawled his companion. "I have no strength to carry anyone with an epileptic fit." At this moment, the blind beggar leapt into the air yelling.

"I must be running mad. I can see! Are these not three men hanging on the crosses? The one in the middle, the one whose foot I smote, he looks like an angel. His blood has restored my sight. This is the Saviour! This is the horn of salvation foretold by the prophets. What calamity have I called on my head." He ran forward like a man possessed and clung to the base of the Cross; tears running down his cheeks,

"My Lord, my Saviour, good Rabbi," he wailed. "Please forgive me. I have sinned; I mocked him; I slapped him. Who will purge me of my sin?"

While this tirade was going on, the mocker stood dumbfounded.

"If the old rogue, the beggar, could really see, then he is no sinner. What disaster have I called on my head; I mocked him. What does it all portend? The world is coming to an end," he moaned with great fear in his voice.

Suddenly, a great darkness engulfed the entire surroundings; utter silence prevailed. Then a loud pealing clash of thunder, like the roaring of a thousand lions, shattered the silence. This was followed by a heavy downpour of rain accompanied by lightning that lit up the scene. The precious blood of the Saviour mingled with the pool of water formed at the base of the cross.

The wretch, the blind beggar, no longer blind, was rolling in the pool of blood stained water. He was moaning, "Please cleanse me, Saviour. Wash away my guilt. Cleanse me from head to toe. Wash away all my mockery and misdeeds. Great Saviour, giver of life, light and sight imbue me with new life so that I may live to testify to this miracle throughout the world."

Suddenly the old man telling me the wonderfully strange story of the last miracle had got up abruptly and was walking away from me. At this point I came to myself. I quickly got up and ran after him. "Sir," I said. "Thank you; thank you Sir." I then asked the old man why old Pa Green, the Sunday School Superintendent or the Vicar had not told us this story.

"My boy, they could not have told you what they did not know. It was told to me by an angel long ago. I was ordered in the early hours this morning to pass it onto you because you are destined to become a preacher of the Gospel. May the good Lord bless you and all that is yours. May you serve long and faithfully in his vineyard."

All I could say to this unbelievable story was, "God bless you too, Sir." I stood there surprised and overwhelmed as I saw the old man walking away. He was still shaking, hugging himself and looking into thin air as one seeing things unseen by human eyes.

I KNOW
A story from Europe

The morning was misty and frosty. The road was deserted except for a man and a horse. The unkempt man, clad in shabby clothes, was leading an old horse and as he shuffled along he appeared to be muttering to himself. A closer look, however, revealed that he was talking to the horse. "Old and loyal friend, I am sorry that it has come to this, I had hoped that we would continue the journey together until we both dropped dead. I am afraid this cannot be so. I have not even a penny in my pocket, let alone enough to buy food for both of us this morning. Hopefully at the end of this journey I shall receive something to help me keep body and soul together for perhaps another week. After that I shall lay me down in old Bernard's disused barn and sleep for ever. For the sake of old friendship I am sure you will not grudge Ted one more week."

To this speech the old horse, understandably, could not make a response, except to roll its sorrowful eyes and neigh from time to time. Ted continued, "Never mind old pal, we shall soon arrive at the yard and good-byes will be said." He stopped to caress the horse; he gently stroked its neck while tears were streaming down his sallow cheeks. Horse and man shared a common grief. Completely engrossed in the heartbreaking farewell, he was oblivious of his surroundings. He was awakened when he heard a voice.

"Who are you, my man? And what are you doing abroad so early on such a raw morning as this?" said a man standing in front of him.

"It is only fair that I should take a befitting farewell from an old and loyal friend like Tack," Ted answered.

"Why so?" the man asked.

"Tack and I spent so many years together in the rag-and-bone trade. Now he is old and broken-down; we are both broken-hearted. I can no longer afford to feed him and he is too old to be put to work. I am taking him to the knacker's yard to be put to sleep. It's only natural that I should feel sorry, dejected and lonely," he moaned.

"Can I make you a bargain?" the man asked.

"What may that be?" Ted replied suspiciously.

"I need an old horse just like yours and I wish to buy it," the man replied.

"How can you joke at a time like this?" Ted interrupted.

"I am in real earnest; I shall pay you handsomely. If you are interested in my offer here is my card. All you need to do is report at the address shown on it at seven o'clock this evening".

"How do I know that you are serious? And what do we eat, Tack and me, between now and dusk?"

"Here is a sovereign for a start; come at seven tonight and put me to the test."

Ted looked at the gold coin, bewildered. He muttered to himself, "Is this man a crank or an imbecile?" He later consoled himself by saying, "I shall spend another day with Tack with good meals for both of us to go with it; besides, I shall have a bottle of good beer". He then turned back and shuffled along with Tack in tow.

For the rest of the morning and all afternoon Ted was restless: he was forever asking passers-by for the time and the right direction of the address shown on the card. At last it was half past six. He walked along with Tack, this time with a spring in his step. Was he not about to come into money? Or was this a cruel jest? All too soon he concluded, "I shall find out the truth of the matter; before we know it old Ted may come into a fortune."

And so he arrived at no. 29 ... Street. He could not believe his eyes or senses. Before him was a long stretch of high wall. The iron entrance gate was securely locked. He hesitated before timidly pulling the bell. Soon he could hear the clanging of the bell in the distance. After a few minutes a man appeared at the gate. Unceremoniously he told Ted, "Be off with you my man; what do you mean by pulling the bell and disturbing me?"

"I am here to see the owner of this house," Ted said.

"What owner?" the surly young man countered. "You must be out of your mind; this is Sir Jacob's mansion. As if Sir Jacob would receive the likes of you."

"And so what?" Ted replied. "He gave me this card and asked me to report here at seven. It is only a minute or two to seven and I do not want to be late."

Still hesitant, the man took the card. After looking at it he exclaimed, "I'll be damned! It's indeed Sir Jacob's card. Wait while I tell Mr. James, the butler." The gate clanged shut.

A few minutes after, Ted could hear the sound of feet approaching. The gate opened and he was invited in by the young man. "Come in, Mr. James will see you" he said. Ted's face lighted up and the expression on his face seemed to be saying, "I told you so." Up they went along the pathway. As they turned a bend he saw before him a large building, in front of which was a lush green lawn. The hedges were neatly trimmed and the flower beds were like pictures he had seen. At the main door stood an elderly man with grey hair. He was elegantly dressed and he had an incredulous look on his face.

"How did you come by this card?" the butler asked. "The owner, I presume, gave it to me this morning," Ted replied. With disbelief still showing on his face Mr. James asked, "What did the gentleman who gave you the card look like?" Ted was about to burst out with indignation when the gentleman himself, Sir Jacob appeared behind the butler.

"James, allow the man to come in; I asked him to come. I have been waiting for him this last half hour," said Sir Jacob.

"Very well, Sir Jacob. I shall ask the groom to tie up his horse and then bring him in," replied James.

"That will not be necessary," said Sir Jacob. "Bring both man and horse in."

Consternation was written on the faces of both Ted and the butler. "Whoever heard such a thing before; asking this unkempt tramp with a funny horse into the hallway of a rich man's home?" muttered the butler. After a discreet cough, he invited the pair in. Sir Jacob walked towards the grand staircase and said, "Follow me." Ted looked perplexed and fixed his eyes on the butler who was staring at Sir Jacob.

"Quickly, I have no time to waste," said Sir Jacob. "Hurry, bring them up the stairs." At this point both Ted and the butler felt convinced of the insanity of Sir Jacob and they were torn between the urge to scream or to make a dash for the door. Sir Jacob, without as much of a backward glance, continued to walk up the stairs and he proceeded along the carpeted corridor. When he looked back he was surprised to see Ted and the horse so far behind. As for the butler, he was rooted to the bottom of the staircase. "Make it snappy my man," Sir Jacob said, "everything must be completed before eight." Then Sir Jacob stopped in front of a white door with a brass handle. He pushed the door wide open and invited both man and beast in.

Ted was now in a quandary; he wanted to rush out of the door as he was convinced that he was with a maniac. He thought he must be correct, as the butler, maintaining a stony silence, kept away from both of them. Ted was awakened from his reverie when Sir Jacob said, "Come across into the bathroom."

"May the holy angels protect me," Ted muttered. Moving as in a dream he walked across the elegant room and found himself in a marble panelled bathroom. A dressing table with gilded mirror was to the left just beneath the two wide windows and a marble bath was to the right.

"Please, quickly haul up the horse into the bath," said Sir

Jacob. Ted obeyed like a man hypnotized. Just as he was about to scream two things occurred. The butler, who had hitherto maintained his distance, peeped into the bathroom and about the same time Sir Jacob calmly pulled out from his pocket a pistol Ted flew towards the door and fell into the arms of the butler who was rooted to the floor petrified. When the shot rang out the two made for the corridor and scampered down the stairs. They were firmly resolved to reach the garden before the pistol was turned on them.

Somehow at the bottom of the staircase, they both stopped and looked upwards. There was Sir Jacob smiling contentedly to himself and slowly walking down towards them. Again they made a dash for the main door. Then Sir Jacob called, "James, please bring our visitor into my study."

"Yes, Sir Jacob," he replied mechanically. Ted knocked at the door of the study and was asked to come in. He peeped into the room before venturing in; he then took off his cap which had all along remained glued to his head. Sir Jacob sat on a satin covered chair and was counting some money from a box unto the oak table. When he finished counting he pushed the money towards Ted. "Count it, my man, it's all there; the fifty gold sovereigns belong to you. I wish you the joy of them and I thank you warmly from the bottom of my heart."

Ted was more puzzled than ever. Without touching the money he said:

"Gov, may I ask a question?"

"Sure, ask." Sir Jacob replied. "Why do you want to give fifty sovereigns away for an old nag which by the way, you have since shot dead."

For answer Sir Jacob chuckled to himself and said, "It is a pity, my man, that you will not be here at eight o'clock when my brother Thomas, Mr Know All, returns from the city. He will in his usual way, come up the staircase with his jaunty strides. He will enter the bathroom to wash imaginary dirt from his shapely hands. For once, he will be unable to continue with his daily ritual. Instead, he will make for the staircase, now jumping two, perhaps three stairs at a time. He will burst into the drawing room puffing with a frightened almost demented look and he will whisper, "Jay, there is a dead horse in my bath." It is a pity you will not be here to see it all and hear me say calmly and soberly with a flourish of my hand, "I know."

THE FRUIT OF PATIENCE

The attractive little town of Bafe nestles neatly within a cluster of hillocks, and with its sixteen hills, sixteen rivers and streams there had long been speculation that the number sixteen is significant for the community. The old legend arose from the prediction of Adifase, a renowned *babalawo* (diviner, follower and devotee of Orunmila or Ifa, the Yoruba god of wisdom and divination), popularly known as *Baba olomo merindinlogun* (father of sixteen) who lived during the reign of Awujale Obanta. He had foretold that *erindinlogun* (16) would bring Bafe great good fortune in the distant future and this had further heightened the great expectations of successive generations of Bafeans.

Bafe has many orchards. Gunsennodu, an *olubafe* from the old times, planted the first one in between the Ibu and Omidu rivers. Since then many more have been established. Bafe's sheltered climate is ideal for growing fruits such as avocado, orange, mango, banana, pitanga (Brazil cherry), pineapple, different kinds of berries, as well as others not mentioned in this story. Unsurprisingly, Bafe's fruit market is the most popular in the area. Traders and others from nearby towns flock to it. Bafe is also a very popular fishing resort. In addition it boasts of many delightful sites good for camping and picnics. All these natural endowments, enhanced by the hospitality of its inhabitants, have made Bafe a favourite place to visit.

Bafe's strategic location has also helped its development. It is midway between the two most prominent towns in the region; and it is only seven miles away from the headquarters of the three foremost churches in the district. The head of one of them, a white priest, an eloquent speaker who is fluent in Yoruba, attracts many people to the church's services; thus, members of its congregation also visit Bafe regularly for fruit as well as for *afon*, African breadfruit, a food well known for its curative qualities.

135

One of the best known landmarks in Bafe is Baba Tapa's compound, a cluster of houses at Idera, on the slope of one of the hills to the north of the town. This compound houses not only members of Baba Tapa's family but also his various businesses and residences for his managers and workers. Baba Tapa's main business is rearing a special breed of fleshy, hornless cattle; the locals call them *eranla*. He also raises ducks, guinea fowl, and pigeons.

Baba Tapa has two mills, one for grinding rice and one for corn. His rice farm is the largest in the district. Reports say that he is a good, God-fearing person and a benevolent employer who pays great attention to the welfare of his staff and their families. In those days this was rare and it was highly appreciated, especially as there was poverty among farmers and other people in a rural area such as Bafe. No wonder everyone admires Baba Tapa and sings his praises.

The river Alase flows through his grazing land. On its bank is a pleasant garden and an orchard adjacent to his rice farm. But by far the most valuable and priceless possession Baba Tapa has is his stunningly beautiful daughter, Omodara, popularly known as Dara. Everyone asserts that she is extremely graceful and attractive; they all extol her humility and her charm.

At first, many thought that Baba Tapa was not a native of Bafe but one of the elders in the town who knew him as a child says otherwise. He explains that Alimi (Baba Tapa's given name) is the son of the well-known Omolaja of Mapagha compound. The present site of Baba Tapa's compound used to be Mapagha's farmland. Alimi, a handsome boy in his late teens left Bafe some forty years earlier to study Arabic in Bida and having become a renowned Arabic scholar he moved on to Mokwa. He was fortunate to have as his wife one of the daughters of Sheik Saidu, a Mokwa chieftain and scholar. He was Alimi's tutor, mentor and father-in-law. Alimi's wife was said to be the prettiest girl in Mokwa at that time. Out of the many suitors seeking her hand in marriage, she, with the support of her parents, chose Alimi because of his humility, his learning and fear of God. Omodora, a carbon copy of her mother, is equally beautiful and adorable.

Since Alimi's return to Bafe he has become very attached to the town and he is foremost in his moral and financial support for the development of the town. He is therefore very popular with both the elders and the youth, for whom he is a role model. He sponsors many of the bright young students of the town and the children of his workers at Bafe's leading secondary school. All his employees are said to be extremely loyal and hardworking, no doubt in return for his goodness and generosity.

Understandably, Dara has many suitors. Alimi is extremely wealthy, having previously been a successful merchant in Mokwa. He and his wife want their daughter to marry a good, God-fearing man who will make Dara happy and also be a good son to them; the more so as Dara is their only child. Many of the suitors come bringing costly and rare objects as gifts. These presents are carefully stored away. However, Baba Tapa appears to be in no hurry to give his daughter away in marriage. Eager suitors became disenchanted and frustrated but there was nothing they can do but await Baba Tapa's pleasure.

Dara appears in public only very rarely, except that she occasionally visits the weekly market with her many friends who often visit her at Alimi's place. Bafe market occupies an important place in the life of the town. Apart from the special weekly market there is a daily market which is held in the morning and evening. The market is not just a place for buying and selling: young people meet there, especially at the night market, where the *sakara* music group performs regularly. The latest news from far and near is also exchanged there. The weekly market days in Bafe are like festivals, and many young men from neighbouring towns come to gaze at Dara's beauty, as well as at her pretty companions. One of the old women, a trader in the market once observed: "Everyone flocks to our market not just to buy our farm products but also to feed their eyes, and some perhaps with beating hearts in search of the rare flower," an allusion to Dara.

One market day, Obaleke, the first son of Oba Adeolu and the most eligible bachelor in Bafe, comes to the market with his friends to luxuriate in Dara's beauty. One of them calls attention to Dara's manner of walking: "Look at the way she glides; see her shapely feet as well as her well sculptured figure; some extra time must have been spent in her making." Yet another, pointing towards her, says, "Look how she is smiling at that poor old woman whom she asks to sit beside her - it's unbelievable. Her teeth are like white pebbles on a river bed. Isn't she bewitching? Her simple but elegant *buba* and *iro* with her head-tie stylishly perched on her head like a bird ready to soar into the air make her wonderful to behold." The usually quiet Muse adds: "Her companions are also very beautiful, but she is by far the prettiest of them all."

On this day, Dara and her companions make many purchases and all the porters are vying with each other to carry her baskets.

One of his companions says to Obaleke ,"Why don't you try to woo and win her; she will make a lovely wife." Obaleke merely smiles without making any comment. His silence and inaction appear strange to his companions as it is an open secret that he loves Dara. At last Dara and her friends complete their purchases and are leaving. Quite a crowd follow them. They all watch until the wrought iron gate of Baba Tapa's compound shuts behind them.

Soon after that visit to the market, news spreads that Dara is ill. Everyone anxiously follows the reports of her ailment. Her affliction lingers for some time. Then comes the horrifying news: Dara is dead! The whole town and the entire district are in a state of shock. Everyone is devastated. The mourning that follows is deep and moving. Baba Tapa's compound is besieged by streams of sombre visitors. Condolences pour in from far and near. Three months later Alimi announces that Dara's many suitors are to come and collect their valuable presents. Some come while others do not respond.

After another six weeks Alimi makes yet another announcement. On this occasion only one fails to respond. Rumour is widespread that Obaleke was one of the suitors. Reports also say that Alimi, for reasons best known to himself, had previously but politely refused an approach from the palace on his behalf.

After a long and thorough search, Alimi discovers the identity and whereabouts of the elusive wooer. Alimi then sends for him. The handsome young man, Olorunleke, eventually puts in an appearance. He apologises for the delay in his coming, adding that since the announcement of Dara's death he had been in deep mourning and was in no mood to communicate with the outside world or receive visitors. He had been praying day and night for the repose of Dara's soul. These are his exact words: "From the day I first set eyes on Dara on one of her visits to the market, something tells me that she is my future wife. Although her beauty was stunning, it was her humility in dealing with people that won my heart. The way she talked to all and sundry including the beggars and the market women was indescribable." He adds: "Dara, unlike her friends, did not walk, she floated. The way she interacted with others was remarkable. I remember watching her help a young girl whose basket of oranges fell off her head. That vivid picture showing her spontaneous willingness to help a lowly person has remained in my memory ever since." He gives Baba Tapa, Dara's mother, and other members of the household his deep condolences and prays that God in his mercy will console them. When leaving Alimi asks him to collect his many gifts and presents to Dara. His response is: "They are no longer mine. They were my gifts to Dara. Please dispose of them as you wish and give the proceeds to the poor." In bidding him goodbye Alimi says, "Although Dara has now passed away, we would like to have your friendship. Please visit us from time to time."

Alimi then starts to make enquiries about Leke and his background. He discovers that he is the last son of Oba Ajagbe who had died a few years before then. At the hottest point in the struggle for the appointment of Ajagbe's successor as king, Leke and his mother quietly slipped out of town to a new home where they now live. Here, God had blessed him and he was popular with all his neighbours. Leke, who before all these happenings was single and seemed to be a confirmed bachelor, had heard of Dara's beauty. So he visited Bafe market to see for himself whether or not her beauty had been exaggerated. On the announcement of Dara's death he, like everyone else, was devastated.

Leke has now become a frequent visitor to Baba Tapa's compound. One day Alimi says to him "I want you to assist me in a new venture. Please come tomorrow so we can discuss it." On the following day Alimi invites Leke to inspect the farm where he grows various herbs and trees.

"This is my new venture," he says to Leke. The farm is located at the farthest end of the vast compound, towards the area where the Alase river disappears underground. They go through a low hedge into a pleasant shrubbery. Beyond is a wooded area and an orchard. It is a peaceful place with various kinds of fruit trees. The orchard is unique in that it contains fruits that are not known in the locality, some of them being hybrids. Right in the middle of the orchard is a cottage with stone walls. These are covered with various creeping plants: bougainvillea of various colours, morning glory with delicate shades of purple and honeysuckle in yellow and pink. On its left are different kinds of fruit trees: orange, tangerine, lemon, avocado and pawpaw; they are all ripe and inviting. In the distance is a cluster of plantains and bananas.

Alimi and Leke make their way to the rear of the bungalow

where the herb garden is located. Many kinds of sweet smelling scents pervade the area. Several other fruit trees dot the orchard, providing shade. Different varieties of herbs are in neat rows beneath the trees; some are in rockeries, while others spread downwards towards the river bank. They come upon workers who are busy weeding and trimming. One is driving new stakes into the ground. Alimi explains to Leke, "The stakes are for the creeping thyme plants; the gravel mulch is to inhibit weeds, nourish and to enable the thyme to gain a foothold". Leke whispers quietly to himself, "This is a little garden of Eden."

Alimi continues with his explanation pointing out the types of herbs, their properties, the time to plant them, their care and handling, and when to harvest them as well as their uses. "These to the right are for the kitchen. Look at those small spring onions, it is a rare species from Senegal. Those to the left are for medicinal purposes." It all sounds interesting to Leke who becomes really absorbed.

"It's getting hot, let's go in for some rest and refreshment," says Alimi taking Leke's *apeji* (wide-brimmed hat). He places it and his own hat on a table as they go into the bungalow. They enter a room which is cool; two of its ends are open-sided. The one to the left opens onto the garden surrounded by a wrought iron fence crafted in beautiful patterns with a decorative archway. Covering it are many creepers; their green tendrils entwine around the iron structure and together with their variegated leaves they give the room a striking look.

The wall to the right has a door that leads into the kitchen. As soon as they sit on the wicker chairs Alimi calls, "Rambe, please bring us something cool to drink as well as the fruit I put on the table this morning." A young lady wearing an apron over her *buba* enters with a tray. Leke is still busy admiring the surroundings, but when a soft and melodious voice says, "Good day Sir." He turns round.

In front of Leke is someone who could be Dara's identical twin. Alimi, seeing the puzzled look on Leke's face introduces her: "This is Rambe, Dara's cousin. She now stays with us to console us. Being first cousins they look very much alike." Leke stammers a greeting while still pondering on how two different persons can be so much alike.

"Rambe, please cut one of the fruits so that my young friend can taste it," Alimi asks.

At first, Leke thinks the fruit is grapefruit, but he then observes that it is much bigger with a more yellowish tinge. When cut the juicy part inside looks pink.

"What is this fruit?" he asks.

"The Ministry of Agriculture from which we obtained the seedling calls it shaddock. Its fruits did not ripen until four years after planting," Alimi replies.

"What exactly is shaddock and where does it come from originally? And why haven't I seen it in the market or heard of it before now?" Leke inquires.

"It is a hybrid of grapefruit and orange. I am told it comes originally from an island in the Pacific Ocean. This is the very first time it has been grown in this area, and because of the long gestation period I have given it the name 'fruit of patience'."

After Rambe leaves the room Leke asks: "Baba Tapa, seriously who is that pretty lady; she is the spitting image of Dara".

"Her name is Rambe; as I said she is Dara's first cousin. Do you like her?"

"Very much, if only for being the cousin of Dara she deserves my liking, perhaps more."

"Well, she is the one who will teach you all about herbs; how to grow and tend them."

"With an instructor like Rambe you can be sure that I shall attend regularly and concentrate," remarks Leke.

Alimi calls Rambe back and formally introduces Leke, stressing that he was one of the suitors of her late cousin.

"He is going to learn all about herbs from you; he is a very patient person and eager to learn. For Dara's sake make sure you teach him all there is to know. I am sure you will be good to him."

"It will give me great delight to teach him all that I know," Rambe replies with an engaging smile.

Leke is mesmerised to see Rambe so close and near. Her bewitching smile reveals two rows of white teeth in between the thin lips; the pert nose, chiselled chin and the dimples on her well rounded cheeks, as well as her hair, braided in Nupe style – all present an enchanting and captivating picture. Leke is dumbstruck. Although he did not have the opportunity to see Dara at such close range, the uncanny likeness between her and Rambe continues to baffle him and linger in his mind.

The Leke who leaves for home that evening, in the frame of mind into which he has been pitched, is both puzzled and elated. From that day on he becomes a regular visitor. Each day he comes to the herb farm with his heart beating fast and butterflies fluttering in his stomach. He takes his lessons very seriously; and so, Leke and Rambe are together for the best part of every day. Dara's mother, Alimi and Rambe become very fond of him. All the other members of the household also like him as he is gentle, courteous and patient.

One evening, just before finishing for the day, Rambe asks: "Leke, do you really like learning about herbs?"

"Of course, you can see that I do. Day by day I like it more and more."

"But do you really like learning all about herbs, or is it because I am the instructor?" Rambe went on.

"For both reasons; I must be honest."

"Do you like me because I look like Dara and remind you of her?" persists Rambe.

Leke responds, "Here, too, I must be honest; initially I liked you for looking like Dara, but as we work together I start to like you more for yourself. Let me confess, I hate going home in the evenings; during the night I long for the morning."

"Thank you for your honest answers and the subtle compliment." A smile flickers on Rambe's face.

"Rambe, what do you find so amusing?"

"It's good to be liked for one's self; and not because one is a substitute for another," Rambe explains, to which Leke responds: "Rambe, you have bewitched me; with your ways and your beauty I cannot but love you. You also have a good and kind heart. Please excuse me for talking like this."

"You do not need to apologise; the feeling is mutual. You too are delightful to know," replies Rambe.

"Rambe, I think you will make a good wife; but do you know that it takes more than beauty to make a good wife?"

"What else does it take?"

"The beauty of the heart is much greater than that of the face; fortunately you have both. You are so kind and caring. You make me feel so much at home. At first, when I behaved clumsily, not understanding the things you explained, you did not laugh at me or make me look foolish. After some time, with your permission I shall ask Alimi's approval to make you a formal proposal. When I do so I shall also teach you my favourite song."

"I am looking forward eagerly to your proposal," Rambe responds, sweetly, adding, "…and your song."

When Leke leaves for home that evening the two young lovers hold hands and gaze into each other's eyes, blissfully in love.

Nine months pass quickly until, one day, Alimi comes to the garden and says to Leke: "When you come tomorrow please come in your best robe as I want you to accompany me to see a respected visitor."

So on the following morning Leke appears in his finest robe. He is overwhelmed to see that the entire household is in a festive mood. When he asks, "What is the special occasion?" Alimi merely tells him that the august visitor has decided to come to the house instead, and a reception is taking place in his honour.

"Where is he?" Leke asks. Alimi's response is *"eniti nwon gbe iyawo bo wa ba ki i ga'run"*, which means 'the groom does not need to tip-toe to see the bride'. "Don't be anxious: the visitor will appear in due course."

Dara's mother enters, in her finest ensemble. All the other members of the household, smartly dressed, are already sitting down. Right in front of their chairs are two others, festooned with decorations: Leke is mystified by the festive atmosphere.

While Leke is still wondering, he hears Alimi telling one of the servants, "Please bring Rambe in and tell Gafar we are almost ready." Soon after, Rambe enters, in a simple but exquisite dress; leading her are sixteen pretty young girls. Alimi asks her to occupy one of the two chairs at the front. He then turns to Leke saying, "My young friend, a few days ago you asked for my approval to your request for Rambe's hand in marriage. You added that for the sake of the late Dara, whom you dearly loved and in whose memory - as well as for Rambe's goodness and beauty - you wished to have her as your wife. Is that still the case?"

Leke is speechless. Before he is able to reply, Alimi, his own mother and some of her friends enter the chamber. Looking from Alimi to Rambe, a bemused Leke asks: "Baba Tapa, am I dreaming?"

At this point, Gafar, the priest, enters and invites Leke saying, "Come and sit here young man; let's get on with it."

Alimi and the entire assemblage burst into hilarious laughter. Dara's mother then intervenes, "Baba Tapa, please speak and relieve Leke of his suspense."

Alimi then takes over.

"I wanted to be sure that Dara married the right man. We were confused when so many suitors started to flock in, the wealthy, the noble, the great and all. I therefore decided to put all the suitors to the test. You, Leke, are the only one who passed the test. You went into deep mourning as if you had lost a wife. You did not want the return of your gifts. I decided to test you further by introducing Rambe to you as Dara's cousin. Both of you have been together these last nine months. Dara's mother and I, and indeed the entire household, watched how the love between both of you grew and developed. Rambe is in fact Dara, and she has confirmed her deep affection for you. You have conquered us all with your character, Leke. Our elders say, *Suru ni baba iwa.* (Patience is the hallmark of character). Anyone with patience will conquer the world; he will inherit the earth. Please continue as you are, humble, approachable, amiable and good to all. Everyone speaks exceedingly well of you. Even the Oba of this town says that you are a better choice for Dara than his own son." He then adds, "That's the trumpet heralding his approach; he is coming to grace this marriage with his royal presence."

Dara's mother, her face a picture of joy, comes dancing forward. Addressing herself to Leke, she says, "You are the only one fit to taste 'the fruit of patience'. May God bless the union between you and Dara."

YOU SWEET ROGUE

Jumoke was widely known, not only in her father's domain, but in the entire district. She was highly educated and as pretty as she was clever and witty. After a convent primary schooling, she went on to complete her secondary studies at a renowned girls' seminary in the city. Soon afterwards, she went to England for her university education. While reading classics she found time to study music and learn about gardening as well. Jumoke as a child and in her early teens was precocious. During her university days she was described as being dashing and daring, which was unusual for a female at that time; she was nevertheless able to take care of herself. As a result, no-one, male or female, could get the better of her. On her return home she became the toast of many eligible bachelors.

Since her parents had moved to the countryside when her father became an *oba* (king), she preferred to spend most of her time there. She had, in any case, always been a child of nature: she loved the forests and the country environment. That she was living away from the city presented no difficulty to her many admirers. They all came calling: the wealthy professionals, the affluent business men, and the politicians. But to everybody's surprise, especially her parents', she refused to make a choice out of all these suitors. She declined to shackle herself in any steady relationship, as she put it.

One day, a handsome and extremely cultured prince came and asked leave of her parents to court her. As the father of the young man was well known and highly respected, the parents gave the prince a warm welcome. But when the prince arrived, Jumoke had gone to a neighbouring town to visit friends. She returned late in the evening just as the prince, who had come all the way from the city, was leaving. His car had just driven out of the compound when he and his driver met Jumoke's car driving in. The prince turned back; and as Jumoke was disappearing up the stairs the mother called her back informing her that a visitor who had waited a long time had returned to see her.

At first, she started making excuses to her mother that she had been out all day and was tired. But her mother was firm with her. She insisted that Jumoke should at least see him and if need be agree another time for the prince to come back. What motivated the *Olori's* unyielding stance was that the prince appeared to her to be a smart and dashing young man who would be compatible with and acceptable to Jumoke. Reluctantly, Jumoke came back and received the prince, in what she called her music room where she played the piano in the evenings or sometimes listened to her stereo. After a short while, the prince left without Jumoke seeing him off as would be expected. When her mother asked her how the meeting had gone, Jumoke said that he was not her type. "You should at least be courteous and listen to him," remonstrated the mother. With an enigmatic smile, Jumoke replied saying, *"Ohun ti enia ko ba ni i je ki nfi runmu,"* (meaning what one would not like to eat, one should not bother to sniff at).

"What on earth are you looking for in a man?" her mother asked in anger. "He comes from a good and royal family. He is a highly educated professional man." Jumoke countered the *Olori's* exasperation: "Mother, he is not my idea of the right man."

Suitors continued to visit her, but she showed no interest in any of them, describing one as a "he-goat"; another as having "the look of a man with roving eyes." She made a lot of rude remarks about the men that came calling on her, and her infuriated parents came to the conclusion that she must really hate men.

Soon thereafter an event occurred which would have far-reaching effects on Jumoke and her family. Her father, a former forestry officer, was also very interested in gardening. He spent a lot of time in the garden and with the gardener whose name was Olu. He had worked for them for over five years and everyone thought that he had become a permanent fixture in the household.

The gardener and another young man, the cook, shared a two bedroom bungalow, separated from the main house by a hedge. Late one evening, the cook reported that the gardener had left home in the morning and not returned. As a result the garden had not been tended or watered; understandably, everyone was worried.

When the gardener still did not show up on the following day *Kabiyesi* arranged for his driver to go to the gardener's home near the city, to see if perhaps he had gone there, but he had not been seen there either. Naturally, everyone both in the Oba's domain and in the city became even more concerned. The *Kabiyesi* and Jumoke, who both loved the garden, were especially disturbed. A report was made to the police; no one answering the description of the gardener had been seen or detained by them. Enquiries at the various hospitals revealed nothing. The search continued locally as well as in the city for some time; but all the efforts proved futile.

About two weeks after the gardener disappeared, a young man, who claimed to be a gardener, came to see *Kabiyesi*. He said that he had heard about the gardener's disappearance and had come to offer his services. It was with a sigh of relief that *Kabiyesi* received him. After examining the young man's references, *Kabiyesi* asked if one of the referees, Mr. Adekunle was the former official of the Forestry Department.

"Yes, *Kabiyesi*, he said that he had worked under you," the young man replied.

"Yes, he did; he must be getting on in years now," *Kabiyesi* remarked.

"Yes, *Kabiyesi*, he is back home in *Idarika*."

"I'll try you for two days; if you are good, the job is yours."

On the first day the new gardener was asked to put the garden in order and trim the hedges. Later, in the evening the gardener invited *Kabiyesi* to inspect his work. He was surprised to see a transformed garden. He was so pleased that he decided to give the new gardener a few more days and then give him formal employment. He was asked to return the next morning.

When *Kabiyesi* looked out of his window early the next morning, he was amazed to see the gardener already at work. In the early evening *Kabiyesi* came out to inspect the garden. He was surprised to see that a new hedge of ixora had been planted to screen off an area on the north side.

"Whatever is that for?" *Kabiyesi* asked.

"I am making a new compost heap which will later be buried in a pit; it will then be covered in black earth. A few weeks after that I shall spread the earth before planting some herbs on it."

"What do you know about herbs?" *Kabiyesi* asked.

"I used to look after the herb garden at the city council nursery. It strikes me that herbs such as thyme, spring onions and garlic will thrive in this soil."

Kabiyesi was impressed with the young man's answers and by the end of that week he had decided to employ him and give him a room in the servants' quarters. A good rapport developed between *Kabiyesi* and the gardener. While inspecting the garden a few days later Kabiyesi asked the gardener his name.

"My name, *Kabiyesi*, is awkward and, to be frank, I am ashamed of it: it is '*Ewunren*[12]'" he whispered. "I suggest, *Kabiyesi*, that you just call me 'gardener'." he added with a mischievous smile. "*Kabiyesi*, it won't be nice and it may be embarrassing to be called that name, especially by *Olori* and the Princess. Please tell everyone to call me gardener; I won't mind."

"If that is what you wish, so be it," *Kabiyesi* agreed.

Within two months the entire compound had been transformed by the quiet and hardworking gardener. New flower beds had been put in place; the previously neglected rose garden took on a new look; colourful creepers had been planted; and a new rockery with ferns and lilies decorated the alcove beneath the ancient

[12] A euphemism for penis.

looking *Iroko* tree. The whole compound smelled sweet; both *Kabiyesi* and Jumoke were delighted.

The quiet gardener was scarcely ever seen; he kept himself to himself. One day Jumoke was practising on the piano and seemed to be having difficulties with some notes. Suddenly she heard a guitar playing the same tune she was struggling to master; but the guitar was playing the right notes and rhythm. She quietly went out to the front of the house where she saw the guitarist strumming away, unaware that he was being watched. Quietly, she moved closer and discovered it was the gardener who was playing the guitar. She coughed quietly to attract his attention, and the guitarist spun round to see who was there. On seeing her, the gardener greeted her and was about to leave when Jumoke asked him to stop.

"Where did you learn to play so perfectly?" she asked.

"I went to a music school," replied the young man.

"Please play that tune once again," Jumoke requested.

"The piece is best played if I sit; do you mind if I do so?" the gardener asked.

"Why should I mind?" Jumoke smiled. So the gardener sat and strummed away.

Soon Jumoke joined him, humming at first, then she started to sing in her clear, enchanting voice. When the song ended, Jumoke complimented him.

"You should be a professional musician, not a gardener."

"I enjoy doing both, Princess," the young gardener replied, adding, "It does no harm to combine them. I usually play when I need to take a rest after physical exertion. Excuse me, Princess, I must go back to work now."

His long strides took him behind the tall ixora hedge. Jumoke bent down and examined the guitar; it was a most exquisitely crafted instrument. She wondered to herself how an ordinary gardener could possess such an instrument. Beside the guitar on the pavement was a book, 'Poems by William Wordsworth'. She returned to the music room full of thoughts, wondering what kind of gardener her father had employed. She was also piqued that the gardener did not react more warmly to her compliment.

The following evening the gardener asked the maid to bring four vases so that he could put fresh flowers into them. About an hour later, he returned the four vases with freshly cut flowers beautifully arranged in them. They were left on a table in the front courtyard by the main door.

Later when the *Olori* returned home she could not but notice the eye catching vases. She called the maid to ask where the flowers had come from.

"The gardener must have left them there," the maid said.

"Call him" the *Olori* ordered.

When the gardener entered the *Olori* commented:"These are beautiful flowers; where do they come from?"

"From the flower beds behind the hedge. I planted them especially for cutting so that you can always have beautiful fresh flowers."

"Come and show me the flower beds," the *Olori* asked.

Accompanying the gardener, she walked the full length of the paved pathway before turning to the left into the partly fenced area. Right in front of her were several flower beds in neat rows, a riot of colours. To her observation "These were not here before," he answered, "You are right *Olori*, I planted them about three months ago, soon after I started working here."

"This is incredible; what's behind that lower hedge?" Olori asked, pointing in the direction of the new fence.

"That's the new herb garden."

The *Olori*'s curiosity was aroused; and for the first time since the new gardener started work with them she went round the garden and, escorted by the gardener, she meticulously inspected the entire grounds.

"The lawns are greener; they look like carpets." she remarked.

"*Olori*, I keep working on them; the new sprinklers which *Kabiyesi* procured at my request have started yielding results."

"Come inside with me" she said.

"*Olori*, please give me two minutes to take off my working boots and wash my hands," the gardener asked politely.

The *Olori* was sitting in a chair when the gardener eventually entered as the maid was putting down the tea tray.

"Sit down, young man." She then poured a cup of tea, turned to the gardener.

"Would you like sugar and milk?"

He was taken aback. "It's very kind of you *Olori*; a little milk, no sugar please."

"I want you to be frank and open with me; why is a young man, well-educated and highly cultured like you working as a gardener? I have been watching you. I became intrigued when my daughter told me the other day that you explained to her how to play an intricate note on the keyboard. She also added that your display on the guitar is that of a maestro; you also read poetry, she told me. You are so detached and aloof. You just don't fit. Tell me why you took this job."

The gardener smiled. "I am enjoying the work; I love gardening. Music is my hobby and although I am good on the piano, the guitar and xylophone are my favourite instruments. *Olori*, by the time I leave the palace you will have the best garden and lawns in the district."

The *Olori*, highly amused, remarked "You have not answered my question; by the way what's your name?"

"If you do not mind Olori I would rather not tell you my name." The gardener answered. "I am not being rude or disobedient," he added apologetically.

"That's absurd, why?" *Olori* exclaimed.

"You may feel that it is offensive," the gardener replied,

averting his eyes.

"Why so, your name is your own," the Olori pressed him.

"It's a bit unusual," is all the young man would say.

"All the same, tell me," Olori insisted.

"*Olori*, you are old enough to be my mother. I'll give you my name only on one condition: the others must not know it. I do not wish to be an object of ridicule."

More intrigued, *Olori* promised she would not divulge the name.

"My name is Potty," the young man said sheepishly.

"Unbelievable! You don't mean potty as in the one used by children?" asked the *Olori*.

"Exactly, *Olori*. My old nurse told me that when I was small I was fond of my potty; it was always difficult to divest me of it. She then started calling me Potty. After that everyone in the household started using the name. I was told that I did not mind the name; rather I liked it. I grew up with the name and it stuck."

"You must have come from a wealthy family," the Olori remarked. "What went wrong? Your family must have come down in life. What happened?"

"It's a long story, *Olori*, I do not wish to bore you or waste your time," the gardener said. "I must be off to pick up the bag of manure I ordered from the store before five o'clock. I am most grateful of your appreciation of my work and your interest in me. Please respect my wish; keep my ridiculous name to yourself. Shall we say that it is a secret between mother and son?"

The *Olori* was so stunned and she almost did not realise that the gardener had left the room. She continued to wonder about him. There is a mystery about this young man; we'll find out in time, she thought. Out of curiosity the *Olori* would walk round the compound every evening to admire the work of the artistic gardener, as she often referred to him. Occasionally, she would tease him, when no one was around: "How is Potty today?" she would whisper. "I am fine, *Olori*," he always replied in good humour.

From time to time the puzzle of the gardener got into the *Olori's* mind. *Kabiyesi* and Jumoke have now become wrapped up in the garden, she thought; could the gardener be responsible for the upsurge in their interest, she wondered. After further inner wrestling she came to the conclusion that if everyone seemed happy with the garden, why should she worry about the mystery man.

One day the *Olori* and Jumoke were in the courtyard. They both started to sniff. One of them remarked that the aroma wafting in the air was unusual.

"The aroma is strange to me; what kind of food can it be?"

"I can't identify it," said the *Olori*.

"That's exactly what I am thinking."

"But who could be cooking? The cook asked for the day off and he isn't back."

"The smell is coming from the direction of the servants' quarters," said Jumoke. "I'll check."

When she peeped into the kitchen the gardener was absorbed in carefully turning down the stove; he was so engrossed that he did not realise that he had company.

"What on earth are you cooking?" He looked up with a start, "It's beans, brown beans with crayfish and onions. I am using my grandmother's recipe."

"Beans!" exclaimed Jumoke. "That's not the smell of beans, although I am not very fond of them."

"It is, Princess. This is a special recipe."

"It has an inviting aroma; may I taste it?"

The gardener obliged and scooped a little bit on the wooden spoon and passed it to her. After tasting it she said, "Are you sure these are beans? It does not taste in the least like the stuff served at the Seminary that was called beans. This, is delicious."

"It will be even better after it has simmered for a while on a low heat," the young man told her.

Jumoke was amazed: "Wonders will never cease; what's it that you don't know or can't do?"

"Am I to understand that you are saying that you like my cooking, Princess?" the gardener inquired.

By way of a reply, Jumoke said, "You really are something. By the way, what's your name?" The gardener smiled.

"What's amusing?" asked Jumoke.

"You won't believe it. My name is Beans. Noticing the look of surprise on Jumoke's face, the gardener went on, "Beans, that's my name. I got the name as a toddler. I was always bouncing and jumping up and down. As I grew up everyone used to call me Beans. I liked it, it became my name; and it stuck. It sounds ridiculous, but nice; but Princess, please keep it to yourself. I would not like to be laughed at."

Jumoke smiled and said: "I'll keep your little secret on one condition. Whenever I feel like eating these kind of unusual beans and I ask you to prepare them, you will do so." The gardener agreed saying, "Princess, that will be a great pleasure."

Jumoke then asked, "Can you please teach me how to play the guitar?"

"It will be a delight to do so, Princess; but you will need to get yourself a good guitar." Jumoke said that she would search for one.

The conversation between her and the gardener again triggered off Jumoke's urge to unearth the actual person behind this inscrutable, hard-working gardener.

A week after the beans incident, Jumoke asked the maid to call the gardener. She was in the music room when the gardener entered. "I have now got myself a guitar, exactly like yours. When can we start the lessons?"

"Whenever you wish Princess."

"Why not now?"

And so the guitar lessons started. Every evening, after practising on her piano the gardener would come in; they would play guitar together for an hour, sometimes more. Before long Jumoke was able to produce simple tunes on the guitar. Occasionally, they would perform a duet – with one on the guitar and the other on the piano. At times the joint performance would be vocal; yet, at other times, a mixture of instruments and voices. There was no doubt that a good relationship now existed between Jumoke and her tutor.

At times, when coming for the guitar and music sessions, the gardener would also bring a bouquet of freshly cut, sweet-smelling flowers. On such occasions, Jumoke would feel elated; to her this good gesture on the part of the gardener seemed as if he was courting her. Often her eyes would wander over his soft, almost feminine, fingers as he strummed on the guitar.

On such occasions the persistent urge to unearth the real person behind the gardener's façade would become more pressing. Her sighs would become more frequent; her yearning for a suitor like the gardener would be accentuated. She indulged in daydreams. Often she would wonder … 'What's happening to me?'

If the gardener's visit occurred immediately after such thoughts Jumoke would say teasingly, "How is Mr Beans?"

"Fine Princess, just fine; please keep this pet name to yourself; do not open me to ridicule."

* * *

Kabiyesi had been on a trip. One afternoon, he returned. The household was in a festive mood. The various servants seemed very busy and the general hustle and bustle meant that one did not need to be told that there would be a celebration that night. The gardener had been requested to bring in fresh flowers.

159

He had just started his evening duties when the Princess came out looking for him. With a sparkle in her eyes she said, "The time has come for you to redeem your promise."

"Which promise?" the gardener asked.

"I am in the mood to eat you tonight," she replied mischievously.

"What on earth are you talking about, Princess?"

"I want your special beans, Mr Thickhead. It's celebration time tonight."

"But it takes time to prepare, Princess," the gardener protested.

"You promised. Please go about it right away. I shall wait, no matter how long it takes."

Kabiyesi had invited a few guests. They were all drinking and merry but Jumoke's mother observed that her daughter was just picking at her food as if she was not interested in the meal. Her mother leant sideways and asked, "Why aren't you eating?"

"I am waiting for a special dish," Jumoke whispered, adding hesitantly, "You remember the evening I tasted the gardener's beans? I have asked him to prepare some for me. I have a craving for it."

"You and your ludicrous tastes and whims; beans are most unsuitable for eating late at night. Our elders say *Ewa ki i se ounje a jesun fomode* (It is not good to take beans as supper)."

"Mother, you and your ancient customs."

"Don't you know that beans purge?" her mother asked her. "That's why they are not eaten at night."

"Mother, I have made up my mind - that's what I'm going to eat on this special night," Jumoke responded.

"When Kabiyesi and his guests retire to the room upstairs, I am going to enjoy my meal. I don't mind if you have some of it," she added with glee.

With a sigh, her mother declined the offer.

Some time afterwards, Jumoke sat all alone at the table. In front of her was the dish of beans with a special sauce that the gardener had recommended. She had two helpings and enjoyed it tremendously. Then she sat at the keyboard playing a medley of lively tunes; she was in a kind of mood which she herself did not understand. When, eventually, *Kabiyesi* was seeing his guests out, they all stopped to watch and listen to her, in apparent admiration.

At last the household was quiet. Only one room was lighted. The light was showing from Jumoke's room. She was reading a novel – a romance, compelling and juicy, which Beans had given her with a bouquet of flowers a few days before – and she was determined to finish reading it that night. For no reason she started to think of 'Beans'. What a peculiar name, she thought, remembering that he had said that he would disclose his real name when the time is ripe. Out of curiosity, Jumoke hoped that it would be soon.

There is something about him, she mused: his fingers, so long and sensitive, do not look like those of a gardener. He speaks with a cultured accent. He is so knowledgeable, he has a detached air; sometimes I feel that he towers so much above me. Definitely, there is a mystery about him. If only one of my so-called suitors would be like him; that would be great fun. Fancy the gardener and the Princess, what a pair, what a thought ... she continued to muse.

Just then she thought she heard someone tapping on the French windows that open onto the balcony. There it goes again. She parted the blinds. She could not believe it. This must be a hallucination; it's impossible! I was thinking about him and he seemed to appear all of a sudden.

The 'apparition' smiled and motioned that she should open the French windows. Suddenly, Jumoke felt faint. For a few moments she felt like someone in a trance. How could my thoughts have transported him here? I must be out of my mind, she thought. She looked out again; the apparition was still there, smiling. It looked so real.

As he said nothing she felt certain she was seeing an apparition. When the gentle tapping sounded again, with trepidation tinged with expectation, she withdrew the bolts, top and bottom. She was transfixed, looking dazed, while the apparition knelt at her feet. Jumoke was completely dumbstruck. She felt like someone dreaming, She thought she heard a voice whispering, "No, my Princess, you are not dreaming." All of a sudden Jumoke's hands, held by those of the apparition became limp. She was falling; she slumped on the bed; she had fainted. The apparition started to fan her slowly and steadily. Then she slowly opened her eyes and moaned, "What kind of dream is this."

"No, my Princess, it's not a dream."

"Who are you? Where do you come from? Am I alive or dead?" The apparition sat on the bed, putting her head on its lap. She kept whispering "What is happening? Where am I?"

"In your room; in the palace. Don't be afraid; just keep calm. You were not meant for any of your previous suitors." There was utter silence. Jumoke shut her eyes; and then appeared to be dozing. After a few minutes she slowly opened her eyes and looked around drowsily. Her lips appeared to be moving, but there was no sound.

Again she looked around, this time, wistfully. She then raised her head with her mouth open, like someone in a coma. Suddenly she became animated. There was a look of fear on her face. "Please don't hurt me. I meant no wrong. I was thinking about a loved one," she whispered.

"Who were you thinking of?"

"Beans, our gardener. In a way you look like him, except that you look more smartly dressed; but you have an aura … if only one can be sure; … no, it cannot be."

"He is the one holding you."

She did not know what to believe. What a strange dream, she thought. She felt like screaming, but she was too listless to do so, perhaps too afraid. On her face was a confused look, maybe more like someone groping in the dark.

With the distressed look on her face the gardener held on to her and started to rock her.

"Do not be afraid. Keep calm," she thought the apparition said.

Suddenly Jumoke turned and clung to the apparition. They embraced. They kissed.

"Please hold me more closely. I do not want to wake up just yet; this perfect dream is too sweet to be true. Let it continue undisturbed." The gardener responded with a soothing caress.

They kissed again and again. The gardener lifted her in its arms and gently positioned her in the middle of the bed. They both became lost in a haze … utter silence prevailed. After what seemed like an eternity, Jumoke screamed, while the gardener tried to stifle her scream. With a great effort she shook herself free shouting: "*Ewa, Ewa* (Beans, Beans) you have caught me."

Her mother, sleeping in the next room, thought she heard a scream. She turned. There was the scream again, followed by the words "beans, beans". She screamed back, "Didn't I tell you, you don't eat beans at night. Do not wake the entire household."

"Help me mother; help! help! Beans!"

The *Olori* jumped up. As she opened Jumoke's door she thought she saw a figure disappearing by the French windows. Jumoke, with horror in her eyes, pointed towards the windows still yelling "*Ewa Ewa*" (Beans, Beans). She was frightened; indeed terror showed on her face. "He has got me; Beans, Beans", she still kept shouting, with a terrified look. By the time the mother reached the window, Beans had already disappeared.

The *Olori* herself then became hysterical, shouting, "*Kabiyesi*, help, help! Hold him." *Kabiyesi* jumped out from bed, and came into the corridor.

"Hold who?" he asked.

"Potty" said the wife.

"Where on earth will I find one?"

"No, him, Potty, the gardener."

He quickly ran to the front balcony shouting, "Guards, guards, hold Ewunren. Don't let him go."

As the guards were wondering, the gardener flew past. Thinking that he was running after whoever it was *Kabiyesi* wanted held, the guards ran after the gardener. By the time they got on to the road the gardener had turned into a side street. The two came back breathing heavily.

Kabiyesi was standing by the front door with an expectant look on his face. When the two guards returned they said in unison, "We saw nobody except the gardener."

"Never mind," answered *Kabiyesi*, and slammed the door.

As *Olori* was cleaning Jumoke up, the poor girl was shivering; and she kept on moaning.

"Keep him away from me, keep him away from me. At first he was so gentle with me, so compassionate, so tender .... Then when I clung to him he inflicted so much pain on me but ..."

She had a funny kind of smile on her face, with her dishevelled hair and lingering smirk she looked like a mad woman. She continued to shake and to mumble. Startled and shaken *Olori* held on to her and started to rock her. She then put her back on the bed and covered her up, patting her on the forehead. She continued to hold her and rock her until she dozed off. When she started breathing quietly *Olori* tiptoed out of Jumoke's room.

It was nearing noon when both *Kabiyesi* and *Olori* came down. Both were yawning and looked tired.

"How is she?" asked *Kabiyesi*.

"Thank goodness she is now sleeping quietly."

"What really happened?" asked *Kabiyesi*.

"If what I think is true, then we have a problem," said the Olori very quietly.

"What do you mean?" asked *Kabiyesi*.

"Please send for the gardener." said the *Olori* shouting for the maid. The maid came back to say, "He is not in his room." They were still wondering about this when they heard a car driving in.

"Are you expecting guests?" asked the *Olori*.

"No."

Then the messenger entered and announced the *Oludotun*. Both of them got up to meet him.

"What a surprise *Kabiyesi*. To what do we owe the pleasure of this unannounced visit?"

"I am here to apologise for my son's behaviour."

"We have not seen him; what has he done?"

"Yes, you have; your gardener who disappeared in the early hours of the morning."

"Good gracious, don't say that the young man who posed as our gardener is your son."

"The impudent rascal." said Kabiyesi. The *Olori* slumped into a chair.

"How is your daughter?"

"She is still sleeping."

"My dear brother and sister, we shall make amends. I shall bring him to you to be scolded. He is very much in love with Jumoke."

Later in the evening *Kabiyesi Oludotun* with his *Olori* and a handsome young man called at the palace. The young man prostrated himself before both *Kabiyesi* and *Olori*. "Here I will lie until you give me unreserved pardon. I knew no other way to approach your unapproachable and impossible daughter. She drove me mad."

"Get up my son." said the *Kabiyesi*. A contrite *Adegboyega* rose, only to fall again and hold the feet of the *Olori*.

"Please let me call you mother," he whispered.

"Get up my son. Let's us go up and see her."

"Come in," said the soft voice. She lifted her head up from the pillow.

"Mother, that was a horrible nightmare; it left me devastated. I still feel sore. Oh!

I did not realise we had company."

Mother smiled. The man beside the *Olori* spoke: "I am sorry I disturbed your beauty sleep, Princess. I just could not wait."

Jumoke felt that the nightmare had started again. She was about to scream. "Please do not scream. It's me, Beans. I have come to apologise and to plead my case." Then Adegboyega with a pensive face went down on his knees. Like someone dreaming Jumoke said, "That voice sounds familiar, but it cannot be."

"Yes, it is. I am Beans."

Jumoke's face lighted with a smile. The *Olori*, seeing the joy on Jumoke's face, disappeared quietly. Jumoke jumped up from the bed and with her face beaming with ecstasy, she flew into his arms and sank her head on Adegboyega's chest saying, "You sweet rogue."

PREDESTINED

1) Early Years, Early Love

It is Monday and my first day at St. Peter's School. The previous Friday I had collected my letter of admission that instructed me to go to Standard 5A at eight o'clock. Instead I arrive at a quarter past seven. I find my way to the classroom, sit down and start reading Daniel Defoe's *Robinson Crusoe*. As is my habit, I soon get thoroughly engrossed in it.

"Hello, fine boy; hello, handsome." I hear the last hello sounding as if from afar. I then look up. Standing in front of me is a pretty young girl who must be about my age. I ask if she is talking to me. With a mischievous smile she says, "I guess so, since there are just the two of us here. My name is Wehinmi. You must be the Lagos boy. I saw you coming out of the Headmaster's office last Friday. You are so handsome. You are mine. I shall show them all, right from the beginning."

"What are you talking about? Who are 'them'?" I ask her.

"I am talking about the other girls in Standard 5A. They are a terrible lot. Mope already has a steady boyfriend and she is so crazy about him; there will be no problem there. Anyway, she is much older than us. Joko, although pretty, is dumb; I am not worried about her either. But Celina, although much older, is a great flirt. She will try to entice you if only to put the rest of us off. Felicia, she is a bush girl who does not know right from left.

"But the two I am afraid of," Wehinmi adds, "are the 'terrible Ys' – Yetunde and Yewande; they are pretty all right but they are too clever by half. Besides, they are not able to love anybody but themselves! I am here this early to make sure that I am ahead of them. You are mine, you are my boyfriend."

"Who says so?" I ask the girl.

"I, Wehinmi, say so and I mean it," she responds forcefully.

"Don't tell me that you already have a girlfriend."

"Me, I have no time for any such nonsense, let alone girlfriends. I have an entrance examination to prepare for. Besides, I am behind with my book reading; I still have ten novels to read and I do not want to anger my father."

"What are you reading anyway?"

After looking at my book she asks, "Who is Robinson Crusoe?"

"I shall pass the book to you when I finish reading it."

"To make sure you remember, my name is Wehinmi. I live with my parents on Old Barracks Road which is within walking distance."

"I know", I reply, "we, too, live on that road."

"That's good, we shall walk home together after school. It will be like that every day. I shall not allow any of the other girls to get near you. You are my boyfriend. I have chosen you."

"You are a small girl; what do you know about boyfriends?" I ask.

"I admit that I do not know much – you are my very first boyfriend. The big girls have taken all the best boys."

Just then the assembly bell rings, summoning us to all line up on the school field. After assembly prayers we re-enter the classroom block. Wehinmi sits down next to me and during the break she introduces me to the others.

To the girls she says: "Labi is my boyfriend. I don't want anyone of you flirting with him or dancing around him."

Later, after school, Wehinmi and I walk home together. She never stops talking. In addition to telling me her life story she tells me all about her parents and her younger brother. She discloses her likes and dislikes and asks me a load of questions about myself. I only answer those I feel like answering.

Although she talks too much, I must confess that I rather like her. I wonder if she has cast a spell on me? Saying goodbye, she says, "We shall meet at this junction tomorrow morning at 7". And that becomes our daily routine.

But I do not allow Wehinmi, with all her feminine wiles, to distract me from preparing for the entrance examination. In fact, I become more determined than ever to pass my exams with flying colours. Besides, I already miss Lagos and I am eager to get back there.

One day, Wehinmi asks me to accompany her home after school. As soon as we arrive she shouts excitedly "Mummy, Labi, the Lagos boy, is here." Then a tall lady appears from behind the curtains that divide the room. She is very pretty with a fine complexion. Looking at both of them it occurs to me that when Wehinmi is older they will look like twin sisters.

The lady says with a smile, "Labi, I am so glad to meet you. I know all about you. Wehinmi never stops talking about you. She says you are very clever. She thinks that you will top the class. What have you done to my little girl? You must have cast a spell on her. She has asked me to request you to assist her with her preparations for the entrance exams, especially in English. Is it true that you have read over 30 novels?"

I politely answer as many of these questions as I can. I also promise to assist Wehinmi with her studies. "Have some refreshments," her Mum offers. All the while Wehinmi is dancing round me. Before leaving us, Wehinmi's Mum hugs me and rumples my hair.

In the middle of November a letter from the High School in Lagos arrives. I have the offer of a place the following year. Wehinmi also gets a place but at one of the local girls' schools.

In December, we all go for the holidays. As I stay very near Wehinmi, I still continue to see her. It seems that not only is she very fond of me, but so too is her mother.

Then comes 21 December, the day before I travel to Lagos. Wehinmi insists that I stay all evening with her. As I am about to leave Wehinmi says: "Labi, do not forget that you are mine. Please say that I am yours! Although I am so young, my heart tells me that I shall never belong to anyone else. All I am asking Labi, for now, is for you to tell me. 'Wehinmi, you are mine,' That will make me happy all my life."

Under the circumstances what can I do but agree. I say: "Wehinmi, you are mine and I am yours." She jumps into the air, yelps and hugs me. It is all very emotional. An indescribable sensation passes through my entire body. In all my twelve years, I have never had such a wonderful feeling.

Saying our final goodbye, there are tears in her eyes. "I hope you will write to me" she says. "I know I will write to you," she adds.

I did not set eyes on Wehinmi again for ten years. What's more, I did not recognise her when I eventually did....and she was not able to tell me who she was. It took another six years before we met again.

* * *

During mid-December we moved into our new house at Oko Awo. The house, a bungalow, has two self-contained flats. It has a large portico in the front with a big yard at the back. I have the last bedroom with two windows opening onto the yard. I use my room as bedroom and study, which is useful, for I am studying hard for my A-level exams the following May.

Before getting down to serious studies, I decide to give myself a fortnight's break to enjoy Christmas and the New Year. This break will also allow me to take stock of my six years at the High School, as well as to plan my work for the forthcoming examinations. It will give me time to get ready for a clerical job that I hope to secure at the government offices. The hours of work give me at least four hours for serious studies every day.

We move into the new house before our neighbours. We choose the flat on the right hand side. The other tenants, our neighbours, "Uncle Bayo" and his family arrive in early January. Bayo, is an engineer in his early thirties. He has just returned from Germany where he has been studying and getting work experience. Uncle Bayo has a young cousin, Ade, of about my age. He too works in a government department. The cousin and I become immediate friends from our first meeting. In addition, Uncle Bayo is very companionable, and we all get on very well. Within two months Ade and I have become firm friends. He too is studying for an examination. We study together, sometimes very late into the night.

At weekends we usually just take it easy. Most weekends Uncle Bayo travels home to his village about twenty miles away. His main reason is to see his mother whose health is poor. He usually leaves for the village on Friday evening and returns on Sunday evening. This gives Ade and me lots of freedom over the weekends.

About three months after moving in, Uncle Bayo starts to visit Ibadan quite frequently. Rumour has it that he is courting a young lady he intends to marry. After this had gone on for almost eight months we learn that he and the lady are to become formally engaged. The ceremony will take place in Ibadan where she and her parents live. The wedding will also be in Ibadan four months later. I cannot attend the wedding as the time for my examination is drawing near. Ade who accompanied Uncle Bayo tells us all about the ceremony. "It was a grand affair," he says, "and the bride is so pretty."

The newly-weds went to the north for their two week honeymoon. Another two week's stay at Uncle Bayo's village followed. This was to enable the bride, Eunice, and Uncle Bayo's mother, who could not attend the wedding due to her ill health, to get to know each other. The new couple finally arrive in Lagos about four weeks after the wedding.

The bride was as beautiful as Ade had said she was, and very witty. Everyone within the compound, as well as her other neighbours, grow to be fond of Eunice.

Uncle Bayo formally introduced Eunice at a drinks party, to which all the neighbours, including myself, were invited. When we shook hands I could sense a mischievous twinkle in her eye. Was it my imagination? She also winked at me. I feel there is something familiar about her. I seem to have seen her, or someone like her, before. Eunice says that it is her first time in Lagos and she seems to like it. I conclude that, if indeed it is her first time in Lagos, I could not have met her before. Perhaps it was someone with a slight resemblance, I think to myself.

Uncle Bayo and his wife Eunice go out a lot in the evenings during the week. Some weekends the couple travel to the village to see Uncle Bayo's mother. On other weekends, Uncle Bayo goes alone and two of Eunice's girlfriends come to visit. Ade is always there to keep them company.

One particular weekend Uncle Bayo had gone off to visit his mother but Eunice's two girlfriends did not visit. On the Saturday night after studying until around midnight, I become so sleepy I actually doze off. Something awakens me, and I decide to walk around the yard to stretch my legs to help myself stay awake. I had been walking for a short while when I heard Ade and Eunice talking. For some reason, I decide to move nearer to the window, although not really wanting to eavesdrop. However, I distinctly hear Ade's and Eunice's voices.

Eunice was saying: "I find the whole arrangement rather distasteful; I don't think I want to go through with it; the truth is that I have changed my mind; I can also see that you are as unhappy with the arrangement as I am."

"You are right there," Ade replied. "My fiancée is getting worried."

"Why don't we tell him that we are working on it?"

"But one day, he will surely find out that we have not been doing so," was Ade's answer.

"Let's leave it at that for now," Eunice says.

"Good night" says Ade; and the lights go out.

The following morning was a bright Sunday. Ade came to my room just as I was getting ready to have some rest after working all night. "Good morning Fola, or shall I say good night." he says. "The latter would probably be more appropriate."

"There was a particular exercise I had to crack and as a result I did not sleep," I began to explain. Then Ade asked me if I had seen anything of Eunice that morning, commenting that she seemed to have disappeared. "She cannot have gone far. She will show up soon," I remarked. I then pull the covers over my head, as if to signal I really did need to get some sleep.

At about noon I wake up and go into the yard for my usual morning exercise. Ade is sitting on a stool with a frown on his face. "What's the problem?" I enquire. "Eunice is yet to show up. It's strange; she has never gone out on her own before. I always accompany her whenever she is going out," Ade tells me.

"You don't have to worry; she will be back soon; after all she is an adult," I say.

After lunch, I decide to take a stroll. Returning that evening I find Ade on the portico looking around anxiously. "She has disappeared into thin air. I am scared. It is so strange – she has never gone out on her own before."

While Ade and I are still discussing Eunice's disappearance, Uncle Bayo drives into the yard. He is naturally disturbed when he learns that Eunice has been missing since early morning. We then sit down to discuss how to search for her.The most logical beginning for the search, we agree, is to go to the houses of her two friends. Ade did so immediately. First thing the following day, Uncle Bayo decides that, if necessary, he will go to Ibadan to continue the search. Not until then shall we inform the police.

Eunice has not been seen by her two friends and so Uncle Bayo sets out for Ibadan the next day. She had not been seen there either.

To be absolutely certain, Uncle Bayo called at their village on his way back. No one there has seen her either. When we check, we discover that none of her belongings are missing. All her dresses, bags, shoes, and jewellery are still in her room. Everyone agrees that this is most strange. A thorough search of her room does not yield any other clues. The report to the police also has no result. The compound, indeed the neighbourhood as a whole, shares our concern. It is quite a mystery. The neighbourhood is rife with all sorts of rumours, speculations and theories. Uncle Bayo becomes increasingly worried.

After a year of fruitless effort, the hunt to find Eunice is called off. Although the search has been abandoned, I cannot stop thinking about her. One night, unable to sleep, I again recall that evening when Uncle Bayo introduced her to me – in particular, that mischievous twinkle in her eye when she winked at me. The strange feeling that we had met before still lingered with me, but I questioned how that could be since it was her first visit to Lagos.

I had already dreamt about her twice. Sometimes strange images of her intruded into my thoughts. Is Eunice a real person? Is she from the spirit world? Why does she leave without taking any of her belongings? What a puzzle!

2) London, Phyllis and The Intervening Years

One day a letter arrives for me. It reads:

"My dear lost friend.

At first I thought I had lost you for all times. When suddenly you reappeared in my life I felt new life surging into me. Then came that evening. At first, I just saw your silhouette but when for some minutes you remained still outside the window I was sure that you were listening to everything we were saying. I was moved. I felt that I had betrayed you. That night I changed my mind. There was nothing else I could do but leave. I did not wish to commit any indiscretion. Whatever it was you saw or heard was not what you thought.

Something tells me that I shall still have the opportunity to explain everything to you. Since our first meeting you had always been with me. Whether I was awake or asleep, you were always there. It will always be so since you are mine and I am yours. My word is my bond and I would like to think that you think the same.

Sometimes I thought you did not recognise me. I am almost certain that I was correct, especially as you did not show any sign of recognition. There was a night I was arguing with myself. I consoled myself with the thought that you were just being a gentleman and did not wish to compromise me. Your thoughts will always be in my mind. Please be patient and wait for me. I am yours and yours only. It's me."

I read and reread the letter. It did not make sense to me. Am I reading someone else's letter? I asked myself. But it was clearly addressed to me. Who could the writer be? Why is she writing, as it seems then, in riddles? What am I supposed to do, especially as she does not give me her return address.

Although the letter is not sad, I feel that the writer is in a state of doubt and distress. What should I do? I asked myself again and again. I read the letter several more times thinking that reading it more carefully will give a clue to the writer and why is it not signed. But one night something compels me to read the letter again and a part of it strikes me as strange. It was the part that read:

"Then came that evening. When for some minutes you remained still outside the window I was sure that you were listening to everything we were saying. I was moved. I felt that I had betrayed you. That night I changed my mind. There was nothing else I could do but leave. I did not wish to commit any indiscretion. Whatever it was you saw or heard was not what you thought."

One sentence keeps recurring in my memory – *"I felt that I had betrayed you."* One other point that struck a chord is when she writes, *"I am yours and you are mine!"* I remembered having heard something similar before.

For the first time it occurs to me that Eunice and Wehinmi might be one and the same person. Eunice and Wehinmi's mother were very much alike, but how could it be she married Uncle Bayo? Here is another puzzle. Wehinmi's face started to haunt me. If I was right, what had happened to her? How was I to find out?

After passing my A levels, I concentrate on saving the best part of my earnings for two years. For this reason I had resigned my civil service appointment to join a commercial enterprise. The pay was much better and merit was given recognition. So I started planning my studies abroad.

I eventually achieve that aim. By the time I travel from Lagos, I have already enough savings to pay my tuition fees for the three years. The night before my departure, I have the feeling that I am not alone. Or perhaps I had been dreaming. But I did feel that I was conversing with the writer of the strange letter.

She kept on reminding me that *"we had plighted our troth; do not break your promise. I have not broken mine, although it might appear to be so. My explanations will more than satisfy you when we meet in due course, as we shall. I wish you a pleasant journey and a safe return. I am waiting to receive your embraces."*

It felt so real that from time to time I peer into the dark corners of the room. I am no longer in any doubt that the mystery letter is from Wehinmi. That night my sleep is sound and peaceful. I awake feeling fresh and alive, and on my flight from Lagos to London thoughts of Wehinmi filled my head.

I arrive safely in London, but my temptations start from my very first day. Our group reach the British Council hostel that morning. One student who is returning for a post-graduate course suggests that we accompany him to the Methodist International House where we find a table tennis tournament taking place. I sit there, seemingly watching the game, but my mind is in another place completely.

Unknown to me, I am being watched. Suddenly I feel a gentle nudge; I turned to my right and my eyes met hers. She says, "Hello handsome, a penny for your thoughts." I say hello. "While you are not exactly bored like me I see that your mind is not on the game. Come on, let's go for a walk."

We walk along Inverness Terrace until we reach the Bayswater Road. We cross over into the park and sit down underneath a tree.

"My name is Phyllis. I am a law student from Kingston, Jamaica. For the first time in the six months I've been here I feel homesick. I miss Frank, my boyfriend. Tell me about yourself," she asks me.

"I am Labi. I arrived only this morning from Nigeria. I am not exactly homesick but I'm missing an old friend terribly. I had not seen her for ten years; and when I did, I did not recognise her. A letter she sent jogged my memory and a few other things that have happened have left me confused. I cannot describe my feelings. I feel so sad and sorry. I wonder what I should do."

"Never mind" Phyllis reassures me. "It appears that we are in the same predicament. Let us be friends so that we can console each other. I shall be your source of strength and you shall be mine."

"That's very kind of you," I replied. "I am sure that we can be good friends, provided we do not get carried away." That is how Phyllis and I come to be good friends. In due course, she becomes like a sister to me. But for her my life and my problems could have become much more complicated.

She shielded me from other would-be girlfriends and London's host of husband hunters. Often, to ward off embarrassment, I introduce her as my girlfriend or fiancée as the occasion demanded.

My stay in Britain is fruitful. Throughout the time, my companion and adviser Phyllis is always by my side. Without her I could not have achieved the success I did. When I get my final year results, Phyllis receives the news with mixed emotions.

That evening she says: "My brother achieved an upper second in economics, so I should feel happier than I am now; but I'm not. The thought that you will be on your way to Nigeria shortly has made me feel very sad – but congratulations again and I wish you more successes in the future".

The following day there is a new development. Frank, Phyllis's boyfriend, telephones to say that he will arrive ten days before my return to Nigeria. I have never seen Phyllis so happy and radiant. It was a great consolation for me that Phyllis would have her boyfriend and would not be lonely.

Days later I board the cargo boat for Lagos. The fortnight on the boat goes by quickly. I make new friends on the ship, one being Maxwell, a newly qualified pharmacist from Eku in the mid-west region of Nigeria. We enjoy our short stopovers in Las Palmas, Freetown and Takoradi.

I need only a week's break before starting my new job as a manager with a trading company that has a large Nigerian network. My posting is to the Head Office to take charge of the western and mid-western regions. My first tour is to Ibadan, the company's Area Office for the west region.

On my first night I find the way to Wehinmi's house at Old Barracks Road. Her parents are still living there, but were away. I leave a note for Wehinmi's mother in which I ask her to remember me to Wehinmi.

On my first tour to the mid-west region I visit Benin City, Sapele and Warri. My main mission is to meet the company's distributors and to get to know the area. One afternoon I take time off to visit Maxwell, the pharmacist who had returned to Nigeria with me. He is glad to see me in Eku where he had just completed furnishing his new store and showroom.

I had mentioned to him that I needed to buy some good fabric and head-ties and asked his advice as to the best store in Warri for such goods. He gives me a note for his young relation. After my business rounds the following day I go to the shop. As I enter the shop, a lady is coming out. I could not believe my eyes – it is Eunice, the missing bride. We both stand still. I speak first. "Is that you, Eunice?" She clasps me with both hands, crying and laughing at the same time. Then she lets me go and pushes me backwards to take another good look at me.

"Is it Fola or a ghost?" she exclaims. "Yes, it's me, dear Eunice, but you have a lot of explaining to do! Let's go inside first," I stammer. As I sit down she pats me on the cheeks.

"Fola it is so good to see you," she says. "You look so dazed and puzzled. I shall explain everything, but all in good time. I am on my way home. Let's have something to drink before we go home. We can then talk in a relaxed atmosphere free from interruption."

As she walks, I cannot stop looking at her. She is a spitting image of Wehinmi's mother, so much so that I have no doubt that she is Wehinmi. She is even more beautiful than when I last saw her. It is a short drive from the shop to her house.

"A good meal before we talk or we talk before the meal?" she asks me.

"I would rather have the talk first. I need answers to so many questions," I reply.

3) Wehinmi's Mystery is Explained

"Would you mind if I tell my story from the beginning, that way there will be fewer questions to ask. Agreed?"

"Agreed." I answered.

"Eunice and Wehinmi are one and the same person: you need not puzzle your head over that. My maternal grandmother, who, by the way, wants to meet you, named me Temisan Orisewehinmi. My paternal grandfather named me Omolara and at my baptism I was given the name Eunice. I understand that this was my mother's idea, so my mother prefers to call me Eunice. My

181

mother and Uncle Bayo's mother were classmates at the Women Teacher's Training College at Ibadan when they were young. The friendship continues to this day, despite the rupture caused by my disappearance in Lagos. But we shall get to that in due course.

"For quite some time," Eunice continues, "my mother was pressing that I should get married. I always told her that the only person I had ever loved, and would ever love, was my Labi. My mother would always reply, 'But where is your Labi? He never writes to you. You do not even know if he is still alive'.

"One day mummy said, 'I am expecting a visitor tomorrow. He has just arrived from Germany'. 'Who is he?" I asked. 'What was he doing in Germany?' Mother told me his name was Bayo and he was the first child of an old school friend, Oluyemi. 'But why is he coming here, mum?' I asked. 'You will see when he gets here'.

"The next day, just before noon, an impressive sports car pulled up in front of our house. Out came this tall handsome man. As I was at the front door he came straight to me. 'Good-day, young lady. Is this the house of Mr and Mrs Ede?' When I said it was, he announced that he was expected.

"I led him in and called out for mummy. When mum arrived, the handsome man bowed before they both shook hands. 'You have become a handsome young man. Why aren't you married?' mummy asked. 'I am still searching for the right partner,' answered the visitor. 'Please forgive me,' mum said. 'I get carried away. Please sit down and make yourself comfortable. Bayo, please may I introduce you to my daughter, Eunice.' Turning to me mum explained, 'This is Bayo, the son of my old friend and classmate. Eunice, please get our visitor a drink. Why don't we try the lemonade you have just made?'

"Mum and I went into the kitchen. Mum had a knowing look on her face. I pretended not to notice it. I placed the tray with the jug of lemonade and three glasses on the table and asked to be excused. I sat on a chair in my room pretending to be reading. Then mum entered and said, 'Eunice what does this mean? You have left our guest unattended.'

"Mum, don't you mean your guest. Why should I attend to him? He is here to see you," I replied. 'Eunice, do not be difficult. You know he is here to see you. Yemi and I thought that if both of you meet and grew fond of each other you might get married.'

"'So my Mum is now a matchmaker,' I answered, adding quickly, 'Mum, you know that I already have a man of my own. Besides, two persons don't get married just because they are fond of each other. All the same let us go down and entertain the visitor.'

"Dad was away so just the three of us sat down for lunch. Having eaten, and as quickly as it was polite to do so, Mum excused herself and I was left alone with Bayo. I must say that he impressed me as a charming person with perfect manners – and he fascinated me. He disclosed that his mother had been pressurising him to get married. It was she who suggested that he should pay this visit as something might come of it. 'She told me how beautiful and intelligent you are,' Bayo disclosed, 'and so here I am. All I want for a start is friendship and assurance that we can meet again from time to time. Who knows, it might lead to something.'

"I answered that while I saw nothing wrong with this idea, I felt I had to point out that there could be a problem. I then told him of the understanding that you and I had while we were young. He dismissed it with a wave of the hand. 'How do you think that such a promise between two twelve-year-old kids could be taken seriously?' he queried.

"I replied that in our own case, it was a special and binding agreement. When he asked where the young man was now, I answered truthfully that I did not know. 'Yet you are still hoping that he remembers you and the promise,' he said with sarcasm.

"Uncle Bayo took to visiting us almost every weekend after

our first meeting, often bringing me presents. I honestly became fond of him. Polished men were rare in our area in those days, and he fascinated me. All my friends thought I was very fortunate to have such a suitor. Then one day he sent me a letter informing me that he intended to visit me the next weekend to ask me for a special favour.

"The letter was brought by Ade, a young man who must have been about my age who looked very much like Uncle Bayo. He explained that they were first cousins. He added that many people thought they are brothers. I asked Ade to tell Uncle Bayo that he was welcome to come.

"He arrived on Friday evening. This time he stayed at a small hotel near our home. The hotel had a night-club with the best band in town. He invited me to join him there the following day, a Saturday, and I agreed.

"Just before he took me home he asked how I felt about our relationship. I told him that I felt that it was fine. He pressed me further and asked if it was a positive enough relationship for us to get engaged. I reminded him that he was yet to make a formal proposal. I add that even after that we would need to wait for at least another three months before getting engaged. I set the three month's limit because intuition told me that I might see or hear from you within that time. He agreed rather reluctantly, on the condition that on weekends when he was unable to come, due to visits to his ill mother, Ade could come to keep me company.

"While agreeing I thought to myself that he wanted to install someone to keep an eye on me. The truth was that I enjoyed Ade's company, perhaps even more than Uncle Bayo's in some ways, because Ade and I are about the same age.

"On getting home I find Mum had sat up for me. She asked how the evening had gone. I told her that I enjoyed it as Uncle Bayo is a very good dancer. Mum wanted to know what else happened. My guess was that Uncle Bayo had already hinted to

her that he was going to propose. Mum was disappointed, as I had nothing else to add.

"As agreed, Ade come every other weekend. Like me, Ade is a scrabble fan and good at chess. We, therefore, spent quite a lot of time playing both games. I got to like him more and more. One evening Ade asked me a curious question. He asked me how happy I should be if Uncle Bayo decided to withdraw his suit leaving the coast clear for him. All I said was, 'What a thought!'. I was to recall that incident afterwards.

"Time flew by and with only two weeks out of the three months I had requested from Uncle Bayo left, there was still no news of you. In the meantime my Mum and Bayo's mother started to make preparations for the engagement. Precisely three months following our discussion I got engaged to Uncle Bayo.

"The wedding was fixed for a month after that. On the night of our engagement I asked Uncle B, as I now address him, why he wanted to marry me when he knew full well that my heart was with someone else. He said that he was willing to take the chance. I again stressed that he would be having a body without a heart. He added that he was sure that he would soon sweep me off my feet. It was the most curious engagement that I ever heard of. I thought I was in a dream.

"We had previously agreed that we would go up North for the honeymoon. Uncle B assured me that I would love Jos, Vom, Bukuru and the other towns and places in the region. Then another curious thing occurred. 'How would you like it if I were to give you another three months of grace after the wedding, just in case your Labi turns up after all?' asked Uncle B. I was astounded and asked him what sort of joke that was meant to be. He said he thought it best that we wait for three months to consummate our marriage.

"I looked at him askance believing he must be joking. But no, he was not. Rather he was paving the way for a favour that he wanted, a favour that he was only prepared to ask, he said, the night before our wedding. 'It can be your wedding gift to me,' he said. Instinct told me that he was serious.

"On the evening before the wedding, Uncle B came to the house and we had supper with my parents. Afterwards, he suggested that we take a stroll in the garden as he was ready to ask for his special favour. We took our wine glasses and another bottle. Sitting down underneath a tree I told Uncle B that I was eagerly awaiting his request. Let me say it almost in his words. He said, 'The doctor told my mother that she had between eighteen months and two years to live. She then asked me earnestly to make it possible for her to see a grandchild before she passed away. As I know that I could not gratify that wish, I was in a quandary.' I wanted to interrupt him but he asked to be allowed to finish.

"Continuing with his explanation, he told me: 'While in Germany, my favourite sport was polo. One evening I fell from my horse after a collision with an opponent. It was a very bad fall. I was rushed to the hospital. I had an operation the following day. Before being discharged, the surgeon advised me that my chances of being able to father a child were remote. Of course, I could not tell my mother about this when I got back to Nigeria. When the pressure started about my getting married I began to think about what I could do. It was then that I decided that I would take Ade into my confidence. He was the only person I could tell as I have no brother. I then requested him to help me father just one child provided you would agree. He was horrified. He then raised a very important issue. He said that one day he too would get married. He already had a girlfriend he intended to marry. Supposing he was willing to gratify mine and my mother's request, what sort of explanations could he give to a future wife? We also wondered what your reactions would be. The plan was to confide in your Mum after the baby arrived.

"'If you decide against this arrangement, the marriage will still have to take place. A divorce can then be arranged discreetly after a decent lapse of time, and that will leave you free for your lover boy. What do you say?' I was so flabbergasted by the strange request I could not speak. I had to think fast. After walking around in the garden, I came to a decision. Having logically marshalled my thoughts, I decided that calling the marriage off was not a possibility – the shame would kill my parents. I would talk to Ade. Both of us might agree to go along with this scheme, but there was no way I could sleep with him - or anybody else for that matter.

"But I knew that I could share my bed with Labi, for my spirit was telling me that he was still alive and he would find me soon. Besides, this was a way for me to buy some more time to find him. I was sure that Ade would go along with me.

"I walked back to where I had left Uncle B and told him that the marriage would go ahead. He hugged me and said that God would bless me. Just getting married, he said, would calm his mother down. So we walked back to the house hand-in-hand. Uncle B said good night to my parents and went to his hotel.

"The wedding took place. We enjoyed our stay in the North, wining, dining and dancing each evening. When we arrived at

Uncle Bayo's village, my mother-in-law was so happy. It was as if her grandchild had already arrived. But my trouble started when we got to Lagos. I could not believe it when I saw you; but you did not recognise me. To compound my problem, when I asked Ade your name he said Fola. I just could not figure it out. That night I could not sleep, as my mind was racing so fast.

"I tried to see you alone so that I could speak to you, but there was no chance. For two days I was ill. I was depressed and restless. What could I do? Then it occurred to me that I would ask Ade your full name. When I asked him and he said it was Afolabi, I had such a sense of relief. Unfortunately it was on that evening that I decided to tell Ade to call the whole plan off. That was when I saw you outside our window. I was frightened that you would have heard our conversation and you would have jumped to the wrong conclusions. Ade and I had never been romantically involved. He was in love with Yeside, his fiancée. He was so relieved when I told him to abandon the plan. But I did not tell him about our previous relationship.

"During the night I thought it through. I would leave first thing in the morning while all of you were still sleeping. I would go into hiding. When all the hue and cry had died down I would make contact with you. I had never been so happy in my life. To think that it was Uncle B who brought about our reunion. I knew too that Uncle Bayo would have no objection to us obtaining a divorce. Although I was only a twelve-year-old when I first set eyes on you, I truly fell in love with you. You would not have believed what I was thinking when I saw you leaving the Headmaster's office. Something told me this was my future husband.

"Do you recall the last evening we spent together before you left for Lagos? I almost died of grief. Throughout Christmas and New Year I was ill. I could not tell Mum what the matter was. When all the other girls started bringing their boyfriends, Mum would ask for mine. I always reminded her that she had met and liked you. I assured her that God intended us for each other and it was meant to be. I am not sure that she believed me."

At that point I interrupted her to ask: "When you ran away from Lagos where were you hiding so you could not be found." She asked if I remembered Felicia, our classmate. It was to her she went because no one would think of looking for her there. "Instead of my afro cut I grew my hair and started to plait it. I started accompanying Felicia to Warri and Ashaka were we bought fine materials for sale in Igbara Oke. We would travel all over Ekiti – Ado, Iyin, Aiyedun, Efon…"

Continuing her narrative, Eunice (or should I now call her Wehinmi?), told me: "After one year when the hue and cry had died down I registered at the Polytechnic to study for a degree in Social Science. At the same time Felicia's mother was teaching us how to sew. I eventually ended up in Eku with Daddy's cousin, Maxwell's mother.

She gave me a small shop in Eku. After two years I had saved enough to rent a shop in Warri. I deliberately continued to use my married name to ward off the wolves. I told them that my husband was away in the UK studying. The shop grew. I took the adjoining one and then a third one. I became the largest distributor of George materials and Hayes head-ties. I started doing wholesale business.

"One day on a trip to Benin City I ran into Ronke, our next door neighbour in Lagos. It was she that told me you were away in Britain studying Economics. I begged her not to tell anyone that she had seen me. We became good friends and I gave her goods on credit. She was creditworthy and paid promptly; in addition she kept my secret.

"Before you go on with your questions I have some of my own, otherwise I shall die of anxiety. I hope you have not entangled yourself with any lady? I hope your love for me has grown as mine has. I have never loved anyone else. I knew you were mine because I said it. I bewitched you. More accurately, our union was predestined."

All the time she had been speaking I never stop looking at Wehinmi. When I indicate that I want to say my piece she suggests that we should first take our meal as it was getting late. Before that, however, she embraces me and gives me a kiss, with fervour. The way the kiss was returned assures her that my long wait had not been in vain.

After the meal I tell my story, especially about the stay in London, full of praise and gratitude for Phyllis whom God had sent to assist me. I say that as soon as Wehinmi can obtain a divorce we would get married. At her suggestion we agree that the honeymoon would be in Jos. She reminds him that her grandmother would like to see me. As she lives in Warri we agreed to visit her the next day.

4) A Wise Granny and a Blessed Union

It is mid-morning when we arrive at Granny's compound, and we greet about a dozen relatives before we get to Granny's apartment. As we enter, there she is: a dignified, elegant, old lady. Her white hair had been brushed back tightly on her head and, despite being in her nineties, she is still an attractive woman. She exudes a lively aura and her pretty eyes still sparkle brightly. There can be no doubt of where Wehinmi and her mother take their beauty from.

She greets us very warmly and Wehinmi presents me to the old lady. "Labi, this is Gran. She was looking forward to meeting you. She was the only one who believed that you were real, alive and would come back to me. She was always speaking about you, especially after she had read my palms. She said that I would be eternally indebted to a lady who would save you for me. She went on to say that the woman was someone with honour; and though greatly attracted to you her conscience would not allow her to come between you and the woman you loved."

"Welcome, my son. I knew that you would come one day,"

Gran said. "Often I saw you in my dreams and visions. I took to you from the first time I saw you. I was told that you were Wehinmi's husband. I was assured that it was meant to be."

"Gran", I replied, "Wehinmi and I were about twelve years old when we first met. How could she know at such a tender age that she was in love with me and I with her?"

The old woman answered my question with these words. "My son, there are many things that men do not understand. Although you and Wehinmi were biologically the same age, she was more mature than you. The creator ensures that girls mature far more quickly than boys. When you met you were twelve. Wehinmi had the maturity of a girl of about sixteen. Besides, like me, she is psychic and has the 'gift'. It must have been revealed to her that you were her husband to be. When her mother became worried that she was not interested in boys, I tried to assure her. I told my daughter that Wehinmi had already given her heart, her life and all, to someone who was predestined for her. Wehinmi's mother did not believe me, but I was convinced, and even more so when one day I read Wehinmi's palms when she was here on holiday. There it was clearly written that Labi was to be her husband. Although it was indicated that several years and many miles would separate you both, it had been ordained. "I also saw that both a woman and a man would threaten to come between the two of you; yet you would both overcome all impediments and eventually share the life that had been mapped out for you."

Gran, seeing the puzzled look on my face, adds: "My son, you would not understand since you do not have the gift. Besides, as I said before, the creator has given women from the beginning of time the special attributes that men in their self-conceit call wiles. Men would never understand. Is not the woman the mother of the man? It has always been so and it will always be. A ten-year-old girl can always hold her own against a male twice that age! Men think that they are wise. What they do not know or understand is that women are wiser! When a man sets out thinking that the woman is weaker, he makes himself even more vulnerable. He has let down his guard. While the woman continues to advance, he continues in the self-delusion that he is on top. This is not so. He is truly the lesser partner in any relationship and as a woman gains strength and authority, the man is obliged to give way. For example, take the farce called courtship. The man may think that he is simply getting to know the woman but the reverse is the truth. All along the woman will be indulging in what is known these days as marketing!

"If she has decided to choose the man who is wooing her, she will of course try to present her best face to the man. She allows the man to see what she knows he wants to see; but deep inside her is what is really important. In her basket of wiles are many faces: she puts them on and changes them at will, one face for the one she likes and another for the one she dislikes, yet another one for the one she loves and would ensnare and enslave for life. The poor man is soon blinded by love!

"I will tell you both a story," Gran said to Wehinmi and me without so much as pausing for breath. "There was the case of a courtship that had lasted two whole years. The poor man thought he knew his girl. He thought that she was not the deceptive type who would have three boyfriends at the same time. He saw her as a good, sweet and honest girl who would not hurt a fly. One evening when he was supposed to be at evening class and it was cancelled he decided to delight his sweetheart by paying her an unscheduled visit. He was shocked to find her in the arms of another boyfriend. Soon after that he discovered she was having frequent dates with yet another boy. Not surprisingly, he decided to avoid this girl in future. When this girl was let down by the third boyfriend, she made an attempt to make up with her first boyfriend – but he had learnt his lesson and would have none of it. I must add that there are just a few examples where it has been ordained that a particular boy and girl have been created for each other. Wisdom alone cannot help a man; he needs in addition the grace that comes from above.

"My dear children, I am so happy to see you both. Labi, it is a great joy to see you in real life. Wehinmi you look even more beautiful, radiant and happy. May God bless you both. I have been assured that I shall carry your children in my arms before I am called home. Do come and see me as often as you can. I shall always pray for you. Labi, have a safe journey to Lagos and please do not delay the wedding."

Back at Wehinmi's residence, she invites me into the sitting room. "Now my questions, Labi," she begins. "What exactly was your relationship with Phyllis? Did you fall in love with her? And she with you? Please be entirely frank with me. Did you kiss and cuddle regularly? Did you make love to her?"

I explain that most of this story has already been told but I did add that Phyllis liked me, but simply in a brotherly sense. "Had I given her encouragement the situation could have been different," I told her, "but there was always Frank. Besides, your face, Wehinmi, was always before me."

I admit that I did waiver once, but I was saved. One evening when I was really depressed and thinking about you, I felt sad, lonely and dejected. I thought that Uncle Bayo must have found you and I was just wasting my time. Who should come in just then? It was Phyllis. The moment she came in I knew that all was not well. She flopped into the chair, so unlike her usual self. She looked tired and dispirited. Without speaking, I could almost read her thoughts. She seemed to be saying, my man is not here, your sweetheart is not here, but we are here; we are fond of each other. We are all but in love. Why can't we at least make the best of it and enjoy ourselves instead of making ourselves miserable?

She then said aloud, 'I am a member of this household yet I have never been allowed to spend a night here. No one will put me off tonight. Whether you like it or not, I am going to sleep here tonight. I shall not have a lonely night today'.

I smiled at her affectionately, and went to the kitchen to make a pot of tea. Then I came back and poured two cups, offering her one. Although she accepted it, she looked at me pleadingly. 'Drink your tea first. We shall speak afterwards.' I said. After we had a few sips she stretched her hands across the table. I touched them, so lightly at first. Before I knew it I held them more firmly; then I started to caress them gently and lovingly. The lovely hand with its long fingers was soft and warm. I was all on fire. I wanted to get up and hold her to my chest, to kiss her and show her how much I understood her need and suffering as well as mine. She looked at me pleadingly, she seemed to be telling me her feelings reciprocated my own. However, I restrained myself. If I had risen from my seat we might have done something that we would regret for the rest of our lives. Why I started massaging her hand I simply don't know; perhaps more strangely, I started to hum so softly a West Indian calypso –her favourite - which calmed her so that she started to doze.

I then put her head on my lap while still caressing her. As she continued to sleep, she started to breathe softly and I gently placed her head on a cushion. I then went into the kitchen to cook her favourite dish of *egusi* soup and spinach with *eba*. When the table was set I gently woke her up. 'Phyllis, my dear sister come and eat,' I said. I watched her. 'I have enjoyed it, dear brother. You have saved me and my honour once again. May God bless you. Please telephone for a cab to take me home. Please bear with me. It won't happen again'. 'No, I have felt as you do from time to time; but we have resisted the urge and temptation for so long, why should we give in when we are nearing the finishing tape?' I told her.

"Her boyfriend Frank telephoned the next day. The truth was, he saved us from ourselves. In the frame of mind in which we both found ourselves something might have happened just before my return to Nigeria. That, my darling, is the honest truth regarding Phyllis and myself. It's the whole truth."

Wehinmi insists on returning to Lagos with me. However, I convince her not to. I promise to visit her again soon. She pleads and pleads, saying that after such a long separation we should always now be together. The night preceding my return to Lagos is a most painful one. Wehinmi insists that I should spend the night in her flat instead of going to the Catering Rest House. Somehow we overcome the temptation. We are together until the early hours of the morning. We limit ourselves to kissing and holding each other; it is deliciously painful, bitter and sweet at the same time. It seems inevitable that both of us should travel to and from Lagos and Warri frequently.

On Wehinmi's next visit to Lagos, we visit a lawyer friend. After hearing explanations about the circumstance of the wedding between Bayo and Wehinmi as well as the separation for over four years, the lawyer assures us that she can easily get a divorce. Kunle, the lawyer, telephones Bayo a few days later for an appointment. He goes to the meeting with a draft divorce settlement. When Bayo reads it and hears that Wehinmi and I are planning to become man and wife, he readily agrees. In addition, he promises to make a very generous wedding present to us in compensation for what he made Wehinmi go through. In due course the divorce comes through and Wehinmi is free to marry me.

The following weekend Wehinmi and I visit Ibadan to see her parents. Wehinmi's mother greets me warmly while recalling the romance between the two kids. She confesses that at the time she thought that it was just a childish infatuation. On hearing about Uncle Bayo's unfortunate predicament, Wehinmi's parents express sympathy for him. They both give their blessings to the proposed union between us. It is at this point that her father confesses that the letters I had sent to Wehinmi were destroyed by him. He then did not think that it was right that two young kids should engage in such correspondence. Wehinmi and I, as well as her mother, express disappointment at this, but in the happy mood of the occasion we do not want to dwell on past mistakes.

And thus, our relationship begins in earnest, a whirlwind kind of courtship followed very soon by the engagement and wedding, after the years of waiting. Ade, Bayo's cousin, is the best man. His wife, Yeside, also comes to the ceremony. For the best part of the time Wehinmi and I hold hands, with our eyes aglow. We then travel to Jos for the honeymoon.

This time it is a real honeymoon. When Wehinmi relates the experiences of her last honeymoon, I feel moved. Both of us feel sorry for Uncle Bayo. Wehinmi said that he was always a real gentleman. Beyond the occasional kisses and embraces, she was never pressured; they even had separate bedrooms.

Wehinmi feels extremely sorry for him. Uncle Bayo was always sad not so much for his own condition but for his mother whose wish for a grandchild he could not gratify. Wehinmi adds that Bayo was always apologetic for the embarrassing situation he had put Wehinmi and Ade through. Wehinmi and I agree that we have no bitterness towards Uncle Bayo. We both assure him of a warm welcome to our home. Bayo's delight at the end of it all is very gratifying.

Gradually Wehinmi quickly settles down in Lagos and she refers to me as her husband and lover. She moves her business base to Lagos and the business keeps growing. Wehinmi's store has become the most popular place for George materials and Hayes head-ties.

Marriage suits both of us extremely well. One evening after our game of scrabble I recall 'the terrible girls' that were our classmates at St Peters School. I ask Wehinmi about them one by one. 'Whatever happened to Mope, the besotted lover?" I ask. "Mope and Jide, her boyfriend, got married." "Jide is now an auto-mechanic and is doing extremely well. As in the past Mope continues to dote on him; only that now he has to compete for her attention with five kids. She has a shop on New Court Road, Ibadan."

"How about the dumb, pretty Joko?" I ask. "She is still pretty but no longer dumb: she caught a very eligible lawyer who is now a judge. She too is the mother of three kids, all boys; and I understand she basks in the admiration of four males," Wehinmi adds with a laugh.

"And the domineering Celina?" I enquire. "She is very much about and has not changed a bit. The last thing I heard about her was that she had just divorced her second husband. Since then she became attached to a much younger man who had lived abroad for many years. I suppose that he needs the guidance of a strong willed flirt like Celina to find his feet. With her young partner Celina may yet become a mother."

"Felicia the 'bush girl'," Wehinmi continues, "has returned home as I already told you. We are the best of friends now and you will get to see her again. We would never have imagined that she of all people would become so close a friend to me. It only goes to show that things and situations should not be taken at face value."

"And the 'terrible Ys'?," I ask. "Yewande and Yetunde continue to be terrible and dangerous. Their beauty continues to attract or rather entrap men, young and old; but marriage and happiness continue to elude them. They have both become widely known as home-breakers. No man or woman is safe from them. They continue to live fast lives, but age is fast catching up with them. Poor girls."

"Why do you call them poor?," I ask. "They are merely reaping what they sowed. Does not the morning show what the day will be like? They were never interested in marriage."

"No, the 'terrible Ys' prefer to hunt for rich men who will

give them good time. Good time girls, that is what they were and still are and that is what they will always be. None of us could have ever foreseen what the future held. But going by what has happened the early beginnings pointed out what was likely to be.

"We, have cause to thank God," concludes Wehinmi. "By the way, are you looking forward to the visit to Grandma tomorrow?" "Yes, very much so. My last visit with her was intriguing."

We wake to a very bright morning and after breakfast set out for Grandma's place in Warri. We drive almost six hours with a short break at Ilesa. When we get there, Grandma is already on the veranda, her favourite relaxing corner. She asks for some more tea to be brought.

"How are you young folks settling down?" the old lady asks us. "Very well, Grandma. I am more in love with him than when I first met him," answers Wehinmi. I add, "Yes Grandma, Wehinmi is indeed a witch. She must have put a love potion in my food. I love her more and more. I cannot bear to let her out of my sight."

"I can very well believe that," Granny says with a giggle, "what with this protruding tummy. When is the young one expected? If only I could travel to Lagos and be around when the baby arrives. Unfortunately I am unable to travel any more. Make sure you send me news the very moment it happens."

After one week in Warri we return to Lagos; we travel in easy stages. We stop for two nights each in Benin City, Akure and Ibadan. After the trip, Wehinmi puts a temporary halt to her travels. She spends more time in bed. I spend a lot of evening time with her. It is nearing six in the evening one Saturday when Wehinmi asks to be taken to the hospital. It is a short labour. The child, a boy, arrives within two hours. I stay on in the hospital until both child and mother are asleep.

Two years later, we have a daughter. Three years after that the twins arrive, a boy and a girl. We then decide that we have a full house and our energy is concentrated on bringing up the children.

Wehinmi is always recalling the past, especially that Monday morning when she and I first met; and the heartache when she thought that I was lost to her. Again fate played a trick on us. When Wehinmi thought that at last she had found me it was not yet so. She had to wait another six years. But both Wehinmi and I have long come to the conclusion that the wait has been worth it. We are a contented and happy couple. It could not be otherwise. Wehinmi has in addition to me four lovely kids, a thriving and successful business, and I am doing extremely well in my own business. We decide to run the two businesses as one in our joint names.

When we reminisce we always conclude by saying that truly God has been gracious to us. Wehinmi adds that it has all come about as a result of genuine love and faithfulness. "Above all, we both have the fear of God in us. In return we have His grace which is all that any marriage can ask for."

VINDICATION

How it started

The bus was pulling up at the terminus as Gbade walked into the square. A smart young lady alighted. She walked ahead of Gbade, daintily picking her steps. She was clearly vivacious and full of life. Gbade had seen her face as she got down from the bus. Firmly imprinted on that face was the consciousness of her beauty and attractiveness.

Her school uniform showed that she was from the Princess College. Gbade quickened his pace and caught up with her. "Good evening, friend", he greeted her. "I bet we are going the same way." Before the young lady could answer he added, "I am Gbade. My tell-tale blazer has shown you that I am from Gregory High."

She answered in a soft and melodious voice that her name was Pero, "I hope that we retain the shield," she added.

"I'm afraid, that's not likely: our boys have prepared most seriously. The shield is ours," Gbade said. "We shall see", Pero answered quietly.

Gbade looked at her again. Her pointed nose and chiselled chin enhanced her beauty. She wore a very confident smile on her face. It was Gbade who spoke again. "I see you wear your beret on the left side, very much unlike your schoolmates."

"I am left handed," Pero answered.

"It's good to see something different," Gbade responded. He could not stop looking at the beauty by his side.

If she was aware of it she gave no indication. "Would you mind if I escort you home after the debate?" asked Gbade.

"Why would you take such trouble since you obviously live on the Island?" Pero replied.

"I will gladly walk you to the moon, if need be," Gbade quickly countered. "We shall see," Pero answered.

Princess College has been famous for years because of its

beautiful lawns and gardens as well as for other good reasons. As they went through the gate, a pleasing fragrance from the roses and other flowers surrounding the lawns pervaded the compound. They walked into the large hall facing the main lawn. It was already half filled.

"Let's move to the front so that we can hear well," Pero said. The event of the evening was the final of the debate competition for Secondary Schools. The trophy had been won for two consecutive years by Princess College. They had high hopes of winning it for the third time running so that they could retain the trophy permanently.

The stage was already set. In the centre was the high table at which the panel of judges would sit. On the two sides were two smaller tables with chairs. Each set had at its front a rostrum. Soon the judges came in with the headmistress of Princess College carrying the coveted shield. As the chairperson, she immediately asked the two contesting pairs to come up to the podium. To Pero's surprise Gbade was one of the main speakers. The speakers were introduced and the rules for the debate were announced. Everyone applauded.Princess College as the defending champion would speak in favour of the motion, while Greg High as the opposing side would speak against.

The two young ladies in their well-groomed uniforms looked stunning; the two boys were wearing well starched trousers and smart brown blazers. The chief proposer of the motion was given a maximum of fifteen minutes to speak, as was the chief opposer in response. Thereafter, the two seconders were given ten minutes each to make rebuttals and additional points.

These were followed by contributions from the floor. The headmistress then summarised the main points made by both sides as well as those from the audience.

At the end of the speeches, loud applause filled the hall. Within the next five minutes, members of the panel of judges appeared to have agreed on the scores; then the audience was asked to vote, if only to confirm the verdict. As with the trend of the speeches, more hands, including those of some of the girls, went up in support of the opposing team. And so, Princess College was not able to retain the shield permanently.

Gbade's partner was a senior boy, a sixth former, and it was he who went forward to collect the shield and shake hands with all the judges. He then shook hands with the two young ladies. He raised the trophy to yet another round of applause.

The headmistress of Princess College rounded up the proceedings by congratulating the winning team, thanking both teams and everybody present. She also advised all the schools and colleges present to start preparations for next year's competition as early as possible. Gbade and his partner came down from the stage hand in hand, the latter still clutching the shield.

Gbade walked down briskly towards the waiting young lady. Although her college had lost, Pero's congratulations and handshake were warm and spontaneous. The look on both faces spoke very clearly: the pair had fallen in love at first sight. Both of them walked silently to the bus stop. The tender glances and smiles were as eloquent as spoken words.

As Pero got into the bus, Gbade followed her. Immediately they sat down they held hands. Gbade felt Pero's soft fingers in his palm. He felt very happy. From the mainland terminus he walked her right to the door of her house. The adventure had started. So it continued afterwards. Before long, everyone began to notice the inseparable pair.

Within two years their love blossomed and by the time Gbade left High School they had pledged undying love to each other. Thus started a courtship that lasted eight long years. It was inevitable that there would be lovers' quarrels. Gbade was a dashing and handsome young-man who was highly gifted. Pero too, with her ever smiling pretty face, always cool and unruffled, was bound to attract the admiration of other young men.

However, their friendship survived with only a partial break of very brief duration. It was a most romantic relationship. They would spend hours together dreaming of a bright and happy future. The support from members of their two families gave the couple a great deal of encouragement. On some weekends during term Gbade and Pero would go for picnics, excursions or dramatic and cultural events with other students from the two colleges and other secondary schools.The pattern and variety of events during the long vacations were different. The two lovers were always together under one pretext or another. They obviously enjoyed each other's company.

During one of the picnics an incident occurred. As the pair walked along a narrow footpath they saw ahead of them three young ladies. One of them was sitting on the ground with her back against a tree. The other two were applying some dressings to her ankle. The injured young lady appeared to be in pain. When Gbade and Pero got to the spot, one of the two girls asked Gbade for help. Gbade deftly removed the bandage and examined the swollen ankle. He said that the crepe bandage had been applied too tightly. In an instant he opened his first aid kit, applied some embrocation and bandaged the injured ankle again. Next he produced his flask of cold water. He applied a little water to the young lady's brow after which he offered her a cup of cold water.

While he was attending to the injured girl, the parties on both sides introduced themselves. They walked down the path led by the two friends. At the rear was the injured girl hopping on one foot with her arms around the shoulders of Gbade and Pero. Just as the two parties were about to take their leave, the injured one, whose name was Nide, said excitedly, "I now remember, you are the troop leader of the second Island Troop which won the First Aid competition last quarter. I thought I had seen the face before. I took part in the competition. I belong to the Third Guide

Company." The three young ladies said thank you and Gbade and Pero left.

Nide walked home in a daze, stopping from time to time. She did not see her aunt who was sitting quietly in the living room. She had almost walked by when the aunt called out. "Nide, whatever is the matter? You look strange. I hope all is well."

"All is well Auntie, except for my injured ankle. We had a wonderful time at the picnic." she answered. "Come and have your meal," invited Auntie Sade. " The table is already set."

Nide was unusually quiet during the meal. She left the table hurriedly pleading tiredness. She flopped onto the bed in her room. Then started talking to herself: "What is happening to me. I feel so excited and happy; but at the same time I feel sad and down". Gbade's picture filled her thoughts. She continued her thinking: "His presence puts new life into me. I would love to be with him every moment of my life. That pretty girl beside him, would she allow it? Because of her, would he have eyes for any other female? I am also pretty. I can hold my own. I'll try. We shall see. The mere thought of him makes me tingle all over. What is this madness that has come over me? Have I fallen in love with him? I am no longer in control of myself. May heaven help me." Try as she might, she could not sleep, thinking of him and the strange effect he had on her.

About a week after the incident, the injured young lady (now without the crepe bandage) visited Gbade's house. She had come to thank him. She repeated the thank you call on two other occasions, much to the amusement and consternation of Gbade. When Gbade mentioned the visit to Pero she smiled mischievously. She joked, "We must be hopeful that no more sprains will occur in the future."

"What is that supposed to mean"? queried Gbade, to which Pero replied, "If a handsome young man will caress my foot while bandaging my ankle, I will oblige and sprain the ankle every other day. I shall of course insist on a good looking first-aider."

"Someone is jealous," observed Gbade.

"Do you blame me? I would not want any pretty and smart young woman dancing round my boyfriend."

"Come off it. What time would I have left when I have to report every morning at Greg High and in the evening I have to present myself dutifully and promptly at seven o'clock at Pero's house," replied Gbade.

"You just watch it. If I ever catch Miss Pretty calling on you again, all hell will be let loose," Pero countered.

"You have nothing to fear, Miss. You already have me on the leash."

Nide Makes Her Move

Nide set out to find out all about Gbade. What she learnt made her to want him more than ever. She was upset when it was also confirmed by many that the pretty Pero of Princess High had been his sweetheart for some time. Everyone spoke of the suitability of the two being lovers. "What a lovely pair," they all said. The more she heard, the more disconsolate she became.

"I know what to do," she said to herself. She had found out that every Tuesday without fail Pero attended netball practice at the High between five and six in the evening. "Next Tuesday at five, the coast will be clear," she thought. "That will be the time to pay Gbade a visit."

So she was there on the following Tuesday on the dot of five. Gbade was in his room doing his homework when he was informed by his younger brother, teasingly, that a 'charming lady' was waiting for him in the living room. 'Who could that be?' he wondered. As he entered, there she was, sitting calmly. She stood up and flashed a bewitching smile at him. Before Gbade could speak she went on, "I have been extremely busy and so I could not repeat my visit before now. By the way, my name is Omonide. My friends call me Nide. I hope you too will call me that."

"It's an unusual name," Gbade answered, "but it sounds pretty. My name is Gbade. Shall we go out into the garden so that we can sit on the bench under the tree?"

Nide agreed to this. After they were comfortably seated she said, "I have come to see you. I need advice."

"What is it? I will be delighted to help if I can," replied Gbade.

"How do I start?" "Yes, I am listening."

"From the day I set my eyes on you, life for me has not been the same," Nide confided. "I am both happy and unhappy. I wish I could be with you every minute of my life. Sometimes I find it difficult to breathe for thinking of you."

Gbade raised his hand as if wanting to speak. "Please hear me out. Do not interrupt me," Nide pleaded. "I know it is not modest for a lady to speak to a gentleman in this manner, but I must. I have had many agonising hours. The truth is that I had never in all my life felt like I do and have done since setting eyes on you. I was smitten the moment I set eyes on you. Although I had suspected it, I became sure in my mind that I was in love with you. I am madly in love. But something tells me that I have come too late. Something tells me that if you had not earlier met a girl named Pero, things might have been different. What do I do now? Please advise me."

Gbade looked at her quizzically but tenderly. He was in a quandary. His look was full of pity and dismay. For many minutes he did not speak. When he did, it was in a tremulous voice. "Dear young lady I am sorry, terribly sorry that you should feel that way about me. I have already given my love to Pero. She has all of me. We have promised undying love for each other."

Nide looked pale and faint. "I understand," she said. "Please do not harbour any ill feeling towards me. I am not a bad girl. I had never fallen in love before. But I had always known that, when I do, it would overwhelm me. It has. I love you and I always will. Please remember me sometimes and pray for me. Perhaps you would like to have me as a sister. In that capacity I can be in your company and hers at times. That will make me happy, very happy. Think about it. One day I shall be interested to hear what you think of that proposal."

Before Gbade could think of a suitable answer, she had got up and walked away. For many minutes Gbade sat all alone beneath the tree. He knew that what the girl said was true. He could feel it. He knew that she was in earnest. He was overcome with pity. Two in love with the same man. What a hopeless and helpless tangle. What will become of the poor girl? He had a premonition that something would happen. If only one could see the future? The poor girl. May heaven send her someone else to love. What will Pero say?" These were the thoughts that ran through his mind. He looked at his watch. He was already running late. Pero would expect him at the school gate to walk her home after netball.

He dashed off for Princess College. He arrived just in time. Pero and her friends were just coming out. "You are puffing dear. What happened? You should have left home earlier. Have you seen a ghost? Aren't you pleased to see me? You look dazed." He had no answer to the barrage of questions. What could he say? Pero looked at him with amused puzzlement. Both of them decided to let the matter rest.

When Pero finished at Princess College she decided to attend a Teacher Training College some hundred miles away from home. While Gbade was in support of her taking the course, he had some misgivings. Understandably, he thought that his sweetheart might be snatched from him by some enterprising young men far away from home. The possibility looked stronger as there was a university near the Teacher Training College. Besides, this was Pero's first trip away from home. The only redeeming feature was that Tara, Pero's classmate at Princess College, was also going to the same college. With Pero and Tara acting as chaperones to each other Gbade felt that he had a measure of security. That thought also gave him comfort.

The course was to last four years. All too soon the first two years flew by. During this period the two love birds travelled frequently between the two towns to see each other. Whenever they were together it was all bliss and happiness. The constant partings, however, brought pain and sadness.

Two years after Pero went to the Teacher's College Gbade won a government scholarship to study in England for four years. Both of them were in a dilemma. Students of the Teacher Training College were not allowed to get married during their period of training. Pregnancy while at college had always resulted in expulsion. To make matters worse, there were frequent stories of smart English girls ensnaring young African men.

Two weeks before Gbade's departure for England, Pero sent an urgent message to him to come over to the college. On arrival she clung to him with an anguished face. She came straight to the point. "Unless we get married secretly, before your departure, this may be goodbye forever."

"Why should that be"? Gbade asked.

"What with all the stories about girls in England, I cannot afford to lose you," Pero answered. After consulting the parents on both sides, a registry marriage took place ten days before Gbade's departure. Fortunately the customary enquiries on both sides had previously been made. Needless to say, given the circumstances, the marriage was not consummated. The night before Gbade's departure was a most agonising one for the couple. They kissed, cuddled, hugged and clung to each other for hours.

And so Gbade flew off to England. Thus began two years of further separation. This time, four thousand rather than one hundred miles separated them. The two years felt like ten. Letters of endearment and protestations of enduring loyalty flew backwards and forwards. It was a very sad and trying period for both of them.

Life dragged on until that July morning when Pero flew into London to join her husband. The joyful reunion defied description. As Pero emerged from the immigration department at the airport, she and Gbade rushed into each other's arms, hugging and kissing. For minutes they clung together without speaking. Then Pero started to cry. Gbade was startled "Why all this crying, now that we are together at last?" He calmed her down and steered her towards the waiting taxi. Gbade had eighteen months to complete his course when Pero arrived in London.

The couple both hoped to return home with a baby, or at least with Pero pregnant. But try as they might there was no sign of pregnancy. They, as well as relations on both sides back home, were disappointed. The couple had to wait ten years before their first child, a girl, arrived. They later had two other children, one boy and another girl. Gbade and Pero were quite well and happy, especially as both of them were progressing well in their careers. Gbade was already a director in his company while Pero had become the headmistress of her school. All their children were brilliant and got on splendidly in their studies.

Everything was going smoothly until one fateful evening when Gbade went to his club. Some members were commiserating with one of their colleagues who had just got married. It was discovered that the new bride was not a virgin. The naïve Gbade was unable to join in the conversation due to his ignorance of the subject. When all the others, except the affected member who was still brooding over his mug of beer, had left, Gbade moved closer to him.

Gbade asked why he was so sure that his wife was not a virgin. With a look of disgust he answered that there had been no obstruction, no screaming and no pain. She just clung to him and appeared to be enjoying herself. "When I, as the affronted husband, asked what it all meant, her attitude and answer were even more devastating." "She asked me, 'Do you expect a lady of my age not to have had sexual experience? Wake up my man; these are modern times'."

The whole episode set Gbade thinking. Although his own wife at their first encounter had not spoken like that, but as far as he could recall there was no impediment whatsoever; neither was there any blood nor screams, nor did his wife complain about any pain. He really loved his wife and did not want the peace within their home disturbed. For this reason he made no reference to this episode.

However, Gbade became resentful. Distrust of his wife started to creep in. He was often moody and kept aloof most of the time. He stayed out more than he normally did and when at home he busied himself with his books. Husband and wife started to drift apart. It was Pero who called attention to this new development. She came and nestled by him on the settee. "Darling, I feel neglected. It's not like you to stay out late day after day. You used to be the home type and I know that you really enjoyed the time we spent together. Now whenever you are home you bury yourself in the study. What have I done to upset you? Please hold me in your arms and kiss me. Your neglect of me is killing me slowly," Pero remonstrated.

Gbade was normally a forthright person and he could not lie. He narrated the episode at the club and referred to their first sexual encounter. He ended on the note that he was most unhappy. He reminded her that during their courtship she was always restraining him so that they could have a most enjoyable and befitting consummation after marriage. He again confessed his ignorance of such matters as he had had no sexual experience before that first encounter in London. What he gathered after making enquiries from his friends in the medical profession made him doubtful as to his wife's truthfulness and chastity. "I was told that a bloodless consummation was just not possible," he ended with a doleful face.

"Supposing there had been an accident," countered Pero.

"What sort of accident?" asked Gbade, adding, "Please do not trivialize this issue or treat me like a fool." Pero claimed to have read about such an accident in a book some time ago.

"Please Pero let us end this conversation. I do not want the peace in this home shattered. Our children and junior relations look up to us. Even if we are not happy as a couple let us pretend to be. When we got married we did so for better or for worse. I am prepared to accept my lot. I shall leave you to your conscience."

The discontent lingered for quite a while. It was a most trying period for both of them. During that period all they could do was to pray.

Late one night Gbade and Pero were watching a film on the television. In it a tyrant who was chieftain of a village had detained some young women who were protesting against the ill-treatment of their menfolk who were opposed to him. The most beautiful of the women was the fiancée of the leader of the dissidents.While all the other girls were herded into a hut, the tyrant ordered that this girl be brought to his quarters. He raped and defiled her before sending her home. At this point, for an inexplicable reason, Gbade looked at Pero. Their eyes met. Although no words were uttered, the look in Gbade's eyes were as good as spoken words. He seemed to be asking, "Was that what happened?" Then, utter silence.

After the film ended Pero got up and tenderly embraced Gbade. While still clinging to him she said very quietly and in a subdued tone: "Darling I have always been faithful to you." Gbade was bewildered. All he could say at that point was, "My good wife, I believe you."

When Gbade eventually went to bed, he could not sleep. All sorts of thoughts went through his mind. Could Pero have been raped? Or in a moment of temptation, during the long separation, could she have succumbed to someone else due to loneliness? Although the great love for his wife eventually prevailed, the doubts and mistrust of the past resurfaced. It lingered for some time. The resultant effect was renewed heartache for both Gbade and Pero.

Some nights after the television film, Gbade was woken up by Pero. She told him that he had been shouting aloud in his sleep. "Stop violating her; stop this defilement. She is my wife". These were the words Pero said Gbade had shouted. "What was happening"? Pero asked.

"I was dreaming. It was such a bad dream. May God preserve us and sustain the peace in this home." Although pressed by Pero, Gbade did not say anything further.

The unease and tension returned. The following night Gbade had another dream. A total stranger suddenly appeared. He prostrated before him and asked for 'forgiveness for a great wrong he did me and mine.' I could not see the face of the stranger clearly. 'What's wrong? I do not know you nor do I understand what you are talking about.' He then woke up with a start.

When Gbade related this dream to Pero he noticed that she too was startled. In addition there was a look of fear on her face. Gbade's understanding of feminine body language had always been uncanny. The startled look mingled with fear on Pero's face provoked in him a lot of thoughts. On the spur of the moment he asked if Pero could spare some minutes to listen to one of the legends in his family. "Sure," replied Pero, "You know I am interested and would love to know everything about you and your family."

"Sit down then and make yourself comfortable" said Gbade. "When we were kids we used to visit the village often to spend our holidays during the long vacations and my grandfather usually told us stories. I want you to listen to one of them which I found very fascinating."

Gbade then recounted the legend of the Queen's basket[13]: "Labo was the first daughter of Oba Afun and was therefore known as Bere. One morning the Oba did not emerge as usual from his chamber. The courtiers did not know what to do. They asked Bere to enter the royal chamber to find out what was wrong. The king said a horrendous thing had happened. All his powers came from just touching a special basket that had been entrusted to him by the late Queen. 'Without the Queen's basket I am nothing,' he said. 'Every morning when I wake up the first thing I do is to touch the basket.' Because he had weighty issues that day he thought he would obtain extra power and discernment by touching the contents. He opened the basket and found the contents spoiled. Bere pointed out that physical state of the contents could not diminish his powers because they depended on the strength of his faith. She asked him what the packets dropped into the basket contained.

" 'They were the trophies of virtue of our womenfolk. Whenever they got married their *ibale* (the sign that their virginity was intact) were sent home as proof of their virtue and the high standard of their upbringing. This was the white cloth stained by blood during consummation of the marriage. Such brides were respected by their families on both sides and they were given presents. For brides who failed there were awful consequences.

"Asked why the cloths had rotted, the king explained that they used special dyes and that the art of making them had got lost. As Bere knew all about herbs she promised her father that she would find the right ones to solve the problem. The king appointed Bere custodian of the Queen's basket and the king emerged to be greeted by his cheering courtiers."

"What an interesting story," said Pero. Before Gbade could

---

[13] This legend is one of those included in "The Quest for the Rare Leaf and other Yoruba tales" published in parallel with this edition.

reply she went on, "Why have you never told me the story before?"

"I don't know," answered Gbade. After a little pause he added, as if an afterthought, "Maybe it had never occurred to me to tell you. I'm happy that you like it." There was another pause before Gbade added: "As you well know the music that issues forth from an *agidigbo* musical instrument, though melodious and enthralling, is not unlike the proverbs of the elders. Only the wise can interpret them and it takes a very discerning heart to keep in step with its melody."

"You sound very deep in philosophical tonight. Let us go to bed oh Solomon." For the best part of the night Pero was unable to sleep. All sorts of thoughts went through her mind. She tossed and turned in bed. Try as she might, sleep would not come until the early hours of the morning.

Bayo and the curse

Meanwhile a man by the name of Bayo had returned to the town of Agbodu after over three decades away in the big cities. His arrival had been causing a stir and, but for the two recent tragedies that befell him, the occasion would have been one for great celebration. Those who had known him remembered him as the brightest student in Agbodu High School, intellectually gifted, handsome and talkative. Many young ladies as well as their mothers were disappointed when he left for the Teacher Training College about thirty years ago.

Now that he had returned to be the principal of Agbodu High School, the first African to be so appointed, many thought that wonders would start to happen. The stories making the rounds, however, were that the Bayo who had returned was quite a different person. Not only was he extremely sad; he was aloof. Only a distant relation and her pretty young daughter, Tomi, were welcomed as visitors in the principal's house. After school hours

215

he kept mostly indoors. It was said that he was very unhappy.

Apart from the two ladies mentioned, there was a young male student who helped with the house cleaning. All the other chores were left to the two women. It was, therefore, very likely that pretty Tomi should fall in love with Bayo. She and her mother were able to arouse him from his state of lethargy. He started to show affection for Tomi. It was clear that he was fond of her. But that was as far as it went.

It was reported that Bayo had said that for Tomi's sake there would be no talk of union between them. He would not wish the poor girl to be the next victim of the tragedy that inevitably befell any lady who fell in love with him, or was in any way involved with him. Six months before Bayo decided to return home, his only child, a nineteen-year old daughter had been raped and taken her own life. The mother, Bayo's late wife whom he had married secretly had doted on the daughter, pined away and also eventually died. Before Bayo got married to this unfortunate lady he had had a previous attachment. Some three months before the proposed marriage, when Bayo decided to ask for her hand, tragedy struck. The woman had been raped by a notorious philanderer and she had to leave the town because of the stigma. It would seem that any woman who fell in love with Bayo was bound for misfortune or disaster. It was generally believed that a curse had been put on him.

As a result of the pressure exerted on Bayo by Tomi and her mother it was decided that a diviner should be approached to determine the source of Bayo's curse, if it was true that he had one. The diviner's finding made matters worse: it was that in times past Bayo had offended a man, highly favoured by the *irunmales*. It was said that the man was a descendant of one of the important *irunmales*. Unless and until that person lifted the curse on Bayo, any woman who fell in love with him, especially if he reciprocated the love, would also meet disaster. Two other diviners were consulted and they confirmed the findings of the first one.

Tomi and the mother did not relent in their efforts. Eventually they prevailed on Bayo to pursue the course of action advised. It was only then that he confessed that he had raped a young woman a long time back, one of his juniors at the Teacher Training College. The young lady already had a fiancé – he believed – when the sad event occurred. The man and the raped woman later got married. The man in question had become very famous and important. Bayo was ashamed and reluctant to approach Pero, for it was she, and he therefore made no attempt to find the couple.

Now due to the pressure and his eagerness to get married and raise a family Bayo decided to go in search of Pero's friend, Tara. There was, however, another hurdle he had to overcome. When the sad event occurred, Pero had not taken Tara into her confidence due to the shame and stigma of rape. He rightly assumed that Tara's horror when she learned what happened might now alienate her from him.

According to Tomi's mother, Bayo had no alternative than to swallow his pride and tell Tara what he had done and seek her forgiveness; this should open the door for the much-needed assistance. It was Tomi's mother who eventually convinced Bayo to follow her on the visit to Tara. After several visits and much persuasion Tara agreed to broach the matter with Pero.

One Saturday afternoon, just before lunch, the gateman announced the arrival of a visitor for Pero. When Pero enquired who it was, it turned out to be Tara. Gbade and Pero had not seen or heard from Tara for a number of years. They were, therefore, surprised but pleased to see her. The three of them enjoyed a hearty lunch and talked about old times.

Good manners dictated that Gbade should excuse the two friends as they might have confidences to exchange after such a long separation. Besides, Gbade had observed that Tara was not at ease. He guessed that she wanted to be alone with Pero. As soon as Gbade left them, Tara disclosed that her mission was rather delicate and that she suspected that she might be seen as the bringer of bad news. She told her that Bayo, whom she had not seen in years, had come to see her begging to be brought to see Gbade and Pero regarding a very sensitive and pressing matter. Tara further disclosed that when she pressed Bayo, he had confessed the rape. He was in a bad way and desperately needed help.

The aggrieved Pero understandably refused point blank to discuss about Bayo, let alone receive him. She stressed that there was no way she would agree to see him. She was peeved that Bayo had told Tara - and perhaps others - about her predicament.

"Why?" asked Tara, "after all we were his friends."

Pero retorted: "While you and he may be from the same town and are related, I am definitely not his friend. A good man would not have callously raped a lady he regarded as a friend. We were mere college mates. Besides, there is another big hurdle.....I never had the courage to take Gbade into confidence in this difficult matter. Often I thought that Gbade suspected something but I always insisted on my faithfulness to him – which is true. How could I now face him and make such a confession only to help the scoundrel who was the cause of all my trouble? Over and over again Gbade has reaffirmed his love for me; but I always had the feeling that he did not trust me. I would, therefore, not risk wrecking our happiness."

Pero was adamant and refused to give her cooperation. Understandably, she was still hurt, offended and humiliated and she believed that Bayo should be allowed "to stew in his own juice." Pero later told Gbade that Tara left rather disappointed and crestfallen.

The following Saturday Tara repeated her visit, this time accompanied by two women, both of them unknown to Pero.

Fortunately Gbade was not around. Gbade was told later that after much pleading and pressure from the two ladies Pero agreed that Bayo could come. Pero's fears that her secret had become public knowledge was confirmed. Despite the pressure from Tomi and her mother, Bayo continued to refuse to meet Pero. However, after much hesitation, he agreed to see Gbade. He wrote a letter to Gbade with a copy to Pero.

But Bayo tried to be too clever and he withheld the original letter intended for Gbade. Pero's copy was duly sent. This was a subtle attempt to blackmail Pero should the need later arise.

On a fateful Saturday afternoon, when Bayo knew that Gbade would still be away at work, he called on Pero. Predictably he got a very cold welcome. He said he would wait for Gbade no matter how late he got home. Pero felt trapped. She advised that although Bayo could stay in the neighbourhood, she needed two hours to serve her husband's dinner and prepare him for the inevitable. Bayo had no option than to agree. Both of them were caught in the same trap. What eventually saved the day was the deep and abiding affection that had always existed between Gbade and Pero. Before Gbade's arrival, Pero had primed the servants to be extremely careful and be at their best. This was to put Gbade in a good mood.

Pero offered to say the prayer preceding the meal. In addition to thanking the good Lord for the meal as well as the good health to enjoy it, she added her appreciation for the love and care shared by them both. During the meal and after, she talked about what she had done all day and asked Gbade about his day. They spent some time exchanging these pleasantries.

Very sensitive person that he was, Gbade quickly observed that Pero's mood, though good, was unusual. "Darling," he asked gently, "is anything the matter?"

She quickly replied: "Do you remember the other day when you reaffirmed that you would always love me. You went on to say on that occasion that love is patient and kind and you added that it always trusts and protects". At this stage, she got up from her chair, embraced Gbade lovingly and knelt at his feet holding his knees. "Darling," she continued, "I wish to ask you for perhaps the greatest favour I will ever ask. I hope you will grant it. Without your love I have always treasured, my life would be empty."

"What is this all about?" asked Gbade. "You know that in spite of our differences every now and again, I will always love you. We are one now, how could I not love you with all my heart? You are part of me and I hope that I am part of you. Go ahead and ask, you already have whatever you want from me."

"You are too good to me. May the good Lord continue to bless you and our marriage," Pero continued. "You will recall your dream some time ago when you said that the man who came between us would come and ask for forgiveness. In the attempt to cover my shame, I said that no such person existed. But that was not true. Please forgive me. Hold me in your arms. Hold me tightly. The man is here. When he has explained himself you will see that I was blameless. He needs our joint forgiveness. Please for my sake hear what he has to say. May the good Lord guide you."

Gbade lifted her up gently and embraced her tenderly. "I had always been acutely aware there was a barrier between us. Bring the man so that the barrier may be removed for all time."

"Thank you, thank you, my love. I have never been unfaithful to you. Before I invite him in let the words come from my lips first. I was raped! No self-respecting wife would ever admit to such a thing. Pity me. Hear him out before you judge me."

"Who says I want to judge you? Gbade replied. "If I were to do that I would also be judging myself since we are now one body. Darling, stop upsetting yourself. I am convinced of your innocence and goodness. You should have taken me into confidence long before now. We would both have been saved the crises we went through. Please invite the visitor in." At this point Pero asked one

of the servants to go next door and bring Bayo in.

Bayo came in, unsteady on his feet. In an attempt to prostrate himself he fell flat on his face. "Sir, I cannot look you or your good wife in the eyes to make this confession. I need your forgiveness so that I can regain my sanity and start to live a normal life again. Please let me tell it all before you interrupt. I am Bayo. I was three years ahead of Pero and Tara at the Teacher Training College. Although Tara is not a relation of mine, we both come from Agbodu. I have known her from childhood. When she introduced her friend, Pero, to me I fell for her instantly. I became her slave. I decided to woo and win her; but it was never to be. On the first occasion I made my feelings known Pero told me that she could not love me or any man other than her first true love to whom she was already engaged. She told me never to address her on the subject again. She even threatened to withdraw the friendship she had given me because of her friendship with Tara. I gave her my solemn promise never to broach the subject again. Despite that promise, I remained her admirer. I was brooding and waiting. I was always kind and helpful to both Tara and Pero. In time Pero came to regard me as a trusted friend. I was, however, planning and watching.

"As I said previously, Tara and I come from the same town. This allowed me to act and behave as Tara's relation. Two months before my thirtieth birthday, I had asked Tara and Pero to make all the refreshments to be served and to play hostesses at my party. About a week or so before the party, Tara took ill and was confined to the college clinic. It took a lot of entreaties and cajoling to get her discharged two days before the birthday celebration. I manipulated it all because I knew that if Tara could not attend, Pero would not. As Tara was still weak as a result of her illness, a lot of the responsibility fell on Pero. Tara spent a lot of time resting and lying down. This threw Pero and me together a lot. Often Pero would tactfully extricate herself from my 'accidental' embraces. After a stern warning from her, I stopped attempting to embrace her. My fear was that I would drive her away. Considering my secret plan I could not risk that.

"On the fateful day of my birthday party, although Tara got dressed and put on a bold face though, she was still not well. She was forced to sit down most of the time while Pero shouldered all the responsibilities as a good and trusted friend. As the party went on far into the night, it was arranged for Tara and Pero to spend the night in my guest room. As the best student in the final year I was already serving as assistant lecturer and had been given a house in the official quarters. As the evening wore on Tara's condition started to get worse. Fortunately some doctor friends were present. She was given some medication to tide her over until the next morning. A sedative was prescribed for her along with other medicines to ensure that she had a comfortable night.

"Pero and the house help were washing and tidying up and Pero was completely exhausted. I offered to make a chocolate drink to enable us sleep peacefully. Unknown to Pero I had put some of Tara's sedative into her cup. I then suggested that she should lie down for a while on the settee while the house help and I finished the cleaning up. We were to call her when we finished so that she could join Tara in the guest room. Unsuspecting, the poor victim agreed.

"After the house help had gone to the servants' quarters I sat on a chair pretending to be reading a book. I was in fact waiting for the sedative in Pero's drink to take effect. When her breathing had become regular I shook her to see if she was in a deep sleep. I then started to remove her clothes. Pero tried to get up but she could not. Besides, I was already pinning her down firmly. Soon after that, I started fondling and caressing her. At this point Pero let out a blood curdling scream. Alas, no one could hear her. The house help was safely in the servants' quarters many yards away and Tara had been heavily sedated. I had added a little bit to what the doctor had instructed so she was in no position to hear Pero's scream, let alone come to her assistance. After Pero's futile struggle I had my way and raped her. Poor Pero was wailing and weeping profusely. I fled the room."

Gbade now asked, "Pero, what did you do then?" Pero, with her head bowed, answered in a tremulous voice full of emotion. "Although I was sedated, I struggled to a sitting position. I was most uncomfortable. I was in great pain. I managed to get up on my feet and make for the guest room. But then it dawned on me that unless I cleaned the mess on the settee and floor, Tara and the house help would realise what took place. In my anxiety not to leave any trace I forgot my giddiness, agony and anger. I concentrated on cleaning the blood stain from both the settee and the carpet.

"Afterwards I dragged myself to the guest room, taking great care not to wake Tara up. I did not want her to see me in my pitiable condition. I went into the bathroom and struggled to clean myself up. I achieved it, between crying and cursing. I got into bed beside Tara. I was shaking all over. Needless to say

I could not sleep. An indescribable anger possessed me. Much as I would have loved to have fallen into a deep sleep, to make me oblivious, if only temporarily, of my affliction, sleep fled from me. The harder I tried the more wide awake I became. I pinched myself to see if I was indeed awake or perhaps I was in a dream. It was a bad nightmare.

"How could this happen to me? My virginity which I had guarded zealously for over twenty four years had been taken away. Why did Satan choose to visit me in the guise of a man called Bayo? I had been eagerly looking forward to the night when my marriage with Gbade would be consummated. I had already been imagining the big hug of pleasure and approval which Gbade would lavish on me in deep appreciation of my virginity. I was going to flaunt my virginity and dazzle my lover, my husband anew. Now, that could never be. Instead, all that I would get from him was perhaps contempt and derision, if not worse. The shame would be so overwhelming it would kill me. The horror! The disaster! How my life had been changed dramatically. Why was I subjected to such indignity, insult and humiliation? Poor me, my 'ibale' would never be sent back to my parents. My name would be forever blotted out from the list of virtuous women within my husband's family and mine. What a disaster. Could I ever face Gbade again, I asked myself? It was the longest night of my life. I tossed and turned in bed. Help me God, I cried continuously but silently throughout that never to be forgotten, traumatic night.

"It suddenly occurred to me that the cleaning in the lounge might not have been properly done. It would not do to leave any tell-tale signs. I quickly got up and despite my emotional bruise I meticulously cleaned both the settee and the carpet all over again – to wipe away the traces of my shame, as it were. I thought that the exertion would wear me out and help me to sleep. But alas, when I got back into bed, sleep would still not come. And so my thoughts started drifting on and on. Love making, I had heard described, was a most enjoyable sport and a blissful experience between two lovers. Certainly what had happened to me two hours or so before was not love-making. The two parties involved were not even friends, let alone lovers. It was sport all right for one person, the demon, the animal who brutalized and violated me. I swore to myself that one day he would pay for it. Little did I know that I was making a prophesy. My sad experience was accompanied by physical and spiritual pain. An indelible mark was left on my heart. I had been ravished and violated. I felt thoroughly soiled. Unless heaven came to my rescue I would be damned forever. But above all, I asked myself how I might explain it to Gbade, especially with all my preaching over the years for the need to wait patiently for the special night at our honeymoon. I consoled myself by saying that an explanation would not be necessary. Heaven would come to my rescue. What had I done to deserve this ordeal and stigma? Did I sin in a former life? Even if it were so, is this punishment not too harsh? And so, the long night wore on. Yet, I could not sleep.

"In the morning, due to a sense of great shame and the humiliation I did not and could not say a word to Tara. We were driven to our hostel by my devilish tormentor. Throughout the short drive no conversation took place. The others might have attributed the silence to tiredness but I knew otherwise. Fortunately it was a Sunday. I pleaded tiredness and promptly went into my room.

"I got into the bath and scrubbed myself thoroughly, as if to wipe off the previous night's dastardly act. I was weeping, moaning, sighing and cursing my tormentor all the time. I started talking to myself in the bathroom. My life had been ruined. What do I tell my husband? Can I disclose this to anyone, let alone Gbade? Then a terrible thought assailed me. What if I become pregnant? Should I abandon my studies and run away? Should I commit suicide and end it all? I lived the next few weeks in a daze mixed with terror.

Whenever I was alone I would back over the past. Since Gbade's departure for England I had become lonely and miserable.

"Thank God for Tara. With her constant companionship it was not easy for the wolves to get at me. The stupid rule against marriage made it impossible for me to disclose my true status. I was hemmed in.

"I should not forget that two days after the party Bayo came, ostensibly to thank us. He had tactfully kept away from us until then. About a month later he asked to have a few words with me. Tara withdrew from the room. He started by offering apologies for raping me. He said that what he did was caused by genuine love. He could not open the subject of love with me again as I told him that I was already engaged. Besides, I had earlier forbidden him not to talk to me about love or anything else again. He thought that by raping me I would be forced into marrying him as I would not like anybody else to know. As this tirade went on I stared at him with unseeing eyes. I told him that but for the shame and stigma, I would have reported him to the police. I went on to say that if I became pregnant, I would not hesitate to abort the pregnancy. I made it clear to him that I could not marry a man like him under any circumstance. I ended on the note that I might never marry as I would not like to deceive my fiancé or disclose this humiliating and disgraceful occurrence to him or anyone else. I was not even able to tell him I was already married as I thought that it was not beyond his despicable character to tell the college authorities if only to further damage my life. I ended saying that on no account was he to speak to me again. In reply, he said haltingly that there was no risk of pregnancy as he had been well protected. I sent him off with many curses.

"As soon as Tara got well she observed that all was not well with me. When she asked if I was ill I assured her that I was fine. Yet I could not get over the nightmare. I had never been so sad or so wretched in all my life. Traces of this might have shown in my letters to you. As you had always been sensitive and caring you seemed to have observed it too. You in fact raised it in some of your letters. I could not tell you anything. I was always praying to God to vindicate me."

During this lengthy intervention, Bayo kept on groaning, shaking and sweating profusely. At times it appeared that he was warding off some enemies unseen by us. He looked like a trapped animal.

When Pero said to Gbade, "Darling, what shall we do to this wretch?" it was Bayo who answered: "All I need is forgiveness and to be allowed to survive. I have more than paid for the harm I did to you. We heard that your husband has been given special power to meet all the exigencies of life and to react to evil. He has embedded in him the traditional spiritual 'boomerang' which has been tormenting me and smashing all those who loved me for almost three decades. I ask both of you to forgive me in the name of God. To err is human, to forgive divine."

Gbade replied, "Go in peace, Bayo. We have forgiven you wholeheartedly. We shall also remember you in our prayers. We shall ask the Almighty Father to forgive you as well."

When the door closed on Bayo, both of us had a feeling of peace and tranquillity. We knew that the angel of discord and all his minions had left our home forever.

"I clung to my husband as I had never done before," Pero related. "I could not help it. I kept on weeping, with tears flowing down my face. All the while Gbade kept on soothing, kissing and cuddling me. I did not know when he piloted me to bed. The next thing I remembered was finding myself in bed the following morning. My wonderful husband was beside me holding my arms. He had such a tender look, full of love on his face."

"You are unblemished; you are spotless; you are stainless; you are indeed worthy, very worthy, to have your 'maiden token' lodged in the Queen's basket," Gbade told her.

After a long pause Gbade continued in whisper, as if talking to himself. "The essence called love can be so soothing, sweet and blissful. Alas, how a gentle twist of fate may expose its harsher side, a sour taste tinged with bitterness and discord. Yet love normally produces an all-pervading fragrance, softness and bliss. Truly blessed indeed is the couple on whom is bestowed from above that all-embracing, all-conquering, enduring true love." ... and Gbade's face became suffused with a strange tenderness.

"Darling, you are already dressed up. Are we going out?" asked Pero.

"I have been out and returned," answered Gbade.

"Where from? Why did you not wake me up?"

"You were enjoying your sleep and it would have been wicked to disturb you. Besides, I was preparing a surprise for you," Gbade told her.

"What surprise?"

"Why don't you go into the bathroom and freshen up?" Gbade replied.

Pero, all eagerness, quickly jumped up. When she entered their private sitting room, she could barely believe her eyes. The room had been transformed. A table was set for two. There was a bottle of champagne in the bucket. There were flowers everywhere. There was also a large basket of fruit. In her excitement and wonder she asked, "Where did these come from? What is happening?"

"I went out early to buy them. I wanted to surprise you . "We are celebrating."

"But, dear husband, what is the occasion?" asked Pero.

"With the removal of the horrible barrier between us and the return of true peace to our home, with the removal of the prolonged nightmare, we need to celebrate. All the other members of this household have been told not to disturb us. Come into my arms, dear wife."

Pero threw herself into his arms. After they kissed and hugged he led her to the table. Pero wanted to continue speaking but Gbade said, "No more talking until after our brunch."

After the meal was over, the champagne popped and poured, Gbade said, "Now let us continue our conversation. If you permit, I shall start. How do you feel?" Before she could reply, he added: "I need not ask if you slept well because I know you did."

Pero admitted: "It was my first deep, restful sleep since that fateful night when I was defiled by Bayo. I had really never slept since then. Not only did I sleep last night, I was in heaven."

"Darling, you should have taken me into confidence right from the beginning. Problems shared, especially with a loved one, we are told, reduce the burden." Gbade told her.

"That's easier said than done," countered Pero. She went on: "What respectably married woman would confess to having been raped, especially in our peculiar circumstance? I just could not. I was hoping and praying that, God in his good time would, one day, vindicate me."

"You should have trusted me and confided in me. True love engenders trust." He continued by asking: "And why were you crying on the day you arrived in London?"

Pero replied: "I felt suddenly frightened. I thought that you would discover that night that I had been deflowered. I felt trapped."

"That night after the film on the television, why did you say that you had always been faithful?" asked Gbade.

"The way you looked at me provoked a reply. I was not myself when I blurted out whatever it was I said," replied Pero. "Do you remember the night you related your dream about Bayo to me, how startled I was. The look of fear on my face was all too revealing, was it not? I thought I was going to die. Darling, your understanding of feminine body language is too uncanny. From that day I have been treading with great care and trepidation. I hope I never live through such a situation again." After a time,

Pero continued: 'When Bayo, during his confession, referred to the spiritual boomerang embedded in you I was so nervous. I said to myself, 'Could that spiritual boomerang harm me for keeping such a secret from you for so long?''

"My dear, my ancestors who discovered the secret of such protection would not have been so thoughtless or wicked as to make it harm loved ones. Although we possess this unique power or whatever it is, we still love and protect our loved ones. No harm can come to you through or from me," he told her.

"To be absolutely frank, I am sometimes afraid that you can read my thoughts. As I previously observed, your understanding of body language and your interpretation of it is frightening," Pero went on.

Gbade intervened, "Sometimes you had a troubled look. Yes, a strange look mixed with pity for me. At such times I became almost certain that you had a well-guarded secret which somehow affected me, a secret which you did not wish unearthed. On such occasions my heart bled for you because I could see that you were under great stress and really sad."

Pero interjected: "Gbade, if you were in my shoes you would feel exactly the same. Often I have asked myself how I could keep such a secret from my husband, a husband who loves me so dearly and whom I also love so much. It was most painful."

To this Gbade said: "When one keeps secrets, the barrier of distrust would always be there. In such a situation it would have been impossible for a couple to live a normal life. One of them would have been living a lie. Supposing Bayo had not come forward to make the confession, what would have happened?"

"My life would have been so miserable. It would be a life of prolonged agony. I would have been living a lie as you rightly put it. Thank God he came. I also thank the Almighty Father that you really love me and that you are so understanding. I doubt if any other man could have been so accommodating. May God bless you."

"Last night after you went to bed I sat up thinking. I asked myself a lot of questions. One of them was whether not disclosing the rape might have been responsible for the long delay before we had children. Were we being punished because you were not telling the truth?"

"Fancy you saying that," interrupted Pero. "Such a possibility had occurred to me, even before Bayo came. Guilty conscience, I suppose."

Again Gbade intervened: "When I was at the Club last Tuesday I heard of a case almost similar to ours; except that the woman concerned kept on affirming that she was a virgin when she got married, in spite of the facts. She wanted to eat her cake and still have it. Unfortunately for her the truth came out in the end. Her former boyfriend unwittingly let the cat out of the bag. When he became a born again Christian he confessed it to his pastor. Miserable fellow! The pastor turned out to be the brother of the deceived husband. When confronted, in front of her lover, she had to confess. She broke down, cried bitterly and asked for forgiveness. She, like many others, forgot that to avoid discovery one must not indulge in any misconduct."

"I was afraid that something like that could happen to me." admitted Pero. "Imagine your contempt and the derision." But Gbade quickly observed: "Do you think me capable of holding you in contempt? Can you ever expect derision from me? Never. When we got married, we did so for better or for worse; we became one flesh. You ought to have known me by now. Under no circumstance would I have derided you. If I did so, I would be deriding myself."

"Since we are starting a new life, I suggest that we look at the nature of love afresh," said Gbade.

"I agree entirely."

"A detailed examination of love ought to be made to guide us for the future, if only to strengthen our love," Gbade continued. "Why have we given ourselves so many headaches and heartaches. When I gave you my love you and asked for yours in return, I did not ask whether or not you were a virgin. No! Such a thought never even crossed my mind. I just loved you as you were. I must confess though that at the back of my mind was always the assurance that a girl with your background and education must be a virgin. Love is such a great force – when it comes it exerts so much pressure; when it pulls, the magnetic force is so powerful that you cannot resist. It leaves you no time to wonder or ask questions.

"Love is like a gust of wind, which pushes or drives you into the arms of a loved one, when she or he beckons. Love, the true meaning or import of which is yet to be discovered, is a great driving force. It can push you to great heights. It can make you attain the unattainable. It can make you achieve the seemingly impossible. Love is the all-conquering force. In the words of Paul the Apostle: 'Love is patient. Love is kind. It does not envy. It does not boast. It is not proud. It is not rude. It is not self-seeking. It is not easily angered. It keeps no records of wrongs. Love does not delight in evil, but rejoices with the truth. It always protects, always perseveres. Love never fails.'

"Now Pero, stretch out both hands and clasp mine as we renew our vows. Let us repeat the words of Saint Paul. Let us resolve to follow them for as long as God gives us life. Let our union be a shining example for all those we come in contact with. May God in his mercy grant our prayers." They both chorused 'Amen.'

"Is all forgiven?" asked Pero. "There is nothing to forgive" answered Gbade.

Thereupon Pero nestled her head on Gbade's chest, and waves of content flowed through the two friends and lovers, now at last truly one.

THE ATONEMENT

How it began

At last, the day for the Annual Anglican Youth Fellowship (AYF) Competition has arrived. As early as five o'clock, long before dawn, I am ready. The buses will leave Obalende bus terminus at seven o'clock prompt. All the AYF members from the various Anglican churches on the island are aware of the arrangements. Normally, walking from St David's church to the terminus takes about twenty minutes. Our house is at the market end of Lewis Street which means an additional ten minute walk. Knowing that I shall linger to watch my favourite squirrels and birds, I set out early.

The usual hustle and bustle of daily life is yet to begin. The road is almost deserted. All is quiet and peaceful. The cool breeze is fresh, clean and soothing – and thanks to the heavy overnight rain, the air is free of dust. Due to the early rains, the elephant grass has grown very tall on both sides of the road. The neatly trimmed hedges are about a foot lower than the elephant grass. The red flowers on the top and sides of the hedges are thick and abundant. The tropical green of the rain-cleansed elephant grass makes a beautiful contrast with the ixora hedges. Behind the tall grass are the flamboyant trees, even taller with their spreading branches covered in yellow flowers.

Sure enough, the grey squirrels are already darting to and fro across the road. The red-eyed turtle doves have already started to twitter, flying from tree to tree; occasionally they touch down looking for seeds and fruits to eat. Watching them is fascinating.

While walking from the church to the police grounds, I see maybe five or six women carrying their wares on their heads going to the market. They sway gracefully as they walk in their multi-coloured dresses. The flower nurseries just beyond the bridge are resplendent with gorgeous flowers and plants. I pause to look at them and at the rockery with the cactuses and African lilies as well as the purple *praecox* that surrounds them. I whisper to myself, "nature is a wonderful artist." The miniature palms interspersed with yucca plants, both *aloifolia* with its mesmerising ivory hue and the light green *rostrala*, looking like bristles of a hedgehog, are stunning. The composite picture is a riot of colour. While I am still admiring this picture of nature in all its glory, the sun peeps out, beaming its light and warmth at me; I feel joyful and I am at peace with myself and the world. Intuition tells me that this will be a special day. I hum a favourite song as I walk along. I then start to think about the day ahead. This will be my first visit to the Posts & Telegraph Institute at Oshodi with its famous picnic sites and playgrounds. I am very keen and hopeful that St David's AYF will win the Archbishop Vining Cup dance competition. Bose and I will represent our branch in the rhumba and waltz as well as the two other steps. We have been practicing daily, working hard at positioning, posture, poise, stance and turns for hours each day for the last three months.

Bose is a dream partner; while I dance, she floats. She excels at all times. It is a delight dancing with her. I hope and pray that Niyi, her excessively jealous boyfriend, will not prevent her from coming to the competition. That would be a disaster. I am still thinking about the enjoyable day ahead as I reach the bus terminus.

I thought that I would be the very first person to arrive, but this is not so. Already standing in front of the first bus are a pair of boys and two girls all wearing the AYF badge. I introduce myself to them as a member from St David's church. They in turn inform me that they belong to the newest AYF branch, from the Trinity Chapel, Alagbon.

Soon the four buses are nearly full, and we start the journey. We stop at various bus stops on the island then four more on the mainland before arriving at Oshodi. We receive a warm welcome from the All Saints branch members who are to be our hosts for the picnic. We are then shown to our bases. Afterwards we are given a half-hour break to look around before we assemble for the devotion. My escort, Bayo, who lives in the neighbourhood, is the current social secretary of All Saints branch. He has used the premises on many occasions so he is able to show me round the compound. Beyond the arena, where the dancing competition is to be held, are the pleasure gardens and playgrounds. The various flower beds and bamboo structures for creeping plants are fantastic. There are different varieties of flowers: hibiscus, buttercup, bachelor's buttons, rose periwinkles, sunflowers, Cana lilies, African lilies and roses of varying colours. The bamboo structures reinforced with steel poles are covered with orange, pink, white and mauve bougainvillea. The garden also contains money plants, morning glory and various kinds of ferns and decorative palms. There are, also, many kinds of trees: Indian Almond, flamboyant, frangipani, and royal palms. There is also a lone Iroko tree, tall, thick and imposing. It looks ancient, dignified and awe-inspiring. It stands in the centre of the landscape like a king – majestic, aloof and magnificent. The half-hour break passes quickly.

The devotion takes place in the open arena enclosed with avocado, grapefruit and orange trees. We sit in a horseshoe formation with the chaplain facing the semi-circle. It is all over in half an hour. Then the elimination contest for the dance competition follows with the judges selecting just six couples to take part in the finals. Bose and I have the highest score. Together with five other pairs, three from the Island and two from the Mainland compete for the coveted cup. I eat lunch very sparingly, mindful of the butterflies in my stomach. The bell summons us, contestants and audience alike, to the main arena. Bose has changed into her flared, pleated lovat skirt to which her white blouse makes a beautiful contrast. She is elegantly poised in the middle of the dance floor as if she is about to soar into the air. I walk briskly to join her. The other five contesting pairs are also in their positions.

Fortunately the contest starts with the rhumba, our favourite step. We dance our hearts out. At one stage it seems as if Bose and I are floating away. At that point the music stops. Bose, the exhibitionist, gives me the nudge; we then give a graceful bow in unison. The applause that follows is long and rapturous, and unsurprisingly we are awarded the highest score of nine. After a short interval, the waltz follows in which Bose and I as well as the couple from All Saints score nine each. But we have the edge as All Saints only scored seven in the rhumba. In the quickstep, thanks to Bose, we score eight with the couple from Ebute-Metta scoring nine; but they still trail behind us as in the previous two steps they scored poorly. In the foxtrot, the last dance, St David's, All Saints and one other pair from the Island score nine each. Bose and I have a total score of 35 and win the competition. All Saints is placed second with 33, and St Peters has 31 in third place. Bose and I receive the coveted Archbishop Vining Cup from the chief judge amidst deafening applause. The impish look in Bose's eyes and her dazzling smile express her pleasure at winning. Bose and I then shake hands with the other two couples. As I shake hands with Temi from All Saints I cannot but notice her hand, which is dainty and extremely soft. My own hand clasps hers for an unduly long time; and as I look into her unique face with its unusually pointed nose and splendidly chiselled chin as well as her twinkling eyes, I become mesmerised.

We both walk slowly away hand in hand towards the barbecue. At first we are both silent; then I break the silence as I introduce myself. "I am Ladi from St David's AYF."

"I am Temi of All Saints AYF. I have a feeling that I have seen you before."

"It's quite possible as I hardly miss any AYF events," I tell her.

On reaching the barbecue spot we deliberately choose a table for two so we can talk together without disturbance. We place our bags to reserve the table and then join the queue for food, with Temi in front so that I can watch her without her noticing. We both receive many congratulations as we choose our food. We then pick our soft drinks and walk back to our table.

My heart is beating fast and I feel dizzy with the thought of being with her. As we sit down we clasp our left hands while picking at our plates with the right hands. I could barely eat as I gaze at her pretty face, her well-rounded cheeks, her pointed nose and chin, her twinkling eyes with their lush eye-lashes, and the crown of abundant hair neatly parted in two in the centre and drawn back into a bun at the back of her well sculptured head. Unlike me, unabashedly examining every inch of Temi's face, she too is examining my face but in a more discreet, ladylike manner. We are both smiling and somewhat quiet. I then suggest we take a walk around the playground. We walk in silence until we reach a cluster of trees and then select a bench beneath them. We sit sideways looking at each other and intuitively we hold hands. The sensation between us is magnetic. The prevailing silence is exceptional. I break the silence saying: "Sweet Temi, a penny for your thoughts."

Temi looks up with a start. "Am I dreaming?" she says quietly.

"Why?" I ask.

"You will not believe it," she answers. "I feel as if we have been transferring our thoughts forwards and backwards, as if in conversation. It would be embarrassing for me to express what I think I heard you say, and my reply!" she adds.

"May I suggest something crazy?"

"Go on, let's have it," she replies with a smile.

I then put my hand into my bag, take out a note pad and tear out two pages, passing one to Temi while keeping the other.

"To avoid any embarrassment, let's write out our thoughts and exchange the pieces of paper," I suggest.

"Agreed."

After a short time, I ask Temi if she is ready.

"Yes, ready," she says. We then exchange our pieces of paper.

"Do you mind if I read yours first?" I ask her.

"No; that's fine," she replies.

"What on earth is the matter with me?' I have fallen head over heels in love with him; the feeling I think is mutual."

"Please read out mine."

"It seems that I have fallen in love with her; this is love at first sight. But supposing she does not reciprocate, what will I do? But I am sure she will."

"This is strange," we both say in unison.

Intuitively, we both stand up and embrace. The kiss that follows is passionate and says a lot. We then both sit back gazing into each other's eyes. When I finally break the silence by saying, "I feel so peaceful," Temi answers, "Me too". For the rest of the evening it is as if we are both in a dream. Instead of getting into the bus in which I came, like someone in a trance I follow Temi into her bus that goes to the Yaba terminus. We both sit side by side, in silence and still holding hands. Throughout the bus ride not a word is uttered. When we reach Yaba, Temi leads me to her home on Agard Street. We find her parents in the front yard.

"At last you're back," her mother says.

"We have been anxious," her father adds. "This is why we are sitting here, waiting for you. Who is this young fellow?"

"He is one of our members from St David's Lafiaji," Temi answers. "He and his partner won the cup for St David's. We came a poor second, after all our hard work and practice. All the same I am happy for him. He volunteered to see me home as it is so late."

After commiserating with Temi for not winning the competition, and saying he is sure she'll do better next year, Temi's father turns to me in a friendly manner: "Thank you young man. What's your name?"

"Good evening Sir. Good evening Ma. I am Ladi Adeolu."

"Which Adeolu would that be?" asks the father.

"My father is a civil servant," I answer. "He works at the old secretariat on the Marina."

"Then you must be S.O.'s son!" Temi's father exclaims.

"Yes, I am."

"It's a very small world. He was my immediate boss before his recent transfer on promotion to the Judicial Department. Yes, you look like him. I hope he is well. Please give him our regards."

"Yes sir, I'll do so. I must be on my way. It is getting late."

By way of goodbye, all Temi could manage with her parents present was a squeeze of my hand, but she whispered, "I'll see you in front of the Ambassador at six tomorrow evening." I feel as if I am floating on air as I walk to the bus stop. Throughout the journey all I can think of is Temi. I get down at Beecroft bus stop mechanically. My dreams that night are all of Temi.

Of course we meet again the next day and thus our relationship blossoms. I become a regular visitor to Temi's house and the friendship between her mother and me gets stronger and stronger. And so Temi becomes my life and we are inseparable.

One evening we are seated on a bench in the park very near Temi's home, one of our favourite meeting places. "I hope you have not forgotten Yeside's birthday party on Saturday evening."

"I have not," Temi replies, "but I won't be able to attend. You remember I told you last week of the death of my aunt back in the village. Mummy thinks that I should accompany her, especially as my Dad will be unable to go. I had to agree as poor Mum never feels at ease going to the village on her own. I am disappointed as Yeside's parties have always been fun. But you go along and enjoy yourself. However, make sure you behave. Don't do anything I wouldn't do."

"As if I would, you naughty girl," is my teasing response.

When I arrive at the party on Saturday, Yeside's guests are already sitting at the tables on the lawn. Yeside takes me round to greet them while introducing me to a few guests that I have never met before. One of them is a very pretty girl, Aduke, who lives in the same compound as Yeside. As there are only three persons at Aduke's table, Yeside suggests that I should join them. In the course of the evening I have a dance with Aduke, who turns out to be a great dancer, almost as good as Bose. We make a handsome pair as we dance. Although I am enjoying the party, I have the urge to go home to catch up with some revision in preparation for the coming exams.

Aduke also walks home to her family's bungalow about the same time. For the first time Aduke seems to notice the beauty of their garden. She walks very slowly and thoughtfully and tells herself: "This is an excellent compound, well laid out and with lots of flowers and trees." She decides to sit on a bench underneath a tree in front of her home. She carefully selects a spot behind a clump of trees as she does not want anyone to see her. Again she looks round the compound, savouring and admiring the lovely surroundings in which she lives. The neighbourhood is well lit by the full moon. There are so many stars in the sky. The breeze from the Marina is cool and it is indeed a most beautiful night.

Shortly after this, Yeside walks past after seeing Ladi off. She is smiling as if she is sharing Aduke's delightful thoughts. At this point Aduke decides to go inside. She opens the door quietly in order not to disturb her cousin, Tara, and her mother who are already in bed.

Aduke tells her Story

My head still buzzing from the party, I undress and get ready for bed, but I cannot sleep and nor do I really want to. I just lie on my bed thinking of what took place at Yeside's house. I feel elated. For most of the night I recollect what happened – how I almost swooned when he asked me for a dance. What a dancer! His posture and elegance, his touch, his smile, his charm and his fashionable clothes. He was so sure of himself, and all the girls were dancing around him.

For half of the night I talked to myself. I had hoped that he would ask me for a second dance; but, oh, how selfish of me. He was easily the most admired man at the party and all the girls wanted to dance with him. All too soon he decided to leave. That was a shame. Did I make the right impression on him? Did he notice me? My heart was pounding all the time when we were together. At last I have found my dream partner, I thought – the one destined for me. There is no doubt that I am in love with him. How I wish that it was already morning. I will ask Yeside all about him.

My thoughts were coming so fast that I could barely breathe. What is happening to me? I asked myself. I felt so excited and happy; but at the same time a little melancholy. I wondered why. And Ladi's image continued to fill my thoughts. His presence seemed to put life into me. I want to be with him every moment of my life, I conclude. But then doubts began to creep in. What chance would I have, what with all those pretty girls buzzing around him? I agonised, before reassuring myself that I am also very attractive, I can hold my own. I shall show them all, I thought. The mere thought of him continued to haunt me. What is this madness that has come over me? There is no doubt about it. I have fallen in love with him. I am no longer in control of myself. May heaven help me. Mercifully, I drift off into sleep at last.

Two mornings after, I am still in a daze. Mum wants to know what is wrong. What can I say? The only answer I can give is, "Nothing, I must be on my way to school". I also avoid my cousin Tara's questioning looks. Later, at school, I could not concentrate during the first two lessons. Even during physical training, which I normally enjoy, I felt listless. I was scolded twice by the games mistress. At break time I keep to myself. It becomes obvious to all the girls that something has happened to me. On the way home, Tolu wants to know what. At first, I would not discuss it but after a lot of coaxing I recount to her my experience of the previous Saturday. Tolu's verdict is: "You are no doubt in love. I have never seen you in this kind of mood. We shall have to find out all about this special boy and see what needs to be done to win him." We both walk on in silence.

After the local cemetery Tolu branches off to go to her own home. When I reach home, only cousin Tara and the maid are in. Mummy is yet to return from her shop. While the maid is getting the meal ready, cousin Tara starts to quiz me. She has been my favourite cousin and constant companion, so I cannot keep anything from her. I recount all that happened at the party the previous Saturday and how I was awake half the night thinking about Ladi. All she said is, "You have been well and truly bitten by the bug. Do be careful. I know that when love comes calling it bites hard. What do you plan to do now?"

"I'll talk to Yeside".

All I could do is to swallow a few mouthfuls of the food on the table before I cross over to Yeside's place. She wants to know if I had enjoyed the party.

"I did, indeed" is my reply. "Since then I have not been myself."

"What do you mean?" asks Yeside.

The words come tumbling out of my mouth. "Who is that young fellow, Ladi? What is his full name? Which school does he attend? How and when can I see him again? Or is he your boyfriend?"

"Take it easy," says Yeside. "Calm down. He is not my boyfriend, at least, not in that way. We belong to the same fellowship in my church. I have known him for many years. He is in the choir, and

he sings like an angel; and he dances like a fairy. He is one of the best in the Sunday school. He is also a great debater. His school is very proud of him. He is greatly liked by all, boys and girls. If you are interested in him, as I suspect, I must add that you are too late. He already has a steady girlfriend, an old school friend of mine. They have been dating for three years."

I felt utterly deflated. I flop into a chair. What a disaster! What is going to happen to me? I feel numb. Suddenly, I feel faint. In fact, I must have passed out. The next thing I remember is Yeside patting me on the back and rubbing my arms. Then she sits beside me, rocking me to and fro. I become blank. After some time I hear myself speaking, "Where am I? What happened?"

"I'll walk you home," Yeside says. I am without feeling whatsoever. How I got back home I do not know.

We enter by the front door and Tara is in the living room, all by herself. She quickly jumps up on seeing us. "What happened? You are looking so pale, Aduke. Yeside, what is the matter?" she asks. They whisper together and then both of them pilot me to my bedroom. My shoes are removed. Cousin Tara goes out and brings some tablets. She passes to me a glass of water and asks me to take the tablets. I must have fallen asleep. When I eventually awake, both Mummy and Tara are with me. "If you do not feel like talking now, don't," says Mummy. "Just rest. Rest your head on my lap." She then starts to rock me like a baby. Very soon I am asleep again. Later that night another cousin, a doctor, enters with a nurse. He examines me thoroughly. With persuasion I take some broth and a slice of bread. I then go back to my bed and sleep.

The next morning I feel a lot better. Cousin Tara is with me. She is looking at me with some anxiety. Then Mother comes in. "My daughter, my baby," she exclaims. "Do not worry. There are many young men around. Ladi is not the only man in the world. Someone else will come for you." But the mere mention of the name, Ladi, puts new life into me. I could only murmur. "It's Ladi I want," I insist. "No other man. I must have him. I cannot love another." I see mother and Tara exchanging looks.

A few days later, I make a further plea to Yeside to arrange another meeting with Ladi. It will afford me an opportunity to plead my case. Yeside refuses bluntly. "Did I not tell you my past relationship with Temi? She was not just a classmate; we were childhood friends. What sort of friend would she think I am to hear that I have been conspiring with you to pinch her boyfriend. Look for help elsewhere."

Yeside's refusal to help me whips up my resolve to do everything possible to avenge my imagined grievance against Temi. "She it was who pinched the man intended for me by providence," I persuade myself. From then on I start collecting all the available information about Temi. In particular, I look for evidence that she is double-dating with a view to using such information to discredit her in Ladi's eyes.

One evening my mother asks me to deliver a parcel to one of her friends. It turns out to be a lucky evening for me. As I approach the address I see Ladi coming out from a nearby house heading in my direction. I quicken my pace so I can speak to him. Fortunately I am very smartly dressed. Switching on what I hoped to be a bewitching and dazzling smile, I say: "Ladi, I haven't seen you since Yeside's party. I hope all is well with you. I am on my way to see your neighbour. Do you mind walking with me." As charming as ever, Ladi replies, "That will be a great pleasure and it's on my way. Good to see you too."

We walk along together. I tell Ladi all about myself. As we approach the house of my mother's friend, I take a bold step. I again refer to Yeside's party expressing how I enjoyed Ladi's company. "I feel as if I had known you all my life. I would like us to be good friends," I tell him. "Why not?" Ladi replies," especially as we are both friends of Yeside."

We part on a friendly note. On a few occasions I contrive to have other 'accidental' meetings with Ladi. On the last of such occasions I told Ladi that when I told Yeside about our friendship she had told me that "Ladi and Temi are inseparable". Ladi confirms that he and Temi have made an irrevocable commitment to each other. He adds that he cannot love anyone else. I was determined to have the last word and said mischievously and seemingly jocularly, "I have noted your commitment and devotion to Temi. However, should Temi at any time disappoint you, please remember that you have Aduke waiting in the wings." Although the tone sounded playful, the message was intended to be serious. In my self-delusion, I feel that I am making progress in winning Ladi's heart.

The following day I discuss the matter with my friend, Tolu. During the discussion Tolu tells me that years back, as children at primary school, Temi, who was then living with her married elder sister, had stayed in the same compound with her, with her elder brother, Debo, and an older sister, Bibayo. Tolu also disclosed that her elder brother Debo was keen on Temi. He had in fact approached her a year earlier try to renew their old childhood friendship. At that time Temi had told Debo that Ladi was her only love. Similarly, when I seek the advice of school friends – Teju, Tolu, Tola and Ronke on the strategy I need to get Ladi to switch his affections and drop Temi in my favour, the girls talk of possible plans. However, I decide to take action to get a rapid result: I cook up a devilish plan. I ask for Tara's assistance. Tara and Gbenga, Ladi's elder brother, had been in a relationship for some time. At my request Tara is to send Gbenga a letter that will require an urgent reply. The urgent reply for delivery to Tara will be sent through Ladi on his way back from school, as Ladi's school and the compound where Tara and I live are on the same road.

My plan is to feign illness at school and return to the house to await Ladi's visit to Tara. I know that Tara, my mother and the maid will all be away from home at that time. Indeed almost the entire compound with its six bungalows will be virtually deserted at that time of the day; that will make the coast clear for me to put my plan into action. Tara agreed, and the next day at school after complaining of a bad - but faked - stomach ache and headache I am sent to the sick-bay. After a while I say I am feeling better and the nursing sister sends me home. Two hours later, Ladi knocks on the door. It is me, and not Tara, who greets him. I have a large towel wrapped around me and say with a sweet smile: "Sorry Ladi, that you had to knock twice. I was in the shower. I was getting ready to go out, but I had promised cousin Tara to delay my outing in order to collect her letter."

As we were about to enter the living room, my bath towel – as a result of my manipulation - slips off me; and conveniently very near the sofa. At that moment my back is towards Ladi. I then turn to face him, saying, "Oops, please forgive me Ladi, how clumsy."

While pretending to struggle to replace my bath wrap I go towards my bedroom but hesitate at the door and say: "Did you not like what you saw?"

"I am not here to watch a nude display," Ladi retorted. "I am a very busy person and I have no time to waste. I shall leave Tara's letter on the sofa and shut the door on my way out." He was clearly shaken and disgusted.

"Please do not leave in such a great haste. I shall be out in a jiffy," I implore him from behind the door. Hastily putting on a very smart frock, I return to him and kneeling say, "Please forgive me, I did not mean to embarrass you."

"You just did. Please get up and sit on a chair," Ladi instructs me. "Supposing Tara or someone else comes in now, what would such a person think."

"Am I forgiven? Then give me a hug, I shall never offend again," I continue in a seductive tone.

"I will do no such thing," he replied angrily, "what do you think you are doing; behaving like a depraved person."

"I am just showing you how much I love you, Ladi," I blurt out.

"No decent and well brought up girl shows love in such a crude way. Stop behaving so badly." Ladi's face was dark with fury.

"Please Ladi, my overwhelming love for you is killing me. Please accept me; I shall be your slave. I shall do anything. Just say you like me. I will have no objection if you just have me and discard me afterwards. I shall be content. I promise to be at your beck and call at any time," I plead, but with no effect.

"You are disgusting," replied Ladi.

He then walked out leaving me alone to mull over what had just happened. "Mr High and Mighty," I say quietly, as my own anger rises. "You have not heard the end of this matter. You will yet have me or pay for your refusal."

At school, Aduke informs her four friends that she no longer has any interest in Ladi. In a tone seemingly full of relief, she tells them: "He is not a man; he is impotent." Her friends look at her in horror. Pressed to tell all, she relates a slanted account of what happened. One of Aduke's friends makes the observation,

"How could a girl so ill yesterday have found the strength and inclination for such a performance."

Promptly Aduke replies, "My illness yesterday was feigned. You no longer need to crack your heads working out a strategy."

"This is a case of sour grapes," taunts another of her friends.

"No, I am dead serious" Aduke counters. Tolu makes the observation that the break period will be over in three minutes and suggests that they wait behind after school to discuss the issue fully.

The five friends have a serious debate when they meet again after school. Teju starts off. She tells me off for having devised such a reckless, shameful and foolish plan, just to snare a boy who is obviously well brought up and who would not dream of involving himself in any form of immoral behaviour. She adds that Aduke has let the group down and should be ashamed of herself; and she made other scathing comments. Aduke maintains that she is right in her assumption and points out that her beauty and her well-proportioned body, as well as her willingness to accept a casual relationship with Ladi, ought to have done the trick. "He must be impotent. No normal male would stand there and react, or rather not react, to my advances as Ladi did."

Tolu, Aduke's best friend, naturally takes her side, saying: "From what Aduke and I have discovered, Ladi would not have hesitated to have Aduke, unless Aduke's accusations are true and he really is impotent." She agrees with Aduke that she should close Ladi's file, forget all about him and find another worthy boyfriend.

Ronke cautions the group, especially Aduke. She advises: "An issue such as the one confronting us cannot be discussed in a casual manner nor considered lightly; there are so many sides to the issue that ought to be given very careful examination." She adds that she had on many occasions met Ladi, who struck her as being sincere and open. The impression she got was that Ladi is someone worthy of trust and respect. "I would expect such a person to rebuff you as he rightly did," Ronke told Aduke. "You deserve what you got; you are envious of what Temi and Ladi have going for them."

Tola made no remark but wore a thoughtful look on her face.

Tolu and Aduke were well aware, all along, that Ronke knew Temi. Aduke had hoped that this discussion would be fully reported to Temi by Ronke, and that Temi would send Ladi packing. Indeed, this was partly the motive for Aduke's underhand plan. For her own part, Tolu thought to herself that Ladi's dismissal would leave the coast clear for Debo, her brother. It was all a sordid conspiracy, such as only the 'saucy five' (as Aduke and her group of school friends were known) would indulge in.

As expected, Tolu reported these developments to Debo and urged him to try his luck again. But she advised him to wait for about two weeks or so before making any move. This was to leave room for Ronke to report the discussion to Temi. Ronke, out of loyalty to her friend, duly did this. She cautioned her to be extremely careful and circumspect in handling the matter, while making the observation that, from the little she knows of Ladi, he appears to be a decent and reliable young man. "I also know that you love him very much. These are good enough reasons for handling the issue delicately and carefully." Temi should not leave herself in a position to be the loser, whatever happens.

She concludes by asking Temi a hypothetical question. "If it's true that he's impotent what will you do?"

"Nothing short of actually making love with him can prove or disprove that," answered Temi, "and I cannot allow any man, no matter how much I love him, to make love to me until after he has married me. To do otherwise would mean disregarding all that my upbringing has taught me. Besides, it is against our traditions and culture."

"What do you intend to do about it?" asks Ronke.

"Let's wait and see," Temi replies. "Matters will sort themselves out."

"As we were talking, what you said some time ago struck me," says Ronke.

"What was that?"

"You complained about the number of girls dancing around Ladi, especially two in particular," Ronke answers. "Supposing he makes love to one of them and she becomes pregnant, where will that leave you?"

"How can an impotent boy impregnate a girl?" answers Temi contemptuously. Speaking more seriously Temi adds: "With time things will sort themselves out."

Temi's Drastic Actions

Poor Temi is restless and sleepless that night. Her long , deep meditation ends on a sad note. "Either way I shall lose out. He may sleep with one of the two girls, or even both of them. What if they become pregnant? The only option is to wait, by that I mean that the wedding I had long planned will either have to be put off indefinitely or I shall get stuck with an impotent man, who will then be no man. In the name of God, what would I do? I know what I will do. I shall use the opportunity to call Ladi's attention to his two special admirers and all the other girls. I shall tell him that I do not have the stamina or inclination to fight any rival in the name of love. I shall tell him that our relationship has to be broken off so that I can have peace of mind. After watching for a brief period I will know if he truly loves me and me alone. God will also reveal whether or not he is really a complete man. It will, however, break my heart to call off the relationship, such a sweet relationship. May heaven help me." She has a rough and sleepless night.

The following evening Ladi shows up as usual. Temi's behaviour is peculiar. As he is leaving, Temi informs him that she has decided that in view of his many female admirers, their relationship should be broken off. She stresses that she is serious and Ladi is not to visit her again. Ladi is stunned and shocked. To stop herself from crying Temi quickly turns round and runs into the house. Ladi remains rooted to the spot for some time; then he leaves in bewilderment.

It is another sleepless night for Temi. "What on earth have I done? I hope that I have not lost the man I truly and deeply love. This game of love is both mad and dangerous," she thinks to herself. Similarly, Ladi could not sleep. All sorts of thoughts run through his mind. He feels numb and half dead. The following three weeks are bleak and sad. Pride prevents him from calling on Temi to beg her to reconsider her decision. He is, in addition, deeply hurt especially as he has previously told Temi that there was no truth in the allegations.

One evening, returning from an outing, Temi is accosted by Debo. Temi reminds him that she had previously informed him that she already has a steady boyfriend. Debo replies that he has decided to have another try as "old friends are better than new; besides, the situation might have changed."

"No, it has not changed," Temi replies. Then Debo starts calling on her daily, pleading to be given a chance. Temi points out that it is impossible for a girl to love two boys at the same time. Debo, however, persists. He then brings a card inviting Temi to a literary event. Out of boredom and to soothe her jaded nerves - as well as to teach Ladi a lesson - she accepts. Debo interprets this to be an act of capitulation on the part of Temi. He decides to exploit the situation. As he takes up the old tale, Temi with her jaded nerves blurts out that she does not love him. "I already have a steady boyfriend with whom I am deeply in love. Please keep away from me," she ends in exasperation.

Back home, a very troubled Temi sits on her favourite bench beneath the Indian Almond tree, thinking and fretting. She has not seen Ladi for three weeks. If only he would come I shall be rescued from the unwanted attentions of suitors like Debo. She is silently asking: "Has Ladi lost interest?" forgetting that it was she who asked him to stop coming. She becomes even more restless and troubled. Although she does not wish to discuss her problem with anyone, it is so obvious, even to her, that she needs advice, and urgently, otherwise she may go crazy. At the same time she does not wish to relent or pay Ladi a visit. She is truly in a dilemma.

For quite some time, Auntie Agnes, a tutor living in the same compound with Temi, has been watching her. Temi's usual smiles have vanished. Once a singing nightingale, she has now lost her voice. Auntie Agnes has come to the conclusion that something must be wrong. "At the risk of being called a nosey-parker, I shall speak to her," she concludes. In any case Auntie Agnes has in the past taken a keen interest in her, especially in her studies. Seeing Temi sitting on the bench with a forlorn look she approaches her and says: "Temi, I have noticed your attitude and demeanour lately. They are so unlike the Temi we all know. Do you have some problems? You never know, I may be able to help. You no longer smile or sing. You are less sociable, locking yourself up in your room on the pretext that you are studying. Besides, I have not seen your Ladi around for some time. What is the problem? Please take me into your confidence."

Temi sighs before replying. "I do have a problem, but I would rather not bother you." Pressed by Auntie Agnes, she explains that she had asked Ladi not to come again, but living without him is proving difficult. "It has not been easy. I have been going through hell," she explains in a broken voice.

"Why did you send Ladi away?" asks Auntie Agnes. "He has too many female admirers, they dance round him all the time. The rumour is that he is romantically linked with two of them," replies Temi.

"Did you confront him with these accusations? If so, what was his explanation?"

"He said that they were not true and that I am his only love."

"Obviously, you did not believe him," Auntie Agnes persists. "Why not? True love always trusts."

Temi hesitates but decides against telling Auntie Agnes about the matter of impotence. "You cannot go on like this," Auntie Agnes advises. "What do you plan to do? Why don't you send for him if you cannot go to him yourself," she suggests.

"I cannot. I cannot eat my words."

"You made a mistake by acting on unproved accusations. Own up and accept your mistake. Do not stress yourself unnecessarily," concludes Auntie Agnes, before taking her leave.

Temi, dejected and worried, continues to ponder what to do. Her thoughts are interrupted by her young cousin, Sola. "Auntie Temi, I have been looking for you all over the place. I have been standing here for quite some time without your noticing me. What is it? Can you spare a few minutes? I want to speak to you,"

"Yes, sit down," Temi says.

"I have not seen Uncle Ladi here for some time," Sola tells her. "I hope he is quite well. I had meant to go to the island in search of him; but I thought I'd talk to you first before doing so." Before Temi could answer, he continues. "Besides, I have seen that hungry looking boy who comes asking for you. He has been here two or three times. I saw you with him the other day near the football field. Don't tell me you want to replace Uncle Ladi with him."

Embarrassed by Sola's comment and jolted out of her inertia, Temi thinks this maybe a good chance to extricate herself. Sola had thought that Auntie Temi would flare up but instead she says, "I want you to do me a favour, Sola. I want you to go immediately to Ladi's place. Tell him that Auntie Temi is dying to see him. Please do not say I sent you. Go without delay."

Sola immediately runs as fast as he can to the bus terminus. When the visitor comes in Ladi cannot believe it: it is Sola, Temi's young cousin. Ladi hardly knows what to think, but after hearing what Sola has to say he hugs Sola and tells him that he will come over to the mainland later in the evening.

Ladi goes out of his way to look as smart and presentable as he can. Unknown to him Temi is doing exactly the same thing. With her hair neatly brushed and caught into a bun at the back, she sits demurely beneath her favourite tree, pretending to be reading a novel. Every so often, she looks towards the main gate. The moment the gate opens she jumps up and runs to meet Ladi. They fall into each other's arms with tears of joy running down their cheeks. Barely able to speak, Temi leads Ladi to the bench on which she has been sitting.

Unbeknown to the two lovers, Auntie Agnes and Sola are watching from one of the windows on the top floor. Looking at each other they both smile, smiles of happiness and contentment at having helped the two lovers to be reconciled. Still holding hands, Temi tells Ladi just how sad she has been, feeling almost suicidal. "I missed you so much. I was forever blaming myself for sending you away."

Ladi consoles her while confessing that he too had been despondent. "When Sola came to see me, my heart started pounding. After telling me that you wanted to see me again, I hugged him for bringing the news that I had been praying to hear. May God bless him for being the bearer of such good news. Now here we are together once again. It has been a nightmare; a very bad dream."

Temi wants to know what has been happening to Ladi. "I suppose that my two rivals have been dancing for joy in the hope that the coast was clear for them," she whispers.

"How can you utter such words? Ladi asks. "It has been a very sad experience. Whenever I got back from school I locked myself in my room to study, but could barely read a word for thinking of you. I felt very ashamed. How would I face the world? It is not funny for a popular young man like me, the head boy of my school, to have been dropped by his girlfriend? I could have never lived it down. It would have hounded me for the rest of my life. I had once sworn to myself that if any girl were to break off a relationship with me, I would never make up with her. Look at me now though, racing back to you. I suppose that you and your friends would have been laughing at me behind my back, saying that the almighty Ladi had been cut down to size. I should perpetually hang my head down in shame."

"What are you talking about," Temi interposes. "I am the one who crawled back. Sola came to you at my request. With all the pain and heart-ache, I had to come off my high horse. I could not afford to lose you. I missed you terribly. It has been a great ordeal."

"Never mind," says Ladi, embracing her fondly. "Let us put the bad dream behind us. Let us march on into a good and joyous future. As if all I was going through was not bad enough, Aduke came along and offered her shoulders for me to cry on. The cheek of it!"

"Same here, Debo came several times saying that he heard that the situation had changed and that I needed someone to look after me," says Temi. "Of course he was sent packing."

When Ladi eventually gets up to leave for home, she sees him off intending to accompany him as far as the football field; but instead she ends up at the bus terminus. As a result Ladi has to accompany her back home. At last she says, "Good night my love. When shall I see you tomorrow?"

"I shall be a bit late because I have to see the doctor tomorrow" replies Ladi.

"I hope it's nothing serious," Temi inquires. "No, it's just that my prospective employer wants a medical report as part of their procedure before I start the job. They want me to start work on Monday immediately after the exams."

The following day, on his way back from the doctor whose

surgery is on the mainland, Ladi calls at Temi's home. "How did it go?" she asks.

"It all went well. As I previously told you, it's the routine medical examination for new entrants. The original copy of the report will be sent to my prospective employers direct. I have been given this copy for my records.".

"May I read it?" Temi asks, excitedly. The envelope is handed to her. She reads it carefully and slowly. Huge relief shows on her face as she reads the doctors remark that "the applicant is a very healthy young man without any deformity or abnormality."

Thus the two lovers resume their courtship. With this new beginning their love grows stronger. It seems all too soon when, seven years after Ladi and Temilade first met at the AYF picnic, their formal engagement and marriage ceremony takes place in a whirl just before Ladi travels to London for further studies. It is fully eighteen months later when Temi joins him. After four years in London, they return home to Nigeria together.

* * *

After the five friends – Aduke, Tola, Tolu, Teju and Ronke – finished at High School only the last three keep in close touch with one another. Aduke stays aloof from her former friends most of the time, though she gets in touch with them occasionally. As always, she is constantly scheming and planning some fresh devilry. Following her offer of a shoulder for Ladi to cry on, which was firmly rebuffed, she starts to watch the movements of Ladi and Temi. She vows to take revenge on both of them - on Ladi, the heartless creature who spurned her love, and on Temi who in her fertile imagination remained the snatcher of the man intended for her by providence. She continues to spy on Ladi and Temi by setting up an elaborate network of informants to monitor their movements both at home and in London.

Pursuing her latest plans Aduke decides to pay a visit to London, taking the opportunity to make some business contacts. Whilst in London she telephones Tinuke, her mother's first cousin. Tinuke was married many years ago to a Swiss national who had lived in West Africa for years. Both of them had decided to retire and live in Zurich. Tinuke has one daughter, Otolorin, generally known as Oto. As Tinuke would like her daughter to marry a Nigerian, she broaches the subject with Aduke. Aduke responds positively to this proposition and promises to look after Oto and be her guardian when she comes to Lagos. Soon afterwards, Aduke returns to Nigeria and is pleased to receive a letter from Tinuke with the news that Oto would soon arrive in Lagos. From the accompanying photograph of Oto, the little girl Aduke had previously seen about twenty years before, has grown into a very pretty young lady. At last Aduke will have a companion, like a younger sister, to live with her. Before Oto's arrival Aduke commissions an interior decorator to look at the bedroom and the adjoining lounge that she has in mind for Oto's use. She is determined to make her feel at home. Oto will be the key to a plan she is hatching.

At last, Oto arrives. Aduke is delighted and even the maid is surprised to see her in such a good mood. As Oto appears in the airport terminal, Aduke greets her: "My dear child, you have grown into a beauty. I am delighted to have you stay with me. I hope you will like it here." Later, with Oto's suitcases in the boot of the car, they drive into the city making light conversation. Oto comments on the development of Lagos with all the new skyscrapers. Reaching Aduke's home, Oto is impressed by the apartment and after unpacking her bags she and Aduke share a meal and continue their conversation. "Your mother's letter says that you are a very competent secretary with working knowledge of English, French and German. How did you come to learn French and German?" Aduke asks.

Oto points out that having schooled in Zurich she learnt to speak and write the two languages reasonably well. "Auntie, have you started looking around for a suitable opening for me?" Aduke replies that she has, and an advertisement in that day's paper may prove suitable. After reading the advert, Oto agrees that the job advertised may be just right for her. "It reads as if it has me in mind." She prepares her c.v. and application letter the following morning which Aduke's driver delivers to the address indicated. A week later Oto is invited for a test and interview. The evening before the interview Aduke has a long talk with Oto. She ends by saying, "Please dress modestly and with care. Use minimal makeup. It is crucial you get this position as secretary to the new manager. When you do I shall advise you further on what you should do."

After the test and first interview, Oto and two others are short-listed for the personnel manager's final interview. After that interview, Oto's papers and those of the other short-listed applicants are passed to the manager. They are asked to report the following day. Aduke gives Oto another pep talk. "So far so good," she tells Oto. "I have selected a very pretty but formal dress for you. I must complimentyouonyourdresssense. This frock is the type a good and sensible manager will appreciate. The dress is your opening gambit, so to speak, and first impressions count. When you are presented to the young manager, be respectful and courteous without being subservient. Relax and feel at home. Exude all the charm and confidence you can. You cannot fail to succeed. I want you to capture and captivate him from the very start."

"Why all this fuss, Auntie," asks Oto. "If I am finally selected I shall only be the manager's secretary, not his wife or mistress. Auntie, you are purring like a cat. You look so excited. What exactly is happening?" But Aduke just ignores her and continues with her instructions. "You must be on your best behaviour, demure, correct and proper. I am sure that you will get the job. When you are eventually appointed you must be diligent. Your conduct must be exemplary. With your looks, all the men will be wanting to get to know you. Please do not flirt with any of them. Concentrate on your work and on pleasing the manager. He's the one who must fall for you. If you follow all my instructions, you will within a few months have him eating out of the palm of your hand."

Oto is shocked at Auntie Aduke's scheming, and begins to wonder if there is a secret motive for her aunt's interest. The next day Oto returns to the house at lunchtime and tells Aduke that she has been given the job. She shows her the letter of appointment and Aduke is delighted. "Congratulations, my dear. This is just the beginning," she comments. "When you assume your duties next Monday, make yourself indispensable. Make the manager dependent on you for his continued success."

Oto is astounded. She asks Aduke: "Auntie, what are we talking about? The position of secretary or something else?"

"At the appropriate time I shall explain" is Aduke's cryptic answer. When Oto starts the new job, she follows Aduke's instructions to the letter. As predicted by Aduke, she captivates everyone in the establishment, including the manager, proving herself punctual and very efficient.

The manager travels a lot. Whenever he returns, reports have to be prepared, and this means that Oto often has to work late. The manager is a well-mannered and polished man, and always very proper in his dealings with Oto. He sees Oto not just as a personal assistant but as a young sister. Even Temi, the manager's wife, respects her. As a result, both of them treat Oto as a member of their family.

One evening, Aduke confides in Oto about what she refers to as her previous relationship with Ladi, Oto's boss. Of course, she gives her a twisted version of what really happened. According to her, Ladi was her boyfriend and they were very much in love. Everything was going well until Temi came along and stole him from her. She had been waiting for an opportunity to take her revenge; and now is the time. For extra effect, Aduke resorts to crocodile tears as she relates her story, in order to gain Oto's sympathy. She urges Oto to be particularly nice to Ladi so that he can be enticed into an affair that will drive a wedge between Temi and him.

Aduke's convincing acting persuades Oto to go along with her Aunt's plan. She starts to make subtle advances to her boss. On one occasion Ladi calls attention to a rare lapse and asks what has come over her. "Until recently you have been a perfect secretary," Ladi tells her. "You dressed modestly and your manners, demeanour and work were first class. But in the last week or so something has come over you. Look at your dress, it is outrageous! What is the matter? Do you have any problems? Unless you change and become your old self I will have to replace you." Oto is contrite and apologises. Before long, however, she relapses. Ladi has to remind her that their relationship should remain strictly that of employer and employee. The irony of the situation is that Oto has actually fallen for Ladi, and now there is no way that she can bring herself to harm him. She tells Aduke about her feelings and how she now regrets being part of the conspiracy to destroy Ladi and Temi's marriage.

Shortly after explaining the situation to Aduke, she resigns her appointment, packs her belongings and returns to her parents in Zurich. Aduke sees Oto's conduct as a betrayal and becomes even more bitter and frustrated. Her previous love for Ladi has turned into a vitriolic hatred; she is determined to do anything to harm Ladi and Temi. Totally obsessed with Ladi, she refuses to consider marriage. Instead she throws herself into her business, intent on making serious money to entice Ladi, if only to spite Temi.

Aduke refuses several marriage proposals until, after pressure from her ageing mother, she marries a man fifteen years older than herself. It is a most unhappy marriage but as far as Aduke is concerned, the marriage is to kill time until such time as she can be in a position to take over Ladi and inflict her revenge. Her husband is wealthy, and when he suddenly dies he leaves Aduke a rich widow. The union of wealth and wickedness breeds disaster. Aduke's unhappy marriage produced a son, Folarin, the image of his father. He in turn gets married to Feyi, a young, clever, pretty lady from a good but impoverished family. True to form, Aduke makes Feyi's life very difficult. Aduke's daughter-in-law is an engineer with a promising future but her mother-in-law insists she becomes her personal assistant in the trading business.

Out of frustration, the young couple leave Nigeria for South Africa where they have a child. One day the child becomes ill and is taken to hospital where it is discovered that she has a very rare blood disease. The best treatment for the disease can only be given by a specialist at an expensive hospital. As the cost of the treatment is above their means, they lose hope. However, in the hospital Feyi meets a fellow Nigerian, a Mrs.

Oye, who visits them in their home and learns of Feyi and Folarin's predicament. Later, the Nigerian lady tells her husband, an engineer, all about Feyi's child and the help needed for her treatment. A few days after, the couple pay another visit to Feyi and inform her that a deposit has been made to the specialist hospital for the child's treatment. After three months treatment, the child's health improves and the kindness brings the two families closer.

Aduke is very unhappy and lonely despite her great wealth. Her frustration worsens daily. Alone and unloved, she starts to miss her son and his family. Out of desperation she decides to pay them a visit. She is pleasantly surprised at the very warm welcome she is given by her son and daughter-in-law. In due course she learns about the generosity and kindness of the Oyes. One evening Folarin and Feyi invite the Oyes and their parents to dinner, since Aduke had expressed the wish to meet and personally thank them for being so good and generous to her son and his family.

Aduke is stunned to discover that her daughter-in-law's benefactors are in fact Ladi and Temi, her arch enemies, who had moved to South Africa. At first she is dumb and taciturn; but gradually she thaws as Ladi and Temi engage her and the others in conversation. In the end they all manage to have a fairly pleasant evening together and Aduke becomes warmer towards the visitors. After Ladi and Temi leave, Feyi who is naturally observant asks her mother-in-law if she had previously met Ladi and Temi. Aduke says she had briefly met them several years ago without going into details.

Soon afterwards she retires to her room. It is only natural that Aduke should be moved. All her life she has been envious of Ladi and Temi. She has done her best to harm them as well as to destroy their happy marriage. In return they have repaid her wickedness and hatred with the kindness and generosity shown towards her son's family and especially to her granddaughter. But for them, the family might have lost the child. Aduke is overcome by remorse. For the best part of that night she reviews her life, past and present. She realises how wicked she has been. What she thought of as a love affair she now clearly realises was just unreciprocated love. Whereas she fell head over heels in love with Ladi, he had never at any time returned the love nor did he try to convey such an impression. She had been a victim of self-delusion. Whilst agreeing that she is envious of the healthy relationship between Ladi and Temi, she also agrees that her hatred of them over the years has no basis or justification. She is struck by remorse. She resolves to confess her misdeeds and sins to Ladi and Temi. Not only would she ask for their forgiveness she would seek advice on how to atone for her sins. It is a completely different Aduke who wakes up in the morning.

Later that afternoon Aduke asks Feyi to telephone Temi. Aduke's explanation is that she wishes to thank them for the visit as well as for their kindness towards her daughter-in-law and her granddaughter. Not only is she very friendly over the telephone but she arranges a meeting with them for the next day. She goes on her own to see Ladi and Temi and is warmly received by both of them. After tea she announces the purpose of her visit. In an impassioned speech she expresses her sorrow and apologies: "Ladi and Temi, I am here to offer unreserved apologies for my wickedness and all the harm I have done to you. I am full of remorse. I want to confess my other misdeeds, those that you do not even know about. I am hoping that after I have made a full confession you will find it in your hearts to forgive me. I am sure that God will show me what I need to do to atone for my sins."

When Ladi gestures to be allowed to reply, Aduke asks him to hear her out. "I am eager to get it all off my chest. After that I shall listen to what you and Temi may have to say. I thank you greatly for the mercy and kindness you showed to those you thought were total strangers. From what I have been told by my son and daughter-in-law, I believe that you would have acted in the same way even if you had known who the child's grandmother was. I also wish to express my appreciation for the way you received me yesterday, even after you knew my relationship with Feyi and her daughter. To my shame I have to confess the other evils I had done against you. You remember the dream flat in Golders Green in London you very much liked and wanted to rent and how it all fell through at the last moment. I caused that. I got to know about it from Zacc, my boyfriend, and asked him not to let it to you. On your return to Nigeria I planted Dele, your steward, in your household. Your precious medication, the hormone treatment from France that got missing was thrown away by him on my instructions. The many accidents in the home you had during his stay with you were contrived by me. The worst was that I planted Oto in your office, Ladi. My plan was for her to seduce you and to ruin your marriage.

" I am really ashamed of myself. When I get back to Lagos I shall see my priest and seek his advice on how best I can atone for my many sins. While I have been going steadily downhill, both of you have been rising higher. I was consorting with and learning from the devil; whereas all the time you had made the fear of God your watchword. Now I have seen the error of my ways. I have destroyed myself through envy, frustration, hatred and the pursuit of revenge. I ruined myself for the sake of what I thought was love; it was self-delusion. Please forgive me and may God have mercy on me. I must leave now; please do not tell Folarin and Feyi what I have told you. May God bless you for keeping my confession secret. Again, thank you for your kindness to my family, especially my granddaughter. Who knows, but for your timely assistance she might have died."

Ladi's brief reply was, "Aduke, we feel really sorry for you," adding "We shall always remember you in our prayers. God will help you turn a new leaf. We harbour no resentment or animosity against you. The Almighty Father will forgive you. May His mercy rest and abide with all of us."

After returning to Lagos, Aduke loses no time to visit her priest. She confesses to him: "I have offended against the heavenly Father and my neighbours. I have sinned. I wish to make atonement. I have come so that you can pray for me, advise and point me in the right direction towards making the atonement." She recounts everything from the beginning to the end and then the priest prays for her. He then asks if she has any specific idea in mind for her atonement. She answers that she had thought of volunteering her time to charity, working at a home for blind, disabled, or deaf and dumb people; or at an orphanage or an institute for the homeless or destitute. She was willing to give financial support to any charity the church might advise. After a short pause, her priest informs her about a new home that caters for troubled girls. Among other things the girls learn trades and homecraft at the institution with the intention of giving them a positive role in society. Although the home works under the supervision of the Diocese, it is privately financed. Aduke immediately expresses her interest in this home, remembering that she was once a troubled girl herself. She thinks to herself: "If these girls can be prevented from making the same mistakes that I made, then that is a duty I must perform." The priest then gives her a letter of introduction to Mother Olga Mary, the director of the girls' home.

Arriving at the girls' home the next day, she is asked to wait a few minutes for Mother Olga Mary, and while waiting she browses through several Christian magazines and literature on the racks and tables. While waiting she recalls her school days and especially her friends, Tolu, Teju, Tola and Ronke. She wonders what has become of them. She becomes engrossed in her own thoughts when Mother Olga Mary arrives.

"Good morning, I am Mother Olga Mary. What can I do for

you?" In response Aduke hands her the letter of introduction. After reading the letter Mother Olga Mary invites Aduke into her office. On sitting down Aduke is taken aback when the Mother says, "Aduke it has been a long time. What has been happening to you? You do not look your usual self although it has been ages since we last met." Surprised, Aduke answers, "Mother have you mistaken me for someone else? I don't remember that we have ever met."

"Really" replies Mother Mary "Think back and remember your school days. Do you remember the band of five, 'the saucy five' of which you were the undisputed leader."

"Of course I do, but how would you know about them."

"Well, I should know about them because I was one of them. Do you remember the shy one who spoke only when necessary?"

With this she stares hard at Mother Mary. Suddenly she exclaims: "My goodness, Tola. What a pleasant surprise!" Mother Olga Mary responds saying, "Yes, it's me. Now, tell me your story. I understand that you are a very successful business woman and very wealthy. Why on earth, with all of that, would you want to serve in this home and work without pay?"

"It's a long story."

"Let's talk about it," says Mother Olga Mary, adding, "I am so pleased to see you after all these years but I have never seen you before in such a sombre mood. It's quite a turn around. Fancy, the usually gay and mischievous Aduke. It's unbelievable. Aduke, it is good to see you, although in what appears to be a sorry circumstance. Please tell me your story; take your time and go at your own pace. I promise not to interrupt you except when necessary."

"Oh Tola, pardon me, Mother Olga Mary, you are a very busy person, would you have the time now to listen to a long, dreary and wicked story. The story of a once normal girl who chose to be wicked and selfish and got herself entangled with the devil; as was to be expected she got herself landed in a big mess."

"Please Aduke no self-pity. Tell your story unvarnished and the merciful Father will show us a way out of what you called a mess."

Aduke gives a deep sigh. "I am sure you will remember the handsome Ladi with the captivating smile whom I fell hopelessly in love with when we were in the third form," recalls Aduke falteringly with a wistful look.

"How could I or any of us forget him? Did we not spend days plotting how we could lure him into the net of the irrepressible Aduke," answers Mother Olga Mary. "When I told you all at the time that I no longer cared for him," Aduke continues, "it was a great lie. I was burning for him. I was literally on fire. I have never loved like that before or ever since; indeed, I had never been in love until then. All day I would think about him. I would dream about him all night. At night, every night all my dreams were of him. I have come to realise that love is like fire. When fire is lit for a good purpose and when it is carefully and patiently tended, its controlled flame gives light and warmth; but when allowed to grow wild, the fire gets out of hand. It causes a lot of harm, destroying everything in its path. I became possessed. Ladi permeated my very life and existence. I lived and breathed for him. I did all I could to entice him. He did not even notice me. He was wrapped up in his love and admiration for Temilade. In my disappointment and anguish I swore to do everything within my power to spoil their relationship.

"Then one cool evening I was at the dancing school when Florence ran in – you remember Florence, the little imp. She was a year behind us. She was my messenger of sorts. I was on the floor with the chief instructor, Mr. B., who was showing me how to execute the 'Cuban Top' - and there was Florence frantically waving and gesticulating. She was making faces and hopping up and down. Fortunately Mr. B. had his back towards her. I thought that whatever news Florence was trying to convey to me must be important and urgent. I asked Mr. B. to be excused and quickly followed Florence towards the toilets..but instead of entering the ladies Florence made for the snack bar. Flopping onto a chair she signalled to me to take a seat. I had hardly sat down when she said, 'Guess what?'

"I retorted that I was not interested in taking part in any guessing game, adding, 'If you have news please let's have it. Can't you see that I am dying of anxiety?' 'Ladi and Temi got married this morning,' she finally blurted out. 'What sort of silly joke is that?" I asked.

"Before she could answer I added, 'Why did we not know they were going to be married? Someone who was invited would at least have told us.'

" 'I was told that they got married by special licence at the Central Registry,' said Florence. 'How can you be so sure?' I asked. 'Deji, my elder brother works at the Registry. He saw them and watched the ceremony from the window.' A great silence ensued. Florence then said, 'Aduke, say something.' I did not utter a word. 'Come on,' said Florence again.

"When there was no reply she looked sideways to see what was happening. It was at that precise moment that I was slumping down. In a flash Florence rushed to break the fall by catching me with both hands. In the process both of us crashed against the wall. Florence was breathing heavily. My head was cupped in her arms. Florence said I looked grey. My eyes dilated. I became perfectly still and made no sound at all. Though terribly alarmed, Florence had the presence of mind to let me down gently onto the bare floor. She dashed frantically into the ladies' room and came out with water and sprinkled it over me. After a few minutes I coughed; then I sneezed. Florence now bent over me gently, wiping my face and arms. She then sat on the hard floor placing my head on her lap and yelled for the snack bar attendant. Between both of them I was gently laid on the couch in the bar. 'What happened?' asked the attendant. 'She slipped and fell, hitting her head against the pillar. Her thick braided hair cushioned the blow,' Florence answered promptly. 'She is much better now. I'll get a taxi and take her home.'

"Then Mr. B. came into the bar. 'What happened?' he too asked. 'I was all the while waiting for her on the dancing floor.' When Mr. B. heard Florence's account he became understandably worried. 'Shall we take her to the hospital?' he asked. At this point I said almost inaudibly that I was fine and would prefer to go home. Mr. B. then drove us both to our house. Fortunately nobody was at home. Florence piloted me into my bedroom. We both sat down, not saying a word. It was Florence who broke the silence. 'The marriage has put a stop to it all. You can now settle down and get yourself another boyfriend'. 'No way!' I shouted hoarsely: 'Temi has won this particular battle but the war continues.' 'What do you want to do? What can you do?' asked Florence. 'A lot,' I snapped. 'I shall give them a fight. I shall give them hell. I even offered to be his concubine but he spurned me. He will pay.' 'Just be careful,' whispered Florence. On this note she quietly left to go home."

Aduke continues: "I had almost perfected my plans when I learnt Ladi had left for London. Later Temi went to join him. I then decided to pursue them. In the meantime I had requested a cousin employed at the Student Affairs Section in London to find out for me Ladi's residential address, which he did. I got to London two months after Temi's arrival. I got there just in the nick of time. Ladi wanted to take a lease on a super flat in Golders Green. He was just about to pay the rent. Zacc, my boyfriend then, who was besotted with me, was in charge of the letting agency. At my prompting he aborted the lease. Ladi and Temi were very disappointed.

"I did all sorts of things to make them uncomfortable. On their

271

return to Nigeria I planted a steward in their home. He caused them a lot of distress. In the end he was sacked. I planted a sweet young lady in Ladi's office, employed as his secretary. I had previously primed her. She was to seduce Ladi with a view to wrecking their marriage; but it did not work. The bond of love between Ladi and Temi was really strong and extraordinary. It was brought home to me what a strong, binding tie true love could be. The poor girl returned to Europe badly bruised and with a broken heart; she had in the process fallen in love with Ladi. "I tried all sorts of tricks but to no avail. I became frustrated and angry. I cursed my lot. I fumed. I raved. I became completely exhausted and tired of living."

At this point Mother Olga Mary asks Aduke to pause for a while and calls for refreshments. Aduke then continues unburdening her heart, disclosing to Mother Olga Mary that she eventually got married and that it was a loveless union arranged to pacify her mother. "I was rescued by fate from the unwanted marriage," explained Aduke, "as my husband, who was fifteen years older than me, died. Fortunately, he left me his fortune. We had produced a son. I did not get on with my son or his wife. My churlish behaviour towards them drove them away from Nigeria.

"I was then left high and dry. I got fed up with myself in spite of my wealth. I did not know where to turn. Out of boredom and loneliness I went in search of my son and his family. I eventually caught up with them in Cape Town. I was horrified to discover that my granddaughter had been gravely ill. I was told that her life was saved by the timely assistance of a Nigerian couple. I was shattered and mortified when I found out the identity of the persons involved. Would you believe, Mother Mary, that my family's benefactors were none other than Ladi and Temi? I became thoroughly ashamed. I came to the conclusion that fate was not quite finished with me. I was filled with remorse. I became truly penitent and, as a result, I went to my priest who sent me to you. So here I am seeking ways to atone for my many sins and wickedness." At this juncture Aduke bursts out in tears, weeping like a child, her chest heaving as she sobs her heart out. Bitter tears roll down her cheeks.

Mother Olga Mary allows her to cry to her heart's content. After some time, Mother Olga Mary holds her in her arms just as she had done in the old days, consoling her. She prays for her, asking God to grant her inner peace and time to make atonement for her sins. Aduke then calms down. She asks Mother Olga Mary how much it costs to maintain the school each year. She wants to be allowed to contribute a substantial sum towards it. But Mother Olga Mary informs her that the existing sponsors are wealthy and may not wish to have any assistance. When she insists that Mother Olga Mary introduce her to the benefactors to see if some arrangement could be made for her to contribute, she returns home much relieved and in a far better frame of mind.

A few days later Mother Olga Mary contacts Aduke to confirm that the two benefactors have agreed to see her the following day to discuss the matter. Aduke arrives in good time and as they are discussing the good old days, the two benefactors arrive. Aduke is completely astounded to discover that they were none other than Ladi and Temi.

There is no problem in reaching an understanding as to how Aduke could help finance the girls' home as well as her role in the running of the home. It was agreed that she would be Mother Olga Mary's assistant in running the home. A second similar home was to be established in a town twenty miles away. The financing of the new project would be borne equally by Ladi and Temi on the one hand and by Aduke on the other. The arrangement would work perfectly well.

Aduke becomes a conscientious worker within the home. The young girls benefit tremendously from Aduke's contributions both in her teaching and financial support. She always defers to

Mother Olga Mary as the head of the institution and in the process Aduke becomes humbler, wiser and more approachable. She never ceases to amaze and impress both Mother Olga Mary and Father Anthony, her priest. Her relationship with Ladi and Temi has changed completely and unbelievably. They are like a brother and sisters.

In due course with the help of her solicitor Aduke sets up a trust fund for all her charitable works. She becomes more of a worker within the church rather than the socialite she was before. She becomes known for her good works and kind deeds. The complete change in her is really impressive. She has been transformed into a totally different person. Mother Olga Mary is so impressed with the changed Aduke, so much that she wishes to show her off to the three other members of their group, Tolu, Teju and Ronke. She goes to a great length to trace them. They are invited to attend a surprise party that the home is hosting to honour Aduke's birthday.

On the day, Aduke is ushered into the room where her former classmates are already seated. They are all pleased to see Aduke and impressed to learn of Aduke's philanthropic work which has been widely publicised. They are amazed that the frivolous and mischievous Aduke has metamorphosed into such a generous spirit. On the following day they have lunch together. They reminisce about old school days and discuss what they have been doing since they parted. Ronke was a secretary; now retired, she offers to assist at the girl's home, two days a week. Teju, a medical doctor, offers free medical services. Tolu, who is a full time housewife, offers to teach homecraft.

Now that the relationship between Aduke and her son and his wife has improved, both of them return home to Nigeria. Thus Aduke has the privilege of enjoying her old age surrounded by members of her family. When she dies she leaves half of all her possessions to a foundation that will continue to run all her charities. The remaining half is left to her son and other members of her family.

Three years after Aduke's death a new chapel built in her memory by her son at the girls' home is dedicated. Thus Aduke, the mischievous, irresponsible and irrepressible girl, the vengeful and wicked woman, died as a God-fearing and highly respected philanthropist. She had indeed atoned for all her sins. Even in death her work of atonement still continues.

Design Management: OsanNimu
Illustration: Phil Wrigglesworth
Graphic Design: Leo Cooper, Angela Lyons
Design Direction: Ayodeji Alaka
Printed in the UK by TJ International